For Julian
the bibliographer! —

Henry

20. 6. 74

Russica

RUSSICA

Русская коллекция
в Нобелевской библиотеке
Шведской Академии

Избранный каталог
1766–1936

Составление:
Катаржина Грубер и Бенгт Янгфельдт
Редактор:
Катаржина Грубер

Almqvist & Wiksell International
Stockholm/Sweden

RUSSICA

The Russian Collection
in the Nobel Library of the
Swedish Academy

A Selective Catalogue
1766–1936

Compiled by
Katarzyna Gruber and Bengt Jangfeldt
Edited by
Katarzyna Gruber

Almqvist & Wiksell International
Stockholm / Sweden

The transliteration of the Russian alphabet
follows the international library system:

e = e
ë = e
ж = ž
з = z
ц = c
ч = č
ш = š
щ = šč
ь = '
ъ = "
ы = y
э = ė
ю = ju
я = ja

Index and lay-out: Michał Bron Jr
Указатель и оформление: М. М. Брон

© 1994. Svenska Akademiens Nobelbibliotek, Stockholm
ISBN 91-22-01619-8
Printed in Sweden by Graphic Systems AB, Göteborg 1994

The Russian Collection in the Nobel Library of the Swedish Academy

The Nobel Library of the Swedish Academy was founded in 1901 in connection with the establishment of the Nobel Prize for Literature (in accordance with Alfred Nobel's will of 1896). The statutes of the Nobel Foundation of 1900 stipulated the creation within the Swedish Academy of a Nobel Committee and a Nobel Library.

As laid down in its regulations, the Nobel Library collects contemporary literature and works on contemporary writers in different languages, and at present it is probably the largest collection of modern literature and literary criticism in Scandinavia.

For its extensive collections of works in Russian and the other Slavic languages the Nobel Library is primarily indebted to the Swedish Slavist Alfred Jensen (1859–1921). Jensen worked from the foundation of the Nobel Library until his death as the Nobel Institute's specialist on "Slavic literary works," with instructions to "examine issues relating to the prize, submit surveys of recently published works outside Sweden and execute translations of foreign works."

At the end of the 19th and the beginning of the 20th century Alfred Jensen was Sweden's leading Slavist. He was a polyglot and made important contributions as a translator from the Slavic languages. In 1896–97 he published two volumes of descriptions of journeys in the Slavic countries (*Slavia*), in 1898 *Ryska skaldeporträtt. Kultur- och litteraturhistoriska bilder från Ryssland* (Portraits of Russian Writers. Sketches from the Literary and Cultural History of Russia) covering the period from the 18th century up until the middle of the 19th century, and in 1908 a three-volume *Rysk kulturhistoria* (A History of Russian Culture). Among his translations should be mentioned *Eugene Onegin* (1889) and other works by Puškin, Lermontov's *The Demon* and other poems (1893), Gogol's *Taras Bul'ba* (1883), Dostoevskij's *Diary of a Writer* (1915) and *Poor Folk* (1920), Turgenev's *Senilia* (1883), Aleksandr Herzen's political works (1916), the anthologies *Ryska berättelser* (Russian Narratives; 1910) and *Rysk litteratur* (Russian Literature; 1912). He also translated Polish poets in the four-volume *Polska skalder* (Polish Writers), published 1899–1906, and *Pan Tadeusz* by Mickiewicz in 1898. In addition he translated the Czech poet Jaroslav Vrchlický, to whom he also devoted a study (*Jaroslav Vrchlický. En litterär studie*, 1904), which was translated into Czech two years after publication in Swedish. His work on the Ukrainian national poet Taras Ševčenko, *Taras Schewtschenko. Ein ukrainisches Dichterleben* (Vienna 1916), was published in Ukrainian in 1921.[1]

Jensen followed modern Russian literature attentively and corresponded with several writers, among them Valerij Brjusov, whose letters to Jensen are now in the Royal Library in Stockholm.[2] Brjusov sent Jensen copies of his books with dedications and Jensen wrote an article on Brjusov, who visited Sweden several times and acquired "new impressions and experiences which he is certain to use in his remarkable, impassioned lyric poetry."[3] Another writer who sent dedicated copies of his books to Jensen was Konstantin Bal'mont. The two poets were described by Jensen as "exceptional talents and consummate masters of verse form."[4]

Jensen's surveys of Russian literature testify to the breadth of his reading. He discusses, often censoriously but with considerable insight, modern tendencies within Russian literature: Merežkovskij's "superficial Nietzscheanism and coquettish worship of beauty," the symbolists' cult of the ego, the "cruel naturalism" and cynicism in the "sexually oriented, pornographic" works of Arcybašev, Andreev, Ajzman and Anatolij Kamenskij, the poems of Michail Kuzmin with their tinge of homosexuality, "which in its somewhat veiled form is even more loathsome to the majority while perhaps inviting to a few," the "fumbling opacity" of Andrej Belyj, and so on. In "the most recent tendencies" in Russian literature Jensen saw "a great deal of immaturity, presumption, affectation, and unsoundness," but he also observed "a vitality" and a "bold search for new subjects and ideals," which in its turn "reveals an ardent, even if misdirected need to reform society and build something new on the ruins of the old."[5]

Despite his dismissive attitude to contemporary Russian literature, Jensen made sure that the Nobel Library acquired a large number of the works of the authors of that generation. The acquisitions were of course governed by Jensen's own tastes. There are, for example, several of the works of the now forgotten Nikolaj Krašeninnikov (whose novel *The Misses* is seen by Jensen as "a gleam of light [...] in the darkness of pessimism"[6]), while the most important works of Andrej Belyj were not acquired until after Jensen's death. One can also see that the authors who were at some time discussed in connection with the Nobel Prize are represented extensively in the library—Maksim Gor'kij, Dmitrij Merežkovskij, and Ivan Bunin (who was awarded the prize in 1933).

In addition to the books from the beginning of this century, the Nobel Library owns a number of books published before the foundation of the Nobel Institute—works by Catherine II, Nikolaj Novikov, Gavrila Deržavin, Denis Fonvizin, Fedor Dostoevskij—and after the overthrow of the monarchy. The oldest printed work in Russian in the library is Lomonosov's *Drevnjaja russkaja istorija*, published in St. Petersburg in 1766. Other rarities are Nikolaj Karamzin's history of Russia in a German translation (1820–33) and a second edition of Astolphe de Custine's *La Russie en 1839* (Brussels 1844). A rare book from a later period is the notorious report by M. Lacis on the Cheka's "struggle against the counter-revolution" (*Črez-vyčajnye Komissii po bor'be s kontr-revoljuciej*, Moscow 1921). Among important journals mention should be made of *Letopis' Doma Literatorov* (Petersburg 1921–22), *Russkaja Kniga* and *Novaja Russkaja Kniga* (Berlin 1921–23), and *Sovremennye zapiski* (Paris 1920–39). Considerable sections of the Nobel Library's Russian collection have been acquired by donation. A donation of historical interest was made in 1920 when the library received thirty-one of the first books published by the Soviet-Russian State Publisher (Gosizdat) after its foundation in 1919 (among them Majakovskij's *Skazka o dezertire* [The Tale of a Deserter]) through the agency of the Russian Trade Delegation in Stockholm.

The bibliography covers books by Russian authors—and by foreign authors writing on Russian subjects—from the end of the 18th century until the Second World War, as well as journals (mainly from this century). It is of course far from comprehensive. The selection is based on an assessment of the rarity, significance and (in)accessibility of the titles.

Bengt Jangfeldt

1. A complete list of Alfred Jensen's works can be found in the article on Jensen by Artur Almhult in *Svenskt biografiskt lexikon*, XX, 1984, pp. 166-68.
2. The letters have been published by Nils Åke Nilsson: "Eight Letters from Valerij Brjusov to Alfred Jensen", *Studia slavica Gunnaro Gunnarsson sexagenario dedicata*, Uppsala 1960, pp. 70-81.
3. Alfred Jensen, "En rysk världstragedi", *Ord och Bild*, 1906: 11, p. 620.
4. Alfred Jensen, "Nyaste strömningar i den ryska litteraturen", *Finsk Tidskrift*, LXXIII, 1912, p. 266.
5. *Loc. cit.*, passim.
6. *Loc. cit.*, p. 281.

Русская коллекция в Нобелевской библиотеке Шведской Академии

Нобелевская библиотека Шведской Академии была основана в 1901 г. в связи с учреждением Нобелевской премии по литературе (в соответствии с завещанием Альфреда Нобеля от 1896 г.). Уставом Нобелевского фонда от 1900 г. было установлено, что при Шведской Академии должны быть созданы Нобелевский комитет и Нобелевская библиотека.

В соответствии с регламентом комитета, Нобелевская библиотека собирает современную художественную литературу и произведения о современных писателях на разных языках и является на сегодняшний день чуть ли не самым крупным собранием современной литературы и истории литературы в Скандинавии.

Своей богатой коллекцией *slavica* и *russica* библиотека обязана в первую очередь шведскому слависту Alfred Jensen (1859–1921), который работал специалистом Нобелевского института по славянской литературе со дня основания библиотеки до своей смерти. В его обязанности входили "подготовка вопросов, связанных с премией, составление отчетов о новых работах, вышедших за границей, и осуществление переводов иностранных публикаций".

Альфред Енсен был ведущим славистом Швеции конца xix — начала xx-го столетия. Он имел огромное значение для собрания славянской беллетристики в Нобелевской библиотеке и внес решающий вклад как переводчик и популяризатор славянской литературы. Енсен был полиглотом и большим знатоком литературы различных славянских стран. В 1896–97 гг. вышли два тома путевых заметок, *Slavia*, в 1898 г. *Ryska skaldeporträtt. Kultur- och litteraturhistoriska bilder från Ryssland från 1700-talet fram till 1800-talets mitt* (Портреты русских писателей. Культурные и историко-литературные картины России с 18-го века до середины 19-го) и в 1908 г. *Rysk kulturhistoria* (История русской культуры) в трех томах. Среди его переводов с русского языка следует в первую очередь назвать *Евгений Онегин* (1889) и другие произведения Пушкина, *Демон* и другие стихи Лермонтова (1893), *Тарас Бульба* Гоголя (1883), *Дневник писателя* (1915) и *Бедные люди* (1920) Достоевского, *Senilia* Тургенева (1883), политические статьи Александра Герцена (1916), сборники *Ryska berättelser* (Русские рассказы), 1916, и *Rysk litteratur* (Русская литература), 1912. Он переводил и польских поэтов (*Polska skalder* [Польские писатели], тт. 1–4, 1899–1906, *Pan Tadeusz* Мицкевича, 1898), и чешского поэта Ярослава Врхлицкого, о котором он написал книгу *Jaroslav*

Vrchlický. En litterär studie (Ярослав Врхлицкий. Литературное исследование), 1904, переведенную на чешский язык два года спустя. Его книга о Тарасе Шевченко, *Taras Schewtschenko. Ein ukrainisches Dichterleben* (Wien 1916), вышла на украинском языке в 1921 г.[1]

Енсен внимательно следил за новой русской литературой и переписывался со многими писателями, в том числе с В. Брюсовым, чьи письма к Енсену хранятся в Королевской библиотеке в Стокгольме.[2] Брюсов посылал Енсену свои книги с посвящением, и Енсен написал статью о поэте, многократно посещавшем Швецию, где он "приобрел новые познания, которые несомненно использует в своей необычайной, страстной лирике."[3] Среди тех, кто посылал Енсену книги с посвящением, был и Константин Бальмонт. Оба поэта характеризуются Енсеном, как "в высшей степени редкостные таланты и выдающиеся мастера стиха".[4]

Обзоры русской литературы, сделанные Енсеном, свидетельствуют о его начитанности. Он обсуждает — часто осуждающе, но с большой осведомленностью — современные течения в русской литературе: "поверхностное ницшеанство и кокетливое поклонение красоте" Мережковского, эго-культ символистов, "грубый натурализм" и цинизм сексуально-порнографических произведений Арцыбашева, Андреева, Айзмана и Анатолия Каменского, окрашенные гомосексуализмом стихи Михаила Кузмина, "которые в своей несколько завуалированной форме еще более отвратительны большинству и, может быть, привлекательны для некоторых", "колеблющуюся туманность" Андрея Белого и т.д. Енсен видел в "новейших течениях" русской литературы "много незрелости, слишком высокое самомнение, искусственность и болезненность", но он отметил также ее "жизнеспособность" и "смелые поиски новых тем и идеалов", что, в свою очередь, "говорит о горячей, хотя и неправильно направленной потребности переделать общество, построить что-то новое на руинах старого".[5]

Несмотря на свое недоброжелательное отношение к современной русской литературе, Енсен заботился о том, чтобы Нобелевская библиотека приобретала произведения писателей этого поколения. Покупка книг, конечно, во многом зависела от вкусов Енсена. Так, например, в собраниях библиотеки найдется много произведений забытого ныне Николая Крашенинникова (его роман *Барышни* Енсен считал "лучом света [...] во тьме пессимизма"[6]), между тем как самые значительные книги Белого были приобретены только после смерти Енсена. Можно также заметить, что писатели, которые обсуждались в связи с Нобелевской премией, широко представлены в библиотеке: Максим Горький, Дмитрий Мережковский, Иван Бунин (получивший премию в 1933 г.).

Кроме книг начала века, в Нобелевской библиотеке имеется много произведений, изданных как до основания Нобелевского института — Екатерины II, Н. Новикова, Г. Державина, Д. Фонвизина, Ф. Достоевского — так и после падения царизма. Самое старое русское печатное произведение в библиотеке — *Древняя русская история* Ломоносова, изданная в Санкт-Петербурге в 1766 г. К другим редкостям относятся русская история Н. Карамзина в переводе на немецкий язык (1820–33 гг.) и 2-е издание книги Астольфа де Кюстина *La Russie en 1839* (Bruxelles 1844). К числу редких современных изданий принадлежит знаменитый отчет М. Лациса о "борьбе ЧК с контр-революцией" (*Чрезвычайные Комиссии по борьбе с контр-революцией*, Москва 1921). Среди важных журналов можно указать на *Летопись Дома литераторов* (Петербург 1921–22), *Русскую Книгу* и *Новую Русскую Книгу* (Берлин 1921–23), *Современные записки* (Париж 1920–39). Большая часть собрания русских книг в Нобелевской библиотеке поступила в качестве даров. Исторически интересный дар был сделан в 1920 г., когда библиотека получила через посредство Торгового представительства Р.С.Ф.С.Р в Швеции от советского Государственного издательства тридцать одну из первых книг, изданных основанным в 1919 г. издательством, в том числе *Сказку о дезертире* Маяковского.

Библиография охватывает книги русских писателей, а также иностранных, писавших на русские темы, в период с конца 18-го века до второй мировой войны, также как и журналы (большей частью 20-го века). Разумеется, она далеко не полная. Выбор построен на оценке книг в соответствии с их редкостью, важностью и (не)доступностью.

Бенгт Янгфельдт

1. Полный список произведений Альфреда Енсена есть в статье Artur Almhult о нем в *Svenskt biografiskt lexikon*, XX, 1984, с. 166–68.
2. Письма опубликованы в статье Nils-Åke Nilsson, "Eight Letters from Valerij Brjusov to Alfred Jensen", *Studia slavica Gunnaro Gunnarsson sexagenario dedicata*, Uppsala 1960, с. 70–81.
3. Alfred Jensen, "En rysk världstragedi", *Ord och Bild*, 1906:11, с. 620.
4. Alfred Jensen, "Nyaste strömningar i den ryska litteraturen", *Finsk tidskrift*, LXXIII, 1912, с. 266.
5. *Там же*, passim.
6. *Там же*, с. 281.

Table of Contents
Содержание

BOOKS

Abramov, Jakov Vasil'evič

V. N. Karazin, ego žizn' i obščestvennaja dejatel'nost': biografičeskij očerk Ja. V. Abramova. S portretom Karazina, gravirovannym v Lejpcige Gedanom. S.-Peterburg: Tipogr. T-va Obščestvennaja pol'za, 1891. 96 s. (Žizn' zamečatel'nych ljudej)

Achmatova, Anna
(Anna Andreevna Gorenko)

Belaja staja: stichotvorenija Anny Achmatovoj. 2 izd. S.-Peterburg: Kn-vo Prometej, 1918. 135 s.

Anno domini MCMXXl. Petropolis, 1921. 101 s. (2.000)

Achšarumov, Ivan Dmitrievič

Čužoe imja: roman v trech častjach. S.-Peterburg: Tipografija E. Evdokimova, 1896. xii, 224, 178 s.
S. v-xii: Vl. Sorokin: N. D. Achšarumov. Portr.

Sobranie sočinenij Ivana Dmitrieviča Achšarumova. T. 1-3. S.-Peterburg: Izd. knigoprodavca N. G. Martynova, 1894-1899.
T. 1: Povesti i razskazy. 1894. 362 s.
T. 2: Potomok roda Vetriščevych: roman. 1894. 287 s.
T. 3: Sjurpriz – Dača v usad'be: razskazy; K čemu: roman; Fantazer: komedija. 1899. 421 s.

Aduev, Nikolaj Al'fredovič

Tovarišč Ardatov: povest'-grotesk. Moskva: Izd. Federacija, 1929. 98 s. (3.000)

Afanas'ev, Aleksandr Nikolaevič

Narodnyja russkija legendy sobrannye A. N. Afanas'evym. Moskva: Izd. N. Ščepkina i K. Soldatenkova, 1859. 203 s.

Narodnyja russkija skazki. 3 izd., dopoln. biografičeskim očerkom i ukazateljami pod red. A. E. Gruzinskago. T. 1-2 Moskva: 1897. li, 351, 445, xxiv: ill.
S. v-li: A. N. Afanas'ev: biografičeskij očerk. Portr.

Afanas'ev, Leonid Nikolaevič

Stichotvorenija Leonida Afanas'eva. T. 1-2. S.-Peterburg: Tipogr. V. V. Komarova, 1896–1901.
T. 1: 1885–1895. 1896. 264 s.
T. 2: 1897–1900. 1901. 448 s.

Ajchenval'd, Julij Isaevič

Kritičeskij al'manach. Kn. II: Š. Bodlėr – B. Zajcev – A. Strindberg – M. Meterlink – G. Ibsen – E. Zolja – St. Pšibyševskij – V. Seroševskij. Moskva: Tipogr. Obščestvennaja pol'za, 1910. 187 s.

Poėty i poėtessy.
Aleksandr Blok – N. Gumilev – Anna Achmatova – Mariėtta Šaginjan. Moskva: Severnye dni, 1922. 91 s. (2.000)

Siluėty russkich pisatelej. Vyp. 1-3. Moskva: Izd. Naučnago Slova, 1906-1910.
Vyp. 1: Batjuškov – Krylov – Griboedov – Ryleev – Puškin – Gogol' – Lermontov – Baratynskij – Tjutčev – Sergej Aksakov – Ogarev – Gončarov – Pleščeev i Pomjalovskij (sravnitel'nye charakteristiki) – Gleb Uspenskij – Garšin

– Korolenko – Čechov. 1906. 243 s.

Vyp. 2: Kol'cov – Nekrasov – Majkov – Ščerbina – Fet – Polonskij – Aleksej Tolstoj – Dostoevskij – Lev Tolstoj – Turgenev – Ostrovskij – Slepcov. 1908. 180 s.

Priložemie: Deti u Čechova

Vyp. 3: Kozlov – Venevitinov – Aleksandr Odoevskij – Poležaev – Jazykov – Levitov – Maksim Gor'kij – Leonid Andreev – Valerij Brjusov – Fedor Sologub – Ivan Bunin – Boris Zajcev. 1910. 138 s.

Ajzman, David Jakovlevič

Svetlyj bog: skazka v četyrech dejstvijach. Peterburg: Gos. izd., 1920. 64 s.

Ternovyj kust: p'esa v 4-ch dejstvijach. Peterburg: Gos. izd., 1920. 67 s.

Aksakov, Ivan Sergeevič

Slavjanskij vopros 1860–1886. Stat'i iz "Dnja", "Moskvy", "Moskviča" i "Rusi". Reči v Slavjanskom Komitete v 1876, 1877 i 1878 gg. Moskva: Tipogr. M. G. Volčaninova, 1886. vii, 791 s. (Sočinenija I. S. Aksakova)

Aksakov, Konstantin Sergeevič

Polnoe sobranie sočinenij Konstantina Sergeeviča Aksakova. T. 1-3. Moskva: V Universitetskoj tipogr., 1875–1889.

T. 1, izd. pod red. I. S. Aksakova: Sočinenija istoričeskija. 1889. vii, 599 s.

T. 2: Sočinenija filologičeskija. Č. I. 1875. xii, 660 s.

T. 3: Sočinenija filologičeskija. Č. II: Opyt russkoj grammatiki, 1880. xxxvi, viii, 470, 151 s. (pribavlenie)

Aksakov, Sergej Timofeevič

Semejnaja chronika i Vospominanija S. T. Aksakova. 9 izd. Moskva: Izd. A. A. Karceva, 1898. 436 s.

Sobranie sočinenij S. T. Aksakova. T. 1-6. Moskva: Izd. A. A. Karceva, 1895-1896.

T. 1: Semejnaja chronika i Vospominanija. 1895. 436 s.

T. 2: Detskie gody Bagrova-vnuka, služaščie prodolženiem Semejnoj chroniki. 1895. 324 s.

T. 3: Semejnyja i literaturnyja vospominanija. Očerki, pis'ma, stichotvorenija. 1895. 450 s.

T. 4: Literaturnyja i teatral'nyja vospominanija i Proizvedenija rannjago perioda. 1896. 472 s.

T. 5: Zapiski ob užen'e ryby. 1896. 306 s.: ill.

T. 6: Zapiski ružejnago ochotnika orenburgskoj gubernii. 1896. 32 s.: ill.

—> Slovar' literaturnych tipov: Aksakov...
—> Smirnov, V. D.: Aksakovy...

Aksakovy —> Smirnov, V. D.: Aksakovy, ich žizn'...

Al'bom Puškinskoj vystavki ustroennoj Obščestvom Ljubitelej Rossijskoj Slovesnosti v zalach Istoričeskago muzeja v Moskve 29 maja– 13 ijunja 1899 g. Pod nabljudeniem Komissii O.L.R. po ustrojstvu Puškinskoj vystavki. Moskva: Izd. K. A. Fišer, 1899. 86, 22 s.: ill. [folio]

Al'bov, Michail Nilovič

Povesti i razskazy. 2. dopoln. izd. S.-Peterburg: Knižnyj sklad V. I. Gubinskago, 1888. 513 s.

Den' Itoga – O ljudjach – Konec Nevedomoj ulicy – Dissonans – Iz nenapisannago romana "Prizraki" – Krestonoscy

Rjasa: roman M. Al'bova. S.-Peterburg: Izd. T-va M.O. Vol'f, [n.d.], 384 s.

Ryb'i stony. S.-Peterburg, 1888. 55 s.

Alfavitnyj ukazatel' sovetskich uzakonenij i rasporjaženij po voennomu vedomstvu, ob"javlennych za vremja s 1-go oktjabrja 1918 goda po 1-oe marta 1919 goda. Vypusk 2-oj. Sost. N. Morozov. Moskva: Gos. izd., 1919. 48 s.

Al'ferov, A., Gruzinskij, A.

Sbornik voprosov po istorii russkoj literatury (kurs srednej školy). Izd. desjatoe. Moskva: Knigoizd. Škola, 1915. 86 s.

Al'ferov, A. —> Desjat' čtenij...

Al'manach russkich dejatelej konca XIX stoletija. Izd. Germana Aleksandroviča Gol'dberga. S.-Peterburg: Tipogr. Isidora Gol'dberga, 1897. 1250 s. Portr.

Al'manach Zemlja i fabrika. N° 6. Gos. Akc. Izd. Ob-vo Zemlja i fabrika, 1929. 339 s.
G. K. Nikiforov: Ženščina – A. Gitovič: Ravnovesie - stichi – Ė. Bagrickij: TBC - stichi – Gl. Alekseev: Gribok - rasskaz – N. Ljaško: Jagoda - skazka; Beregovoj slovograj – Nik. Dement'ev: Na koncerte - stichi – Mich. Gerasimov: Gora - stichi – Ivan Erošin: Altaj-

skie pesni; Novoe ruž'e; Čerep – Vasilij Rjachovskij: Chozjain

Almazov, Boris Nikolaevič

Sočinenija B. N. Almazova v trech tomach, s portretom, gravirovannym na stali, i kratkim biografičeskim očerkom. T. 1-3. Moskva: Universitetskaja tipogr., 1892.
T. 1: Stichotvorenija. 460 s.
T. 2: Stichotvorenija. 497 s., vi. Alfavitnyj ukazatel' vsech stichotvorenij
T. 3: Proza: Katen'ka (povest') — Pansion dlja blagorodnych devic (rasskaz) — Stat'i kritičeskija i bibliografičeskija — Stat'i dlja junošestva — Fel'etony iz Moskvitjanina. 668 s.

Altaev, Al. (M. V. Jamščikova) **& Feliče, Ar.** (L. A. Jamščikova)

Ljubov' velikaja: sbornik rasskazov i skazok. Ill. chudožnika V.V. Spasskogo. Peterburg: Gos. izd., 1920. 147 s.: ill.

Pod znamenem "Bašmaka": krest'janskaja vojna v Germanii: istoričeskaja povest' iz XVI veka. Risunki K. N. Fridberga. Peterburg: Gos. izd., 1920. 217 s.: ill.

Amfiteatrov, Aleksandr Valentinovič
(Old Gentleman)

Nedavnie ljudi: Stepan Stambulov – Sofijskoe žit'e-byt'e – O Černjaeve – Pamjati Polonskago – Pamjatnik Carju-Osvoboditelju – Zachar'in – Moskovskij gorodskoj golova Alekseev – Tainstvennaja korrespondencija. S 6 portretami: S. N. Stambulova – Kn. Ferdinanda Bolgarskago – Kn. Borisa Tyrnovskago

– M. G. Černjaeva – M. D. Skobeleva – Imperatora Aleksandra II. S.-Peterburg: Tipogr. T-va Chudož. Reč', 1901. 305 s.: ill.

Otravlennaja sovest': roman – V strane ljubvi. S.-Peterburg: Izd. A. S. Suvorina, 1898. 422 s.

Stoličnaja bezdna: ėtjudy, listki, tipy i kartinki. S.-Peterburg: Izd. T-va. P. Taburno, 1900. 339 s.

Vos'midesjatniki: roman v dvuch tomach. 1-2. 5. izd. Berlin: Izd. Grani, 1923.
    T. 1: Razrušennyja voli. Č. 1: Molodo-zeleno. 316 s. Č. 2. Svadebnyj chmel'. 355 s.
    T. 2: Krach duši. Č. 3: Vlast' tela. 375 s. Č. 4: Solnce zachodit. 332 s. S. 327-332: Spisok sobstvennych imen, prinadležaščich dejstvitel'no suščest-vovavšim ili suščestvujuščim licam, upominaemym v romane "Vos'mide-sjatniki"

Andreev, Leonid Nikolaevič

Car' Golod: predstavlenie v pjati kart-inach s prologom. Risunki E. Lansere. SPB: Izd. Šipovnik, 1908. 126 s.: ill.

Gubernator: povest'. Berlin: J. La-dyschnikow, [n.d.], 68 s.

Mysl': drama v šesti kartinach. Berlin: J. Ladyschnikow, 1922. 68 s.

Polnoe sobranie sočinenij Leonida Andreeva. S portretom avtora. T. 1-8. S.-Peterburg: Izd. T-va A. F. Marks, 1915. T. 8: s. 322-325: Alfavitnyj uka-zatel' sočinenij L. Andreeva

Prekrasnyja Sabinjanki: istoričeskoe proisšestvie v trech častjach. Berlin: J. Ladyschnikow, [n.d.], 38 s.

Razskaz o semi povešennych. S.-Peterburg: Biblioteka Naše čtenie, 1909. 93 s.

Razskazy. T. 1-2. S.-Peterburg: Izd. T-va Znanie, 1901–1906.
    T. 1: 1901. 201 s. Bol'soj šlem – An-geloček – Molčanie – Valja – Razskaz o Sergee Petroviče – Na reke – Lož' – U okna – Žili-byli – V temnuju dal'
    T. 2: 1906. 303 s. Mysl' – V tumane – Žizn' Vasilija Fivejskago – Prizraki – Krasnyj smech.

—> Arabažin, K. I.: Leonid Andreev... —> Bocjanovskij, V. T.: Leonid Andreev... —> Kniga o Leonide Andreeve...

Andreev, L. —> Ščit: literaturnyj sbornik...

Andreevič (pseud.) —> Solov'ev, E. A.

Andreevskij, I. E. —> Ėnciklopedičeskij slovar'...

Andreevskij, Sergej Arkad'evič

Stichotvorenija 1878–1887. 2 izd. S.-Peterburg: Tipogr. A. S. Suvorina, 1898. 306 s.

Annenkova-Bernar', N.
(Družinina, Nina Pavlovna)

Razskazy i očerki. Moskva: Izd. red. žurnala Russkaja mysl', 1901. 463 s.
    Petlja – Jubilej aktrisy – Kara – Ne-zabvennaja – Ona – Sny – Goremyč-naja – Krestnyja – Ne chotel

Annenskaja, Aleksandra Nikitična

N. V. Gogol', ego žizn' i literaturnaja dejatel'nost': biografičeskij očerk A. N. Annenskoj. 2-e izd. S portretom Gogolja, gravirovannym v Lejpcige Gedanom. S.-Peterburg: Tipogr. T-va Obščestvennaja pol'za, 1894. 80 s. (Žizn' zamečatel'nych ljudej)

Annenskij, Innokentij Fedorovič

Kniga otraženij. S.-Peterburg: Tipogr. Trud, 1906. 213 s.
Problema Gogolevskago jumora – Dostoevskij do katastrofy – Umirajuščij Turgenev – Tri social'nych dramy – Drama nastroenij – Bal'mont-lirik

Anton Pavlovič Čechov, ego žizn' i sočinenija: sbornik istoriko-literaturnych statej. Sostavil V. Pokrovskij. Moskva: Tipogr. G. Lissnera i D. Sobko, 1907. 1062 s.

Apollon: literaturnyj al'manach. S.-Peterburg: Knigoizd. Apollon, 1912. 161 s.: ill.
Stichotvorenija Anny Achmatovoj, K. Bal'monta, Aleksandra Bloka, Andreja Belago, N. Gumileva, M. Zenkeviča, Incitatusa, Sergeja Klyčkova, Nikolaja Kljueva, M. Kuzmina, Benedikta Lifšica, O. Mandel'štama, M. Moravskoj, Henri de Régnier (perevod Maks. Vološina)

Apollonov, S.

Stichotvorenija. Moskva: Tipogr. Borisenko i Breslin, 1900. 140 s.

Apraksin, Aleksandr Dmitrievič

Gore i radost': razskazy i povesti. S.-Peterburg: Tipogr. A. S. Suvorina, 1889. 201s.
Krasavec-knjaz' – Bezputnaja žizn' – Terpi ljubja – Mokraja kurica – Mišura – Nerovnja – Opravdannyj

Kain i Avel': roman iz semejnoj chroniki knjazej Sumskich A. D. Apraksina. S.-Peterburg: Tipogr. V. V. Komarova, 1890. 232 s.: ill.

Nezemnyja sozdanija i drugie razskazy. S.-Peterburg: Tipogr. V. V. Komarova, 1890. 165 s.

Aptekman, Osip Vasil'evič

Gleb Ivanovič Uspenskij. Moskva: Kooperativnoe izd. Zadruga 1922. 17s. (1.000)

Apuchtin, Aleksej Nikolaevič

Sočinenija A. N. Apuchtina. 4 posmertnoe, dopoln. izd. s portretom, faksimile i biografičeskim očerkom. S.-Peterburg: Tipogr. A. S. Suvorina, 1900. xxii, 658 s.

Arabažin, Konstantin Ivanovič

Leonid Andreev: itogi tvorčestva. Literaturno-kritičeskij ėtjud. S.-Peterburg: Obščaja Pol'za, 1910. 279 s.

Arcybašev, Michail Petrovič

Dikie: povest'. Berlin: Izd. I. P. Ladyžnikova, 1923. 129 s.

Razskazy. T. 1, 2, 4. S.-Peterburg, 1908.

T. 1: 3 izd. Paša Tumanov – Kuprijan – Podpraporščik Gololobov – Krov' – Smech – Bunt – Žena – Užas. 345 s.

T. 2: 2 izd. dopoln. Iz podvala — Smert' Lande — Teni utra – Krovavoe pjatno — Iz zapisok odnogo čeloveka — Bog. 283 s.

T. 4: Moskva: Moskovskoe knigoizd., 1908. Čelovečeskaja volna — Milliony. 284 s.

Sanin. Berlin, 1909. 342 s.

Aristov, Nikolaj Jakovlevič

Pervyja vremena christianstva v Rossii po cerkovno-istoričeskomu soderžaniju russkich letopisej. S.-Peterburg: Izd. V. K. Simanskago, 1888. 188 s.

Arsen'ev, Aleksandr Vasil'evič

Sbornik stichotvorenij, poëm i razskazov A. V. Arsen'eva. S predisloviem P. I. Vejnberga, vin'etkoj chudožnika V. S. Krjukova i portretom avtora. S.-Peterburg: Izd. A. A. Ivanovoj, 1899. xxx, 162 s.

S. i-xxx: Biografičeskij očerk

Slovar' pisatelej drevnjago perioda russkoj literatury IX-XVII veka (862–1700 gg.). Sostavil A. V. Arsen'ev pod red. O. F. Millera. Priloženie k "karte dlja nagljadnago obozrenija istorii i chronologii russkoj literatury". S.-Peterburg: Izd. knižnago magazina Novago Vremeni, 1882. 136 s.

Arsen'ev, K. K. —> Novyj énciklopedičeskij slovar'...

Aseev, Nikolaj Nikolaevič

Dnevnik poëta. Leningrad: Priboj, 1929. 226 s.

Sobranie stichotvorenij v trech tomach. 2-3. Moskva: Gos. izd., 1928–1931.

T. 2: Stichotvorenija 1925–27 gg. 1928. 184 s.

T. 3: Poëmy i skazki. 1931. 255 s.

T. 4, dopoln.: Stichi polednich let. 1930. 189 s.

Astrov, V. —> Legendy, skazanija... Pod red. Vladimira Astrova...

Auslender, Sergej Abramovič

Zolotyja jabloki: razskazy. Moskva: Knigoizd. Grif, 1908. 215 s.: ill.

Avdeev, Michail Vasil'evič

Sočinenija M. V. Avdeeva. T. 1-2. Sanktpeterburg: Izd. F. Stellovskago, 1868–1870. (Sobranie sočinenij russkich avtorov)

T. 1: Tamarin: roman – Jasnye dni – Gory – Derevenskij vizit – Nynešnjaja ljubov' – Ognennyj zmej – Poezdka na kumys – Porjadočnyj čelovek – Na doroge – Dorožnyja zametki. 1868. 264 s.

T. 2: Podvodnyj kamen' – Mež dvuch ognej – Meščanskaja sem'ja – Pis'ma iz-za granicy. 1870. 330 s.

Avenarius, Vasilij Petrovič

Kniga bylin: svod izbrannych obrazcov russkoj narodnoj épičeskoj poëzii. Sostavil V. P. Avenarius. S portretom pevca bylin Rjabinina, raboty L. A. Serjakova, i risunkami A. V. Prochorova i N. N. Karazina. Izd. pjatoe, pečatannoe so vtorogo bez peremen. Moskva: Izd. knigoprodavca A. D. Stupina, 1898. xxiv, 320, xxxix: ill.

Puščin v sele Michajlovskom: stranica iz žizni Puškina. Peterburg: Gos. izd., 1920. 39 s.

Za careviča: istoričeskaja trilogija V. P. Avenariusa. Č. 1: Tri venca: istoričeskaja povest' iz vremen pervago samozvanca (Pererabotana dlja junošestva iz romana togo-že nazvanija). S 12 otdel'nymi risunkami. S.-Peterburg: Izd. knižnago magazina P. V. Lukovnikova, 1901. 366 s.

Averčenko, Arkadij Timofeevič

Kipjaščij kotel: sbornik razskazov. Konpol': Knigoizd. Kultura G. Pachalova, O. Cigojan i M. Šakaj, 1922. 158 s.

Rasskazy cinika. Praga: Izd. Plamja, 1925. 193 s.

Šutka mecenata: jumoristiceskij roman. Praga: Plamja, 1925. 192 s.

Averkiev, Dmitrij Vasil'evič

Povesti iz sovremennago byta D.V. Averkieva. Izd. tščatel'no peresm. i ispr. v trech tomach. S.-Peterburg: Tipogr. brat. Panteleevych, 1898.
    T. 1: Chmelevaja noč' – Licho. 396 s.
    T. 2: Veču ne byt'. 552 s.
    T. 3: Chudožnik Bezpalov i notarius Podleščikov. 498 s.

Avseenko, Vasilij Grigor'evič

Novye razskazy. S.-Peterburg: Tipogr. M. M. Stasjuleviča, 1899.
    T. 1: V ogne — Kar'era Vjazigina — Svadebnoe putešestvie — Stolknovenie — Ofelija — Noč' — Muž — Illjuzija —

Stepan Stepanovič — Gostinaja. 1899. 439 s. Peterburgskie očerki. T. 1-2. S.-Peterburg: Izd. A. S. Suvorina, 1900. 294, 300 s.

Avvakum, protopop—> Mjakotin, V. A.: Protopop Avvakum... —> Borozdin, A.K.: Protopop Avvakum...

Azbuka krasnoarmejca—> Moor, D., Azbuka krasnoarmejca...

Babel', Isaak Ėmmanuilovič

Istorija moej golubjatni. Pariž: Biblioteka novejših pisatelej, 1927. 63 s.
    Istorija moej golubjatni — Pervaja ljubov' — Ljubka Kozak — U bat'ki našego Machno — Konec Sv. Ipatija

Bachmetev, Evgenij

Sorok mesjacev v belom flote: 18 aprelja 1917 g. – 18 ijulja 1920 g. Rasskaz morjaka. Moskva: Gos. izd., 1921. 31 s. (Krasnaja knižka, 36; 100.000)

Bal'mont, Konstantin Dmitrievič

Belyj zodčij: tainstvo Četyrech Svetil'nikov. S.-Peterburg: Izd. Sirin, 1914. 324 s.

Dar zemli. Pariž: Knigoizd. Russkaja Zemlja, 1921. 159 s.

Fejnyja skazki: detskija pesenki. Moskva: Knigoizd. Grif, 1905. 81 s.

Gamajun: izbrannye stichi. Stokchol'm: Severnye ogni, 1921. 109 s.

Gde moj dom: očerki (1920–1923). Praga: Izd. Plamja, 1924. 182 s.

Gornyja veršiny: sbornik statej. Kn. 1. Moskva: Knigoizd. Grif, 1904. 209 s.

Jasen': videnie dreva. Moskva: Izd. K. F. Nekrasova, 1916. 237 s.

> *Ded.:* Skandinavu Al'fredu Iensenu ot davnišnjago počitatelja bogatoj sagami Skandinavii. K. Bal'mont. Prostory Sibirskich Snegov. 1916, mart

Kraj Ozirisa: egipetskie očerki. Moskva: Izd. M. i S. Sabašnikovych, 1914. 323 s.: ill.

Liturgija krasoty: stichijnye gimny. Moskva: Knigoizd. Grif, 1905. 234 s.

Marevo. Pariž: Izd. Franko-Russkaja Pečat' (Presse Franco-Russe), 1922. 130 s.
    Stichi 1917; 1920–1921; 1921

Moe-ej: Rossija. Praga: Izd. Plamja, 1923. 125 s.

Morskoe svečenie. S.-Peterburg-Moskva: Izd. T-va M. Vol'fe, [n. d.]. 259 s.

Pod novym serpom: roman v trech častjach. Berlin: Knigoizd. Slovo, 1923. 381 s.

Poėzija kak volšebstvo. Moskva: Knigoizd. Skorpion, 1915. 93 s.

> *Ded.:* Glubokouvažaemomu Al'fredu Iensenu ot strastnago počitatelja Skandinavii K. Bal'mont. 1916. II.17. Moskva, Brjusovskij p., 19

Polnoe sobranie stichov. Moskva: Izd. Skorpion 1904–1914.
    T. 1: Pod severnym nebom – V bezbrežnosti – Tišina. 4 izd. 1914. 267 s.
    T. 2: Gorjaščija zdanija – Budem kak Solnce. 1904. 405 s.
    T. 3: Budem kak Solnce. 3 izd. 1908. 234 s.
    T. 8: Zelenyj Vertograd. 2 izd. 1911. 153 s.

Pticy v vozduche: stroki napevnyja. S.P.B.: Izd. Šipovnik, 1908. 228 s.

Severnoe sijanie: stichi o Litve i Rusi. Pariž: Russkoe knižnoe delo Rodnik, 1931. 180 s.

Sobranie liriki. Kniga šestaja.: Tol'ko ljubov – Semicvetnik. Moskva: Izd. V.V. Pašukanisa, 1917. 206 s. (5.000 + 300 numerovannych)

Solnečnaja prjaža: izbornik 1890-1918. Moskva: Izd. M. i S. Sabašnikovych, 1921. 271 s. Portr.
    Izbornik sostavlen samim poėtom 1919 g. Portret risovan s natury togda že M. B. Sabašnikovoj-Vološinoj

> *In K. Bal'mont's hand:* NB. Stranicy, posvjaščennyja Skandinavii: 166, 167, 168, 246

Sonety solnca, meda i luny: pesnja mirov. Moskva: Izd. V.V. Pašukanisa, 1917. 272 s.

Svetlyj čas: izbrannye stichi. Paris: J. Povolozky, 1921. 69 s. (Miniatjurnaja biblioteka)

Vozdušnyj put': razskazy. Berlin: Izd. Ogon'ki, 1923. 199 s.

Žar-ptica: svirel' slavjanina. Moskva:

Knigoizd. Skorpion, 1907. 234 s.

Zlyja čary: kniga zakljatij. Moskva: Izd. žurnala Zolotoe runo, 1906. 116 s.

Zmeinye cvety. Moskva: Knigoizd. Skorpion, 1910. 248 s., xliii, ill.

Zovy drevnosti: gimny, pesni i zamysly drevnich: Egipet — Meksika — Majja — Peru — Chaldeja – Assirija — Indija-Iran — Kitaj — Japonija — Skandina-vija — Éllada — Bretan'. Berlin: Knigo-izd. Slovo, 1923. 319 s.

Quelques poèmes. Trad. du russe par A. de Holstein et René Ghil. Paris & Zürich: Éditions Georges Crès, 1916. 163 s.
    S. 9-24: Préface. S. 153-157: Index bibliographique: Œuvres de Constantin Balmont. 2 portr.

Visions solaires: Mexique — Égypte — Inde — Japon — Océanie. Trad. du russe avec une préface par Ludmila Savitzky. Seule traduction autorisée et approuvée par l'auteur. Ornée d'un portrait. Paris: Éditions Bossard, 1923. 338 s.

Barancevič, Kazimir Stanislavovič

Flirt i drugie razskazy. S.-Peterburg: Vladimirskaja Tipolitografija, 1901. 336 s.

Izgar (Staroe i Novoe): povesti i razska-zy. S.-Peterburg: Tipolitografija Éner-gija, 1905. 286 s.

Ptica nebesnaja: 40 razskazov Sar-mata: jumorističeskij sbornik. Moskva: Izd. 2-e knigoprodavca M. V. Kljukina, 1900. 363 s.

Rodnyja kartinki: 17 razskazov. Mosk-va: Universitetskaja tipogr., 1895. 368 s.

Barankevič, Ivan

Staryj Nil: rasskaz. Moskva: Gos. izd., 1920. 31 s.: ill. (Krasnaja knižka, 2)

Baratynskij, Evgenij Abramovič

Polnoe sobranie sočinenij E. A. Bara-tynskago. S portretom avtora, biografi-ej i ego pis'mami. V Kieve — V Charko-ve: Izd. Knigoprodavca-izdatelja F. A. Iogansona, 1894. viii, 404 s.

Barbjuss, A. —> Barbusse, Henri

Barbusse, Henri

Ogon': dnevnik odnogo vzvoda. Pere-vod s francuzskogo S. V. Gal'perina pod red. E. G. Lundberga. Moskva: Li-teraturno-izdatel'skij Otdel Narodnogo Komissariata po Prosveščeniju, 1919. 381 s.

Barjatinskij, Vladimir Vladimirovič

Vo dni Petra: istoričeskaja p'esa v 4-ch dejstvijach knjazja V. V. Barjatinskago. S.-Peterburg: Izd. A.S. Suvorina, 1900. 160 s.

Barsov, El'pidifor Vasil'evič

Slovo o polku Igoreve kak chudo-žestvennyj pamjatnik kievskoj družin-noj Rusi. T. 1-2. Moskva: V Universi-tetskoj tipogr. (M. Katkov), 1887.
    T. 1. 462, 16 s.; T. 2. 298, 17 s.

Barsov, Nikolaj Ivanovič

Neskoľko izsledovanij istoričeskich i razsuždenij o voprosach sovremennych. S.-Peterburg: Tipogr. M. M. Stasjuleviča, 1899. viii, 378 s.

Barsov, Nikolaj Pavlovič

Očerki russkoj istoričeskoj geografii. Geografija načaľnoj (Nestorovoj) letopisi. Izsledovanie N. P. Barsova, ė.o. Professora i Bibliotekarja Imperatorskago Varšavskago Universiteta. Izd. 2-e, ispravl. i dopol. alfavitnym ukazatelem. Varšava: Tipogr. K. Kovalevskago, 1885. iv, 371 s.

Barsukov, Aleksandr Platonovič

Razskazy iz russkoj istorii XVIII veka. Po archivnym dokumentam. Sanktpeterburg: Tipogr. T-va Obščestvennaja poľza, 1885. 284 s.

Bartenev, Petr Ivanovič —> Devjatnadcatyj vek...

Basanin, Mark

Klub kozackago dvorjanstva. S.-Peterburg: Izd. A. S. Suvorina, 1893. 243 s. (Novaja biblioteka Suvorina)

Novoselkovskoe kladbišče: roman Marka Basanina. S.-Peterburg: Izd. A. S. Suvorina, 1901. (Novaja biblioteka Suvorina)

Basov-Verchojancev, S.
(Sergej Aleksandrovič Basov)

Žadnyj mužik: skazka. Moskva: Gos. izd., 1920. 15 s.: ill. (Krasnaja knižka, 32; 100.000)

Batjuškov, Konstantin Nikolaevič

Sočinenija v proze i stichach Konstantina Batjuškova. Č. 1-2. 2 izd. Sanktpeterburg: V tipogr. I. Glazunova, 1834. 340, 270 s. Portr.

—> Majkov, L.: Batjuškov, ego žizn'...

Baye, Amour Auguste Louis Joseph Berthelot de

Kiev: la mère des villes russes. Vingtquatre gravures hors texte. Paris: Librairie Nilsson, 1896. 40 s., 24 ill.

Bazunov, S. A.

A. S. Dargomyžskij, ego žizn' i muzykaľnaja dejateľnosť: biografičeskij očerk S. A. Bazunova. S portretom Dargomyžskago i muzykaľnym priloženiem, sostojaščim iz vybora ego proizvedenij dlja fortepiano. S.-Peterburg: Tipogr. T-va Obščestvennaja poľza, 1894. 80, 16 s. (Žizn' zamečateľnych ljudej)

M. I. Glinka, ego žizn' i muzykaľnaja dejateľnosť: biografičeskij očerk S. A. Bazunova. S portretom Glinki i muzykaľnym priloženiem, sostojaščim iz vybora ego proizvedenij dlja fortepiano i penija. S.-Peterburg: Tipogr. T-va Obščestvennaja poľza, 1892. 78, 16 s. (Žizn' zamečateľnych ljudej)

A.N. Serov, ego žizn' i muzykal'naja dejatel'nost': biografičeskij očerk S.A. Bazunova. S portretom Serova i muzykal'nym priloženiem, sostojaščim iz vybora ego proizvedenij dlja fortepiano. S.-Peterburg: Tipogr. T-va Obščestvennaja pol'za, 1893. 79, 8 s. (Žizn' zamečatel'nych ljudej)

Bednyj, Dem'jan
(Efim Alekseevič Pridvornyj)

Čitaj Foma, nabirajsja uma. (Dlja junych gramoteev). Moskva: Gos. izd., 1919. 64 s.: ill. (Den' sovetskoj propagandy)

Divo divnoe: skazki. Moskva: Gos izd., 1921. 34 s.: ill

Krasnoarmejcy. Moskva: Gos. izd., 1919. 64 s.: ill.

Kuj železo, poka gorjačo: proletarskie basni. Moskva: Gos. izd., 1919. 55 s.: ill.

Mošna tuga, vsjak ej sluga: basni s illjustracijami chudož. K. N. Fridberga. Peterburg: Gos. izd., 1920. 32 s.: ill.

Mužiki: povest'. Moskva: Gos. izd., 1919. 48 s.: ill.

Pesni prošlogo. Moskva: Gos. izd., 1920. 30 s.: ill.

Vsjak Eremej pro sebja razumej: proletarskie basni. S risunkami chudožnika A. K. Moskva: Gos. izd., 1919. 46 s.: ill. + izd. 1921

Zemlja obetovannaja. Moskva: Gos. izd., 1920. 48 s.: ill.

Belinskij, V. G. —> Protopopov, M.A.: V.G. Belinskij...

Beljaev, Ivan Dmitrievič

Krest'jane na Rusi: izsledovanie o postepennom izmenenii značenija krest'jan v russkom obščestve. Sočinenie I. Beljaeva udostoennoe premij Demidova i gr. Uvarova. Moskva: Tipogr. Obščestva rasprostranenija poleznych knig Mochova, 1891. 296 s.

Beljaeva-Ėkzempljarskaja, S.

Modelirovanie odeždy po zakonam zritel'nogo vosprijatija. Odobreno Naučno-techničeskim sovetom švejnoj promyšlennosti. Moskva-Leningrad: Gizlegprom, 1934. 103 s.: ill.

Belkina, O.

Dezertir: rasskaz. Moskva: Gos. izd., 1920. 31 s.: ill.

Belogolovyj, Nikolaj Andreevič

S. P. Botkin, ego žizn' i medicinskaja dejatel'nost': biografičeskij očerk d-ra N.A. Belogolovogo. S portretom Botkina, gravirovannym v Peterburge K. Adtom. S.-Peterburg: Tipogr. T-va Obščestvennaja pol'za, 1892. 79 s. (Žizn' zamečatel'nych ljudej)

Vospominanija i drugija stat'i. S 3 portretami avtora, portretami P.I. Borisova, A.P. Jušnevskago, A.V. Podžio, Gr. M.T. Loris-Melikova, S.P. Botkina, M.E. Saltykova, vidom mogily N.A. Belogolovago i biogr. očerkom i vospomin. G.A. Džanšieva i V.A. Krylova. 3-e izd. Moskva: Tipo-lit. K.F. Aleksandrova, 1898. xxxviii, 560, x s.

Belokurov, Sergej Alekseevič

O biblioteke Moskovskich Gosudarej v XVI stoletii. Moskva: Tipogr. G. Lissnera i A. Gešelja, 1898. xvi, 336, Dxxvii (priloženija) s.

Belomorskija byliny zapisannya A. Markovym, s predisloviem V. F. Millera. Moskva 1901. 617 s. (Ėtnografičeskij otdel Imperatorskago obščestva ljubitelej estestvoznanija, antropologii i ėtnografii)

Belov, A. A.

Kak tri mužika-bednjaka stali žit' kommunoj. Peterburg: Gos. izd., 1920. 31 s. (Krasnaja knižka, 31; 100.000)

Belov, Evgenij Aleksandrovič

Russkaja istorija do reformy Petra Velikago. S.-Peterburg: Izd. L. F. Panteleeva, 1895. 479, 8 s.

Belyj, Andrej
(Boris Nikolaevič Bugaev)

Korolevna i rycari: skazki. Peterburg: Alkonost, 1919. 56 s.
   Obložka raboty chudožnika N. N. Kuprjanova, marka Ju. P. Annenkova

Kotik Letaev. Peterburg: Ėpocha, 1922. 292 s.

Peterburg: roman. Čast' vtoraja. Berlin: Ėpocha, 1922. 285 s. (3.000)

Serebrjanyj golub: roman. Č. 1-2. Berlin: Ėpocha, 1922. 299, 245 s. (3.000)

Belyja noči: Peterburgskij al'manach. SPB: Izd. T-va Vol'naja tipogr., 1907. 232 s.
   Stichi 28 poėtov

Bem, A. L. —> O Dostoevskom: sbornik...

Ber, Boris Vladimirovič

Stichotvorenija: Bolezni – Svetlyj bog – Priroda i serdce – Prorok – Sčastie – Severnaja legenda. S.-Peterburg: Tipogr. M. M. Stasjuleviča, 1897. ix, 254 s.

Berezovskij, V. V.

Russkaja muzyka: kritiko-istoričeskij očerk nacional'noj muzykal'noj školy v eja predstaviteljach (Glinka – Dargomyžskij – Balakirev, Borodin, Rimskij-Korsakov – Musorgskij – Čajkovskij – Kjui, Glazunov, Ljadov i dr.) – Serov, Rubinštejn i dr. S.-Peterburg: Tipogr. Ju. N. Ėrlich, 1898. xii, 524 s.

Bestužev-Rjumin, Konstantin Nikolaevič

Biografii i charakteristiki: V. N. Tatiščev, A. L. Šlecer, Karamzin, M. P. Pogodin, S. M. Solov'ev, S. V. Eševskij, A. F. Gil'ferding. S.-Peterburg: Tipogr. V. S. Balaševa, 1882. 358 s.

Bezobrazov, Pavel Vladimirovič

S. M. Solov'ev, ego žizn' i naučno-literaturnaja dejatel'nosť: biografičeskij očerk P. V. Bezobrazova. S portretom S. Solov'eva, gravirovannym v Peterburge K. Adtom. S.-Peterburg: Tipogr.

E. Evdokimova, 1894. 80 s. (Žizn' zamečatel'nych ljudej)

Bezymenskij, Aleksandr Il'ič

Pokolenie socializma. Moskva: Moloda-
ja gvardija, 1931. 47 s. (20.000)

Stichi delajut stal': s buksirom "Pravdy" na šturme proryvov zavodov im.
Petrovskogo i Lenina i zavoda "Krasnyj
Putilovec" 20-30 avgusta, 13-19 sen-
tjabrja. Moskva-Leningrad: Gos. izd.
chudožestvennoj literatury, 1930. 90
s. (10.000)

Bezymenskij, A. —> Udar za udarom...

Biblija: sireč knigi svjaščennago pisa-
nija vetchago i novago zaveta. Moskva:
V sinodal'noj tipogr. 1859.

Bil'basov, Vasilij Alekseevič

Istoričeskija monografii. T. 1-5. S.-Pe-
terburg: Tipogr. I. N. Skorochodova,
1901.
    T. 1: Muzej christianskago iskusst-
va — Legendarnyj obraz Kirilla i Mefodija — Ženščina-papa — Monachinja
Rosvita, pisatel'nica X veka — Dokumenty Matveja Parižskago — Čech Jan
Gus iz Gusinca i ego pis'ma iz tjur'my,
izdannyja Ljuterom — Ioanna Bezum-
naja — Abbat Polin'jak i pol'skoe bez-
korolev'e. 568 s.
    T. 2: Pojavlenie russkich na istori-
českoj scene — Pis'mo pervago Lžedi-
mitrija Klimentu VIII — Jurij Križanič
— Pamjati Von-Vizina — Adrian Gri-
bovskij, sostavitel' Zapisok o Ekaterine
II — Meždunarodnyja snošenija Rossii

s Germanieju — Prisoedinenie Kur-
ljandii – Rossija i Anglija v XVIII veke
— Pamjati Imperatricy Ekateriny II —
Zapiski sovremennikov o 1812 gode —
Samarin Gagarinu o Lermontove —
Opeka nad proizvedenijami Puškina —
Nakanun Krymskoj vojny — Narodnaja
škola v Rossii — Srednjaja škola 30 let
nazad — Peterburgskija pis'ma. 589 s.
    T. 3: Pervyja političeskija pis'ma
Ekateriny II — Vocarenie Ekateriny II
— Poslednie gol'štincy — Pochody po
Volge i Dnepru — Morovaja jazva
1770–1774 godov — Ekaterina II i graf
N. P. Rumjancov — Švedskaja vojna
1788–1790 godov — Ekaterina II i V.V.
Kachovskij — Zapiski V. R. Marčenki.
601 s.
    T. 4: Nikita Panin i Mers'e de La-
Riv'er — Ekaterina II i Mel'chior
Grimm — Denis Didro — Knjaz' de-Lin
– Princ Nassau-Zingen. 592 s.
    T. 5: Petr Vinejskij — Svetskij papa
— Rim i Vizantija v Kieve — Doktor-
skaja dissertacija v Kieve — Semilet-
njaja vojna po russkim istočnikam —
Zabytyj Panin —Tajna protivo-nelepa-
go obščestva — Vysylka princa iz Ros-
sii — Doktorskaja dissertacija v Peterburge — Nemirovskij kongress. 488 s.
S. 477-488: Spisok izdanij

Obzor inostrannych sočinenij o Ekaterine II. 1-2. Berlin: Stuhr'sche Buchhandlung, 1896. (Istorija Ekateriny
Vtoroj. T. 12)
    T. 1: 1744–1796. viii, 564 s.
    T. 2: 1797–1896. viii, 576 s.

Biznes: sbornik literaturnogo centra
konstruktivistov pod red. Kornelja Zelinskogo i Il'i Sel'vinskogo. Moskva:
Gos. izd., 1929. 260 s.

K. Zelinskij, I. Sel'vinskij, B. Agapov, N. Aduev, E. Bagrickij, E. Gabrilovič, G. Gauzner, V. Inber, V. Lugovskoj, I. Panov (D. Tumannyj), A. Kvjatkovskij

Blok, Aleksandr Aleksandrovič

Dvenadcat'. S predisloviem P. Suvčinskago. Sofija: Rossijsko-bolgarskoe knigoizd., [1921?]. 36 s.

Dvenadcat' – Skify. 6. izd. Petrograd-Moskva: Izd. Petrograd, 1924. 32 s. Obložka raboty V. D. Zamirajlo

Sobranie sočinenij Aleksandra Bloka. 1-5, 7, 9. Berlin: Épocha, 1923.
T. 1: Stichotvorenija. Kn. pervaja 1898–1904: Ante lucem — Stichi o prekrasnoj dame — Rasput'ja. 249 s. Portr.
T. 2: Stichotvorenija, Kn. vtoraja 1904–1916: Puzyri zemli — Nočnaja fialka — Raznye stichotvorenija — Gorod — Snežnaja maska — Faina — Vol'nye mysli. 283 s. Portr.
T. 3: Stichotvorenija. Kn. tret'ja 1907–1916: Strašnyj mir — Vozmezdie — Jamby — Ital'janskie stichi — Raznye stichotvorenija — Arfy i skripki — Karmen — Solov'inyj sad — Rodina — O čem poet veter. 271 s. Portr.
T. 4: Poemy. Stichotvorenija. Proza 1907–1921: Dvenadcat' — Skify — Poslednie stichotvorenija — Vozmezdie. Proza. 162 s. Portr.
T. 5: Teatr 1906–1919: Balagančik — Korol' na ploščadi — Dialog o ljubvi, poèzii i gosudarstvennoj službe — Neznakomka — Pesnja sud'by — Roza i krest — Ramzes. 388 s. Portr.
T. 7: Stat'i. Kn. pervaja 1906–1921: Liričeskie stat'i — Rossija i intelligencija — Molnii iskusstva — O naznače-

nii poèta. 346 s.
T. 9: Stat'i. Kn. tret'ja 1907–1921: O teatre. 334 s. Portr.

Sobranie stichotvorenij. Kn. 1-3. Moskva: Knigoizd. Musaget, 1911–1912.
Kn.1: Stichi o prekrasnoj dame (1898–1904). 2 izd., ispr. i dopoln., 1921. 208 s.
Kn. 2: Nečajannaja radost' (1904-1906). 2 izd., dopoln., 1912. 151 s.
Kn. 3: Snežnaja noč' (1907–1910). 1912. 194 s.

Stichotvorenija. Kn. 1-3. Berlin: Knigoizd. Slovo, 1922. Cvetnaja obložka raboty N. D. Milioti
Kn. 1: 1898–1904: Ante lucem — Stichi o prekrasnoj dame — Rasput'ja. 254 s. Portr..
Kn. 2: 1904–1908: Vstuplenie — Puzyri zemli — Nočnaja fialka — Raznye stichotvorenija — Gorod — Snežnaja maska — Faina — Volnyja mysl'. 335 s.
Kn. 3: 1907–1916: Strašnyj mir — Vozmezdie — Jamby — Ital'janskie stichi — Raznyja stichotvorenija — Arfy i skripki — Karmen — Solov'inyj sad — Rodina — O čem poet veter. 327 s.

—> Čukovskij, K.I.: Kniga ob Aleksandre Bloke... —> Ob Aleksandre Bloke: stat'i...

Boborykin, Petr Dmitrievič

Sobranie romanov, povestej i razskazov P. D. Boborykina v 12 tomach. T. 1-2, 5-12. S.-Peterburg: Izd. A. F. Marksa, 1897 (Priloženie k žurnalu Niva na 1897 g.)
T. 1: Kitaj-gorod: roman v 5-ti knigach. 423 s.
T. 2: Bez mužej — Psarnja — Ume-

ret'-usnut'… — Pristroilsja — Bezvest-naja. 358 s.

    T. 5: Na uščerbe: roman v 3-ch častjach. 359 s.

    T. 6: Obrečena — Proezdom — Vto-raja ot vody — Ot"ezde. 329 s.

    T. 7: Pereval: roman v 3-ch čast-jach. Č. 1-2. 373 s.

    T. 8: Pereval. Č. 3. — S ubijcej — Gorlenki. 311 s.

    T. 9: Chodok. 384 s.

    T. 10: Poumnel — Izmennik — "Morz" i "Juz". 285 s.

    T. 11: Rannie vyvodki — Trup — Vasilij Terkin. Č. 1. 303 s.

    T. 12: Vasilij Terkin. Č. 2. 355 s.

Bocjanovskij, Vladimir Teofilovič

Leonid Andreev: kritiko-biografičeskij ètjud. S portretom i faksimile L. N. Andreeva. S.-Peterburg: Izd. T-va Lite-ratura i Nauka, 1903. 64 s.

V. V. Veresaev: kritiko-biografičeskij ètjud. S portretom i faksimile V. Vere-saeva. S.-Peterburg: Izd. T-va Literatu-ra i Nauka, 1904. 66 s.

Bogdanovič, Ippolit Fedorovič

Sočinenija Ippolita Fedoroviča Bogda-noviča. Sobrany i izdany Platonom Beketovym. Č. 1-6. Moskva: V tipogr. izdatelja, 1809- 1810.

    Č. 1: 1809. vi, 360 s. S.9-93: Ivan Bogdanovič: O Bogdanoviče i ego soči-nenijach. Portr.

    Č. 2: 1810. 224 s.

    Č. 3. 1810. 290 s.

    Č. 4. 1810. 225 s.

    Č. 5. 1810. 226 s.

    Č. 6. 1810. 166 s.

Bogoraz, Vladimir Germanovič
(pseud. Tan)

Očerki i razskazy. 2-oe dopoln. izd. T. 1-6. S.-Peterburg: Izd. N. Glagoleva, 1904.

    T. 1: Iz chroniki goroda Propadin-ska — Pašen'kina smert'. 284 s.

    T. 2: Po belu svetu. 280 s.

    T. 3: Čukotskie razskazy: kn. 1. 373 s.

    T. 4: Čukotskie razskazy: kn. 2. 301 s.

    T. 5: Russkie v Amerike: kn. 1. 349 s.

    T. 6: Russkie v Amerike: kn. 2. 326 s.

Stichotvorenija. S.-Peterburg: Izd. S. Dorovatovskago i A. Čarušnikova, 1900. 123 s.

Stichotvorenija. 2-oe dopoln. izd. S.-Peterburg: Izd. N. Glagoleva, 1905. 159 s.

    Ded.: G. Iensenu s uvaženiem ot avtora

Bolotov, Andrej Timofeevič

Žizn' i priključenija Andreja Bolotova opisannyja samim im dlja svoich po-tomkov. 1738–1793. T. 1-4. S.-Peter-burg, 1870–1874. 1017, 1120, 1244, 1330, 84 stb.

Bol'šaja sovetskaja ènciklopedija.
Gl. red. O. Ju. Šmidt. T. 1-65. Moskva: Akcionnoe Obščestvo Sovetskaja Ènci-klopedija, 1926–1931.

Boreckaja, Marija
(Marija Vasil'evna Žuravskaja)

Golodnye. Moskva: Gos. izd., 1921, 31

s.: ill. (Krasnaja knižka, 17; 50.000)

Plovučij majak: (archangel'skaja byl'). Moskva: Gos. izd., 1920. 30 s.: ill. (Krasnaja knižka, 37; 100.000)

V lesu dikosti. Moskva: Gos. izd., 1920. 63 s. (Krasnaja knižka, 13)

V železnom kruge. Moskva: Gos. izd., 1920. 31 s.

Borozdin, Aleksandr Kornilievič

Literaturnyja charakteristiki: devjatnadcatyj vek. T. 1-2. S.-Peterburg: Izd. M. V. Pirožkova, 1903–1907.
    T. 1: 1903. 324 s. Portr.
    T. 2: 1905. 357 s. Portr.
    T. 2: Vyp. 2. 1907. 350 s. Portr.

Protopop Avvakum: očerk iz istorii umstvennoj žizni russkago obščestva v XVII veke A. K. Borozdina. S.-Peterburg: Tipogr. V. Demakova, 1898. xiii, 348, 171 (Priloženie)

Botkin, S. P.—> Belogolovyj, N. A.: S. P. Botkin...

Božerjanov, Ivan Nikolaevič

S.-Peterburg v Petrovo vremja: k dvuchsotletiju stolicy 1703–1903. Jubilejnoe izd. Tekst I. N. Božerjanova. S.-Peterburg: Tipogr. Ch. Krauze, 1901. 54 s.: ill. [folio]

Božerjanov, I. N. —> Detstvo, vospitanie i leta junosti russkich imperatorov...

Bražnikov, Lev D.

Idei russkich pisatelej XIX veka: materialy k istorii russkoj literatury: Karamzin, Žukovskij, Krylov, Griboedov, Puškin, Lermontov, Nekrasov, Gogol', Turgenev, Gončarov, Dostoevskij, Saltykov, Graf L. N. Tolstoj. S.-Peterburg: Tipogr. V. Kiršbauma, 1892. viii, 356 s.

Brik, Osip Maksimovič

Barin, pop i kulak: narodnye skazki. Moskva: Gos. izd., 1920. 48 s.: ill. (Krasnaja knižka, 30; 150.000)

Brikner, Aleksandr Gustavovič

Potemkin. Sočinenie A.G. Briknera. S 2 portretami. S.-Peterburg: Izd. K. L. Rikkera, 1891. 276 s.

Briliant, S. M.

Fon-Vizin, ego žizn' i literaturnaja dejatel'nost': biografičeskij očerk S.M. Brilianta. S portretom F. Vizina, gravirovannym po risunku I. Panova. S.-Peterburg: Tipogr. T-va Obščestvennaja pol'za, 1892. 93 s. (Žizn' zamečatel'nych ljudej)

G. R. Deržavin, ego žizn' i literaturnaja dejatel'nost': biografičeskij očerk S. M. Brilianta. S portretom Deržavina, gravirovannym v Lejpcige Gedanom. S.-Peterburg: Tipogr. T-va Obščestvennaja pol'za, 1893. 79 s. (Žizn' zamečatel'nych ljudej)

I. A. Krylov, ego žizn' i literaturnaja dejatel'nost': biografičeskij očerk S. M. Brilianta. S portretom I. A. Krylova, gravirovannym v Lejpcige Gedanom. S.-Peterburg: Tipogr. T-va Obščestvennaja poľza, 1891. 85 s. (Žizn' zamečateľnych ljudej)

Brjančaninov, Nikolaj

Vostok i Zapad. Moskva: Pečatnaja A. Snegirevoj, 1912. 241 s.

Brjusov, Valerij Jakovlevič

Chefs d'œuvres. 2-e izd. s izmenenijami i dopoln. Moskva: Tipogr. É. Lissnera i Ju. Romana, 1896. 90 s.

Dalekie i blizkie: stať i i zametki o russkich poėtach ot Tjutčeva do našich dnej. Moskva: Knigoizd. Skorpion, 1912. 213 s.

Me eum esse: novaja kniga stichov. Moskva: T-vo tipogr. A. I. Mamontova, 1897. 62 s.

Moj Puškin: stať i, issledovanija, nabljudenija. Red. N. K. Piksanova. Moskva-Leningrad: Gos. izd., 1929. 317 s. (2.000)
    Portr. of Brjusov

Ognennyj angel: povesť v XVI glavach. Izd. vtoroe, ispr. i dopoln. primečanijami. Ukrašenija po sovremennym gravjuram. Moskva: Knigoizd. Skorpion, 1909. 374 s.: ill.

Puti i pereputja: sobranie stichov. T. 1-3. Moskva: Knigoizd. Skorpion, 1908-1909.
    T. 1: Junošeskija stichotvorenija — Èto-ja — Tretja straža (1892/1901 g.). 1908. 213 s.: ill.

Ded.: Al'fredu Iensenu v znak uvaženija Valerij Brjusov. 1907.

    T. 2: Rimu i miru — Venok (1901/1905 g.). 1908. 239 s.

Ded.: Mnogouvažaemomu Al'fredu Iensenu družeski Valerij Brjusov. 1908.

    T. 3: Vse napevy. (1906/1909 g.). 1909. 178 s.: ill.

Ded.: Al'fredu Iensenu ot neizmenno predannago i blagodarnago Valerija Brjusova. 1909

Stephanos — Venok: stichi 1903–1905 goda. Moskva: Knigoizd. Skorpion, 1906. 168 s.

Tertia vigilia: kniga novych stichov 1897–1900. Moskva: Izd. Skorpion 1900. 173 s.

Urbi et orbi: Stichi 1900–1903 g. Moskva: Knigoizd. Skorpion, 1903. 190 s.

Zemnaja os': razskazy i dramatičeskija sceny (1901–1906 g.). Vin'etki Vasilija Milioti. Moskva: Knigoizd. Skorpion, 1907. 166 s.

Ded.: Al'fredu Iensenu v znak uvaženija, družestva i priznateľnosti Valerij Brjusov. 1907.

Zemnaja os': razskazy i dramatičeskija sceny (1901–1907 g.). Izd. 2-e, dopoln. Obložka i sem' risunkov Al'berto Martini. Moskva: Knigoizd. Skorpion, 1910. 166 s.: ill. S. 161-166: Bibliografija

Ded.: Mnogouvažaemomu Al'fredu Iensenu ot priznateľnago avtora. 1910. Valerij Brjusov

Brjusov, V. Ja.—>Chudožestvennoe slovo...

Brückner, A. G. —> Brikner, A. G.

Bucinskij, Petr Nikitič

O Bogdane Chmel'nickom. Sočinenie P. N. Bucinskago. Char'kov: Tipogr. M. Zil'berberga, 1882. v, 240, vi s.

Budilovič, Anton Semenovič

Neskol'ko myslej o greko-slavjanskom charaktere dejstvitel'nosti svv. Kirilla i Mefodija. Varšava 1895. 117 s.

Bugaev, Boris Nikolaevič —> Belyj, Andrej

Bulgakov, Fedor Il'ič

Illjustrirovannaja istorija knigopeča-tanija i tipografskago iskusstva. T. 1: S izobretenija knigopečatanija po XVIII vek vključitel'no. S.-Peterburg: Izd. A. S. Suvorina, 1889. viii, 364 s.: ill.
    S 6-ju chromolitografičeskimi i s 8-ju avtotipičeskimi priloženijami, s 270 snimkami istoričeskich šriftov, zaglav-nych listov, tipografičeskich ukrašenij, portretov tipografščikov, pervonačal-nych izdanij zagraničnych i russkich, s 150 inicialami i zastavkami iz slavja-no-russkich rukopisej raznych vekov

Bunin, Ivan Alekseevič

Razskazy. Izd. vtoroe. T. 1-2. S.-Peter-burg: Izd. T-va Znanie, 1903. 286, 222 s.

Burenin, Viktor Petrovič

Byloe: stichotvorenija 1861–1877. Izd. 2-oe. S.-Peterburg: Tipogr. A. S. Suvo-rina, 1897. 416 s.

Chvost. 3 izd. S.-Peterburg: Tipogr. A. S. Suvorina, 1893. 263 s.

Smert' Agrippiny: drama v pjati dejst-vijach V. P. Burenina. S.-Peterburg: Tipogr. A. S. Suvorina, 1888. 200 s.

Burenuška: sbornik rasskazov i sti-chotvorenij. Risunki A. N. Komarova. Izd. T-va I. D. Sytina, [1921?]. 16 s.
    Izd. zaregistrirovano v Otdele Pečati M. S. R. i Kr. D.

Buslaev, Fedor Ivanovič

Moi dosugi sobrannyja iz periodičes-kich izdanij. Melkie sočinenija Fedora Buslaeva v dvuch častjach. Č. 1-2. Moskva: V Sinodal'noj tipogr. 1886. 407, 480 s.

Narodnaja poėzija: istoričeskie očerki. Sanktpeterburg: Tipogr. Imperatorskoj Akademii Nauk, 1887. vi, 501 s.

Bykov, Aleksandr Alekseevič

Patriarch Nikon: biografičeskij očerk A. A. Bykova. S portretom Nikona, gra-virovannym v Lejpcige Gedanom. S.-Peterburg: Tipogr. T-va Obščestven-naja pol'za, 1891. 111 s. (Žizn' zame-čatel'nych ljudej)

Byliny starinki bogatyrskija
Vstupitel'naja stat'ja E. A. Ljackago. 2 izd. Stockholm: Izd. Severnye ogni, 1920. 166 s. (Ryska sägner).

Čajanov, A. V. —> Kremnev, Ivan

Catalogue de la section de Russica ou écrits sur la Russie en langues étrangères. T. 1-2. Supplement. Table méthodique. St.-Petersbourg: Imprimerie de l'Academie Imperiale des Sciences, 1873. 845, 771 s.

Čechov, Anton Pavlovič

"Na pamjatnik A. P. Čechovu": stichi i proza. S.-Peterburg: Tipogr. T-va Obščestvennaja pol'za, 1906. 184 s. 6 portretov A. P. Čechova, faksimile rukopisej Čechova
   1. F. D. Batjuškov: A. P. Čechov po vospominanijam o nem i pis'mam — 2. Stichotvorenija: Posvjaščenie Pleščeva A. P. Čechovu (1888 g.); Pamjati Čechova; Stichotvorenija — 3. Iz perepiski A. P. Čechova

Novye pis'ma (iz sobranija Puškinskogo doma). Pod red. B. L. Modzalevskogo. Peterburg: Izd. Atenej, 1922. 132 s.

Pis'ma A. P. Čechova. Moskva: Izd. M. P. Čechovoj, 1912.
   T. 1: 1876–1887. S illjustracijami. 1912. xxiv, 374 s.

Rab'i duši: rasskazy. Peterburg-Moskva: Gos. izd., 1919. 53 s. (Narodnaja biblioteka. Redakcija V. Veresaeva)
   Kapitanskij mundir — Otstavnoj rab — Smert' činovnika — Tolstyj i tonkij — Meljuzga — Maska — Razmaznja — Bespokojnyj gost' — Mest'
   + izd. 1920

Tri sestry: drama v 4-ch dejstvijach. 2-oe izd. S.-Peterburg: Izd. A. F. Marksa, 1901. 104 s.

—> Anton Pavlovič Čechov, ego žizn'... —> Derman, A. B.: Tvorčeskij portret Čechova

—> Solov'ev, E. A.: Kniga o Maksime Gor'kom i A. P. Čechove...

Čekin, A. (V. Jarockij)

Industrial'nye rabotniki mira: (k charakteristike professional'nogo dviženija Soedinennych Štatov). Moskva: Gos. izd., 1921. 75 s. (Biblioteka Professional'nogo Dviženija. Serija meždunarodnaja, 1; 40.000)

Černyševskij, Nikolaj Gavrilovič

Čto delat'? Roman napisannyj im v zaključenii 1862–1863. Izd. Sovremennika [n.d., S.l.]

Éstetika i poèzija. Éstetičeskija otnošenija iskusstva k dejstvitel'nosti. "O poèzii" Aristotelja. "Pesni raznych narodov". Kritičeskija stat'i o russkoj poèzii: Ogarev, Benediktov, Ščerbina, Pleščeev. Lessing, ego vremja, ego žizn' i dejatel'nost'. (Sovremennik 1854-1861 gg.). Izd. M. N. Černyševskago. S.-Peterburg: Tipogr. i litogr. V. A. Tichonova, 1893. 509 s.

Kritičeskija stat'i: Puškin, Gogol', Turgenev, Ostrovskij, Lev Tolstoj, Ščedrin i dr. (Sovremennik 1854-1861). Izd. M. N. Černyševskago. Vtoroe izd. S.-Peterburg, 1895. 387 s.

Očerki Gogolevskago perioda russkoj literatury. (Sovremennik 1855–1856). Izd. vtoroe M. N. Černyševskago. S.-Peterburg, 1893. 386 s.

Pis'ma bez adresa N. G. Černyševskago. Genève: M. Elpidine, 1890. 44 s.

Zametki o sovremennoj literature 1856-

1862 gg. (Sovremennik 1856-1862 gg.). Zametki o žurnalach — "Vremja" — Novyja povesti — Sočinenija Granovskago —Polemičeskija krasoty —V iz"javlenie priznatel'nosti. Izd. M. N. Černyševskago. S.-Peterburg, 1894. 444 s.

Čertkov, Vladimir Grigor'evič

Uchod Tolstogo. Berlin: Izd. I. P. Ladyžnikova, 1922. 195 s.: ill.

Češichin, V. E. —> Vetrinskij, Č. (pseud.)

Cetlin, Mich.

Dekabristy: sud'ba odnogo pokolenija. Pariž: Sovremennyja zapiski, 1933. 395 s.

Cheraskov, Ivan Michajlovič

Krest'janstvo i revoljucija. Berlin: Izd. T-va I. P. Ladyžnikova, [n.d.]. 66 s. (Social'no-političeskaja biblioteka)

Chmel'nickij, B.—> Bucinskij, P. N.: O Bogdane Chmel'nickom... —> Jakovenko, V. I.: Bogdan Chmel'nickij...

Chomjakov, Aleksej Stepanovič

Polnoe sobranie sočinenij Alekseja Stepanoviča Chomjakova. T. 1-8. Moskva: Universitetskaja tipogr., 1900.
T. 1: Izd. tret'e, dopoln. 408 s. Portr.
T. 2: Sočinenija bogoslovskija. Izd. četvertoe. 524 s. Portr.
T. 3: 482, 11 s. Priloženie: Descrip-

tion of The "Moskovka", a new rotatory steam engine invented and patented by Alexis Khomiakoff of Moscow. London: I. I. Guillaume, 1851
T. 4: Tragedii i stichotvorenija. 419 s. Portret s 1842 g.
T. 5: Zapiski o vsemirnoj istorii. Č. 1-ja. Izd. 3-e, dopoln. 587 s. Portr.
T. 6: Zapiski o vsemirnoj istorii. Č. 2-ja. Izd. 2-oe. 504, 21 s.
T. 7: Zapiski o vsemirnoj istorii. Č. 3-ja. Izd. 3-e. 1906. 503, 17 s.
T. 8: Pis'ma. 480, 58 s.

Stichotvorenija A. S. Chomjakova. 3 izd. Moskva: Tipogr. A. Gatčuka, 1881. 160, iv s.

Chruščov, P.

Tajna i krov': roman. Predislovie A. I. Kuprina. Riga: Literatura, 1927. 238 s. (Naša biblioteka, 20)

Chudožestvennoe slovo. Vremennik N. K. P. Kniga 1-ja. Otvetstvennyj redaktor V. Ja. Brjusov. Moskva: Izd. Narodnogo Komissariata po Prosveščeniju, 1920. 63 s. [folio]
K. Bal'mont, V. Brjusov, B. Pasternak, K. Ašukin, V. Aleksandrovskij, Mich. Gerasimov, Vjačeslav Ivanov, Oleg Leonidov, V. Bakulin, B. Pil'njak, Nikolaj Ašukin, A. Lunačarskij, V. Friče — Bibliografija — Chronika

Cikulenko, A.

Rukovodstvo dlja bibliotekarej Krasnoj Armii. Moskva: Gos. izd., 1920. 31 s. (25.000)

Čirikov, Evgenij Nikolaevič

Ěcho vojny. Moskva: Moskovskoe izd., 1915. 219 s.

Sobranie sočinenij. T. 2, 9-10, 14-15. Moskva: Moskovskoe knigoizd., 1910-1915.
T. 2: 6 izd.: Čužestrancy — Invalidy. 1910. 309 s.
T. 9: Plen strastej čelovečeskich — Rasskazy — Miniatjury. 1910. 306 s.
T. 10: Tichij omut: kartinki dorevoljucionnoj provincii. 1910. 324 s.
T. 14: 4 izd. Žizn' Tarchanova. Č. 2: Izgnanie. 1915. 346 s.
T. 15: 2 izd. Žizn' Tarchanova. Č. 3: Vozvraščenie. 1914. 353 s.

Sočinenija: Razskazy; P'esy. T. 1-4. S.-Peterburg: Tipogr. A. E. Kolpinskago, 1903–1904. 324, 397, 298, 383 s.

Čiževskij, D. M.

Ego veličestvo Trifon: narodnaja drama v 5 dejstvijach. Moskva: Gos. izd., 1920. 32 s. (Krasnaja knižka, 29; 100.000)

Comakion, A. I.

A.A. Ivanov, ego žizn' i chudožestvennaja dejatel'nost': biografičeskij očerk A. I. Comakion. S portretom A. A. Ivanova i gravjuroj s ego kartiny "Javlenie Christa narodu". S.-Peterburg: Tipogr. T-va "Obščestvennaja pol'za", 1894. 86 s. (Žizn' zamečatel'nych ljudej)

Čukovskij, Kornej Ivanovič

Dve duši M. Gor'kogo. Leningrad: Izd. A. F. Marks, 1924. 80 s. (Biblioteka dlja samoobrazovanija; 4.000)

Kniga ob Aleksandre Bloke s priloženiem chronologičeskogo spiska stichotvorenij A. Bloka sostavlennogo E. F. Knipovič. Peterburg: Ěpocha, 1922. 121 s.

Malen'kie deti. Leningrad: Izd. Krasnaja Gazeta, 1928. 95 s.: ill.
Ot avtora — Detskij jazyk — Ěkikiki — Lepye nelepicy

Ot Čechova do našich dnej: literaturnye portrety; charakteristiki. SPB: T-vo Izdatel'skoe Bjuro, 1908. 183 s.
1. Gorod i meščanstvo: A. Čechov; K. Bal'mont; F. Sologub; O. Dymov. 2. Ložnyj individualizm: M. Gor'kij; A. Kamenskij; M. Arcybašev; A. Roslavlev; S. Juškevič; M. Kuzmin. 3. Krizis individualizma: B. Zajcev; L. Andreev; D. Merežkovskij; V. Brjusov. 4. Priloženie: Bal'mont, kak perevodčik Šelli

Čulkov, Georgij Ivanovič

Kremnistyj put'. Moskva: Izd. V. M. Sablina, 1904. 141 s.

Marija Gamil'ton: poěma. Risunki Belkina Beniamina. Peterburg: Izd. Akvilon, 1922. 38 s.: ill. (1.000)

Tajga: drama. S.-Peterburg: Izd. Ory, 1907. 85 s.

Vesnoju na sever: lirika. S.-Peterburg: Knigoizd. Fakely, 1908. 86 s. Obložka M. V. Dobužinskago

Custine, Astolphe-Louis-Léonor de

La Russie en 1839 par le Marquis de Custine. 2. éd., revue, corr. et augm. T. 1-4. Bruxelles: Société Belge de Librairie, 1844. 301, 289, 288, 300 s.

Nikolaevskaja Rossija. Vstupiteľnaja staťja, redakcija i primečanija Sergeja Gessena i An. Predtečenskogo. Perevod s francuzskogo Ja. Gessena i L. Domgera. Moskva: Izd. Vsesojuznogo Obščestva Politkatoržan i Ssyľnoposelencev, 1930. 319 s. (4.000)

Čužak, N. F. —> Literatura fakta...

Cvetaeva, Marina Ivanovna

Molodec: skazka. Praga: Izd. Plamja pod obščim rukovodstvom professora E. A. Ljackago, 1924. 105 s.

Posle Rossii: 1922–1925. Pariž: Izd. I. E. Povolotzky, 1928. 153 s.

Dal', Vladimir Ivanovič

Polnoe sobranie sočinenij Vladimira Dalja (kazaka luganskago). T. 1-10. S.-Peterburg-Moskva: Izd. t-va M. O. Voľf, 1897–1898. Pervoe posmertnoe polnoe izd., dopoln., sverennoe i vnov' prosm. po rukopisjam.
   T. 1: Kritiko-biografičeskij očerk (P. I. Meľnikova) — Pavel Aleksandrovič Igrivyj — Otec s synom — Gde poterjaeš', ne čaeš', gde najdeš', ne znaeš' — Gofmanskaja kaplja — Otstavnoj. 1987. xcv, 325 s.
   T. 2: Nebyvaloe v bylom — Razskaz lezginca Asana — Savelij Grab — Raspoch — Chmeľ, son i jav' — Mičman Poceluev. 1897. 453 s.
   T. 3: Vakch Sidorov Čajkin — Bedovik — Kolbasniki i borodači — Žizn' čeloveka — Peterburgskij dvornik — Den'ščik — Čuchoncy v Pitere — Nachodčivoe pokolenie. 1897. 422 s.
   T. 4: Povesti i razskazy. 1897. 383 s.

   T. 5: Povesti i razskazy. 1897. 343 s.
   T. 6: Soldatskie dosugi — Matrosskie dosugi. 1897. 422 s.
   T. 7: Povesti i razskazy. 1898. 412 s.
   T. 8: Povesti i razskazy. 1898. 306 s.
   T. 9: Russkija skazki. 1898. 312 s.
   T. 10: Pochoždenija Vioľdamura i ego Aršeta — Očerki i staťi. 1898. 599 s., ill.

Tolkovyj slovar' živogo velikorusskago jazyka V. I. Dalja. Izd. Obščestva ljubitelej Rossijskoj slovesnosti, utverždennago pri Imperatorskom Moskovskom Universitete. T. 1-4. Moskva: V tipogr. A. Semena, 1863–1866.

Danilevskij, Grigorij Petrovič

Sočinenija G. P. Danilevskago (1847-1889). 6 izd., dopoln. v vos'mi tomach s portretom avtora. 1-8. S.-Peterburg: Tipogr. M. M. Stasjuleviča, 1890.
   T. 1: Razskazy. 397 s.
   T. 2: Na Indiju pri Petre I — Knjažna Tarakanova — Potemkin na Dunae — Umanskaja reznja — Starosvetskij maljar. 396 s.
   T. 3: Černyj god (Pugačovščina) — Bes na večernicach. 410 s.
   T. 4: Sožžennaja Moskva — 825-j god — Semejnaja starina — Poezdka v Jasnuju Poljanu. 391 s.
   T. 5: Beglye v Novorossii — Volja. 418 s.
   T. 6: Beglyj Lavruška — Sorokopanovka — Novyja mesta — Znakomstvo s Gogolem — Ukrainskija skazki — Stichotvorenija. 396 s.
   T. 7: Devjatyj val — Četyre vremeni goda ukrainskoj ochoty — Stórija o Gospode. 393 s.
   T. 8: Cimbelin — Žizn' i smert' korolja Ričarda treťjago — Ukrainskaja starina. 404 s.

Sočinenija G. P. Danilevskago. Izd. 8-oe, posmertnoe v dvadcati četyrech tomach s portretom avtora. 1-24. S.-Peterburg: Izd. A.F. Marksa, 1901. (Priloženie k žurnalu Niva na 1901 g.)

T.1: S. 5-95: G. P. Danilevskij: biografičeskij očerk

Dargomyžskij, A.S. —> Bazunov, S.A.: A.S. Dargomyžskij...

Daškova, E.P. —> Ogarkov, V.V.: E. P. Daškova...

Daumier, Honoré —> Sergeev, M.S.: Dom'e: Osada...

Davidova, Marija Avgustovna

Stichotvorenija M. Davidovoj. S.-Peterburg: Tipogr. V. Kiršbauma, 1899. 135 s.

Dejč, Lev Grigor'evič

S. M. Kravčinskij. S priloženiem stat'i V. I. Zasulič. Petrograd: Gos. izd. 1919. 64 s. (Istoriko-revoljucionnaja biblioteka)

Delo o patriarche Nikone. Izd. Archeografičeskoj kommissii po dokumentam Moskovskoj sinodaľnoj (byvšej patriaršej) biblioteki. S.-Peterburg 1897. xxxii, 453, 21 s. (Index)

Del'vig, Anton Antonovič

Polnoe sobranie stichotvorenij barona A. Deľviga. S portretom i biografiej. 3 izd. S.-Peterburg: Izd. A. S. Suvorina, 1892. 161 s. (Deševaja biblioteka, 48)

Dement'ev, I. N. —> Kubikov, Ivan Nikolaevič

Demidovy —> Ogarkov, V.V.: Demidovy — osnovateli gornago dela...

Derjabina, S.

Na zare novogo mira: skazka nastojaščego. Moskva: Gos. izd. 1920. 32 s. (Krasnaja knižka, 25; 100.000)

Derman, Abram Borisovič

Tvorčeskij portret Čechova. Moskva: Kooperativnoe izd. Mir, 1929. 348 s. (3.000)

Deržavin, Gavrila Romanovič

Sočinenija Deržavina. S ob"jasniteľnymi primečanijami Ja. Grota. 2-e akademičeskoe izd. (bez risunkov). T. 1-7. Sanktpeterburg: V tipogr. Imperatorskoj Akademii Nauk, 1868–1878.

T. 1: Stichotvorenija: č. 1. 1868. xxxviii, 542 s. Portr.

T. 2: Stichotvorenija: č. 2. 1869. xii, 463 s.

T. 3: Stichotvorenija: č. 3. 1870. xvi, 641 s.

T. 4: Dramatičeskija sočinenija. S ukazatelem k pervym četyrem tomam. 1874. 723 s.

T. 5: Perepiska (1773–1793). 1876. 938 s.

S. 881-938: Alfavitnyj ukazateľ ličnych imen, geografičeskich nazvanij i nekotorych predmetov, upominaemych v tome 5.

T. 6: Perepiska (1794–1816) i "Zapiski". 1876. vi, 840 s.

S. 803-837: Alfavitnyj ukazatel' imen i nekotorych predmetov upominaemych v tome 6; S.838-840: Alfavitnyj spisok lic i mest s kotorymi Deržavin perepisyvalsja ot 1794 po 1816.

T. 7: Sočinenija v proze. 1878. 661 s.

S. 647-661: Alfavitnyj ukazatel' imen i nekotorych predmetov pominaemych v tome 7

—> Briliant, S. M.: G. R. Deržavin...—> Francev, V. A.: Deržavin u slavjan... —> Grot, J. K.: Žizn' Deržavina...

Desjat' čtenij po literature. A. Al'ferov, A. Gruzinskij, F. Nelidov, S. Smirnov. S 29-ju risunkami. Moskva: Izd. A. I. Mamontova, 1895. 248 s.: ill.

Russkie narodnye pevcy — Maksim Grek — Chuliteli nauk v Ekaterininskoj satire XVIII veka — D. I. Fonvizin — S. T. Aksakov — D. V. Grigorovič — V. G. Belinskij — Petruška — Servantes — Defoe

Desnickij, V. A. —> M. Gor'kij: materialy i issledovanija...

Detstvo, vospitanie i leta junosti russkich imperatorov. Izdano k desjatiletiju so dnja roždenija Ego Imperatorskago Vysočestva Naslednika Cesareviča i Velikago Knjazja Alekseja Nikolaeviča. Sostavil I. N. Božerjanov. S.-Peterburg: Tipogr. A. Benke, [1914]. 128 s.: ill. [folio-al'bom]

Devjatnadcatyj vek: istoričeskij sbornik izdavaemyj Petrom Bartenevym (iz-datelem Russkago Archiva). Kn. 1-2. Moskva: Tipogr. F. Ioganson, 1872. T. 1: 494; T. 2: 296, 0242 s.

S. 01-0242: Zapiski očevidca o vojne Rossii protivu Turcii i zapadnych deržav (1853–1855), sočinenie N. I. Ušakova

Diterichs, L. K.

V. G. Perov, ego žizn' i chudožestvennaja dejatel'nost': biografičeskij očerk L. K. Diterichsa. S portretom Perova i 8-ju snimkami s ego proizvedenij. S.-Peterburg: Tipogr. T-va Obščestvennaja pol'za, 1893. 80 s. (Žizn' zamečatel'nych ljudej)

Divil'kovskij, Anatolij Avdeevič

Kak rabotnicy i kest'janki dolžny pomoč' demobilizovannym. Moskva: Gos. izd. 1921. 15 s. (Raboče-krest'janskie listovki, 63; 60.000)

Dmitriev, Fedor Michajlovič

Sočinenija F.M. Dmitreva. T. 1-2. Moskva: T-vo tipogr. A. I. Mamontova, 1899-1900.

T. 1: Istorija sudebnych instancij i graždanskago apelljacionnago sudoproizvodstva ot sudebnika do učreždenija o gubernijach. 1899. 588 s.

T. 2: Stat'i i izsledovanija. 1900. 622 s.

Dmitrievskij, S.

Stalin. Stockholm 1931. 338 s. [in Russian]

Dobroljubov, Nikolaj Aleksandrovič

Sočinenija N. A. Dobroljubova. T. 1-4. Izd. O. N. Popovoj. S.-Peterburg: Tipogr. I. N. Skorochodova, 1896. Izd. pjatoe.
    T. 1. S portretom N.A. Dobroljubova i ego biografiej, sost. A. M. Skabičevskim. lxxxii, 543 s.
    T. 2. 563 s.
    T. 3. 548 s.
    T. 4. 674 s.

—> Skabičevskij, A.M.: N.A. Dobroljubov...

Dobryv, A. P.

Biografii russkich pisatelej srednjago i novago periodov. S alfavitnym ukazatelem proizvedenij pisatelej. Sost. A. P. Dobryv. S.-Peterburg: Stoličnaja tipogr., 1900. 534, 49 s.

Dolinov, Moris Evseevič

Oktjabr': agit-p'esa v odnom dejstvii s prologom. Moskva: Gos. izd., 1920. (Krasnaja knižka, 40; 50.000)

Dom'e, A. —> Daumier, H.

Dostoevskij, Fedor Michajlovič

"Ispoved' Stavrogina": tri nenapečatannye glavy iz romana "Besy" — Plan "Žitija velikogo grešnika". Moskva: Izd. Centrarchiva RSFSR, 1922. vi, 77 s. (Dokumenty po istorii literatury i obščestvennosti. Vyp. pervyj; 10.000)

Netočka Nezvanova: razskaz. V Češskoj Prage: Naša reč', 1920. 166 s.

Polnoe sobranie sočinenij F. M. Dostoevskago. Vnov' prosm. i dopoln. samim avtorom izd. T. 1-3. S.-Peterburg: Izd. i sobstvennost' F. Stellovskago, 1865.
    T. 1: Chozjajka — Gospodin Procharčin — Slaboe serdce — Zapiski iž mertvago doma. Bednye ljudi — Bylyja ljudi — Čestnyj vor. 274 s.
    T. 2: Unižennye i oskorblennye — Krokodil — Skvernyj anekdot — Zapiski iz podpolja — Zimnija zametki o letnich vpečatlenijach. 256 s.
    T. 3: Igrok — Dvojnik — Elka i Svad'ba — Čužaja žena i muž pod krovat'ju — Malen'kij geroj — Netočka Nezvanova — Djadjuškin son — Selo Stepančikovo i ego obitateli. 374 s.

Polnoe sobranie sočinenij F. M. Dostoevskago. Izd. četvertoe. T. 1-12. S.-Peterburg: Tipografija brat. Panteleevych, 1891–1892.
    T. 1: Povesti i razskazy. S. i-xli: Dostoevskij — očerk žizni i dejatel'nosti sost. K. K. Slučevskim. S portretom F. M. Dostoevskago i faksimile. 1892. xli, 528 s.
    T. 2: Povesti i razskazy. 1891. 588 s.
    T. 3: Zapiski iz mertvago doma: roman v dvuch častjach — Povesti i razskazy. 1892. 669 s.
    T. 4: Unižennye i oskorblennye: roman v četyrech častjach s épilogom — Večnyj muž: razskaz. 1891. 476 s.
    T. 5: Prestuplenie i nakazanie: roman v šesti častjach s épilogom. 1891. 512 s.
    T. 6: Idiot: roman v četyrech častjach. 1891. 616 s.
    T. 7: Besy: roman v trech částjach. 1891. 621 s.
    T. 8: Podrostok: roman v trech částjach. 2892. 560 s.
    T. 9: Dnevnik pisatelja za 1873 g. (Iz žurnala "Graždanin" — Kritičeskija stat'i — Političeskija stat'i. 1891. 456 s.

T. 10: Dnevnik pisatelja za 1876 g. 1891. 424 s.

T. 11: Dnevnik pisatelja za 1877 g. 1891. 523 s.

T. 12: Brat'ja Karamazovy: roman v četyrech častjach s épilogom. 1892. 875 s.

Polnoe sobranie sočinenij F. M. Dostoevskago. T. 1-12. S.-Peterburg: Izd. A. F. Marksa, 1894–1895. (Sbornik Nivy. Besplatnoe priloženie k žurnalu Niva)

T. 1: Č. 1-2: Povesti i razskazy. S kritiko-biografičeskim očerkom o F. M. Dostoevskom sost. V. V. Rozanovym i s portretom F. M. Dostoevskago gravirovannym na stali F. A. Brokgauzom. 1894. 528 s.

T. 2: Č. 1-2: Povesti i razskazy. 1894. 604 s.

T. 3: Č. 1: Zapiski iz mertvago doma: roman v dvuch častjach — Skvernyj anekdot: razskaz. 1894. 357 s. Č. 2: Povesti i razskazy. 1894. 353 s.

T. 4: Č. 1: Uniżennye i oskorblennye: roman v četyrech častjach s épilogom. Č. 2: Uniżennye i oskorblennye (Okončanie) — Večnyj muž: razskaz. 1894. 506 s.

T. 5: Prestuplenie i nakazanie. 1894. 546 s.

T. 6: Idiot: roman v četyrech častjach. 1894. 661 s.

T. 7: Besy: roman v trech častjach. 1895. 652 s.

T. 8: Podrostok. 1895. 582 s.

T. 9: Kritičeskija stat'i – Dnevnik pisatelja za 1873 g. (Iz žurnala "Graždanin") – Političeskija stat'i. 1895. 472 s.

T. 10: Dnevnik pisatelja za 1876 g. 1895. 444 s.

T. 11: Dnevnik pisatelja za 1877 g. 1895. 548 s.

T. 12: Brat'ja Karamazovy: roman v četyrech častjach s épilogom. 1895. 920 s.

Polzunkov. S 4 risunkami P. A. Fedotova. Moskva-Leningrad: Gos. izd., 1928. 58 s.: ill.

S. 1-31: Dostoevskij i Fedotov: vstupitel'naja stat'ja V. S. Nečaevoj

—> Dostoevskij i Puškin... —> Grossman, L. P.: Dostoevskij na žiznennom puti... —> O Dostoevskom: sbornik stat'ej... —> Pereverzev, V. F.: Tvorčestvo Dostoevskogo... —> Puškin. Dostoevskij... —> Šestov, L.: Dostoevski und Nietzsche...—> Solov'ev, E. A.: F. Dostoevskij...

Dostoevskij i Puškin: reč' i stat'ja F. M. Dostoevskogo; stat'i A. Volynskogo, K. Leont'eva, Gl. Uspenskogo. Red. A. L. Volynskogo. Sanktpeterburg: Panfeon, 1921. 55 s.

Družinin, Aleksandr Vasil'evič

Polin'ka Saks: povest' A. V. Družinina. S.-Peterburg: Izd. A. S. Suvorina, 1886. 166 s. (Dorožnaja biblioteka)

Družinina, N. P. —>Annenkova-Bernar', N.

Dubrovin, N. F. —> Materialy i čerty k biografii Imperatora Nikolaja I...

Édvards, Al'bert

Tovarišč Ietta. Avtorizovannyj perevod s anglijskogo M. A. D'jakonova s predisloviem Zin. Vengerovoj. Petrograd: Gos. izd., 1919. 268 s.

Éfros, Nikolaj Efimovič

"Na dne". P'esa Maksima Gor'kogo v postanovke Moskovskogo Chudožestvennogo Teatra. Moskva: Gos. izd., 1923. 113 s.: ill.

Vse snimki dlja knigi "Na dne" ispolneny chudožnikami svetopisi M.A. Sacharovym i P.A. Orlovym, v special'nom dlja étogo izd. spektakle, ustroennom Moskovskim Chudožestvennym Teatrom

Éjchenbaum, Boris Michajlovič

Lev Tolstoj. Kn. vtoraja: 60-ye gody. Leningrad-Moskva: Gos. izd. chudožestvennoj literatury, 1931. 424 s. (5.000)

Melodika russkogo liričeskogo sticha. Peterburg: Opojaz, 1922. 199 s.
1. Metodologičeskie voprosy 2. Žukovskij 3. Puškin, Tjutčev, Lermontov 4. Fet

Ekaterina II

Sočinenija Imperatricy Ekateriny II. Red. i primečanija V. F. Solnceva. T. 1-3. S.-Peterburg: Izd. Evg. Evdokimova, 1893. (Ežemesjačnoe priloženie k žurnalu Sever)
T. 1: Dramatičeskija sočinenija. vi, 266 s.
T. 2: Dramatičeskija sočinenija. 288, viii s.
T. 3: Satiričeskija i pedagogičeskija sočinenija — Žurnal'nyja stat'i. 127, xxxii s.

Sočinenija Imperatricy Ekateriny II. T. 1-4. Na osnovanii podlinnych rukopisej i s ob"jasnitel'nymi primečanijami akademika A. N. Pypina. S.-Peterburg: Izd. Imperatorskoj Akademii Nauk, 1901.

T. 1: Dramatičeskija sočinenija. xlvii, 417 s.
T. 2: Dramatičeskija sočinenija. 517 s.
T. 3: Dramatičeskija sočinenija. iii, 455 s.
T. 4: Dramatičeskija sočinenija. iv, 262 s.

—> Bil'basov, V. A.: Obzor inostrannych sočinenij o Ekaterine II... —> Grot, J. K.: Ekaterina II...

Eleovskij, S. (S.N. Milovskij)

Razskazy. S.-Peterburg: Tipogr. N. N. Klobukova, 1904. 382 s.

Éliasberg, Aleksandr i David —> Russkij parnas...

El'pat'evskij, Sergej Jakovlevič

Razskazy. T. 1-3. S.-Peterburg: Izd. T-va Znanie, 1904. 258, 326, 258 s.

Énciklopedičeskij slovar' pod red. I. E. Andreevskago. Izdateli: F. A. Brokgauz (Lejpcig) i I.A. Efron (S.-Peterburg). T. 1-4 + 2 dopoln. S.-Peterburg: Semenovskaja tipo-litografija (I. A. Efron), 1890–1904, 1906.

Éngel'gardt, Michail Aleksandrovič

N. Prževal'skij, ego žizn' i putešestvija: biografičeskij očerk M. A. Éngel'gardta. S portretom Prževal'skago, gravirovannym v Lejpcige Gedanom i s geografičeskoj kartoj. S.-Peterburg: Tipog. I. G. Salova, 1891. 79 s. (Žizn' zamečatel'nych ljudej)

Ėngel'gardt, Nikolaj Aleksandrovič

Istorija russkoj literatury XIX stoletija: kritika, roman, poėzija i drama. T. 1-2. S.-Peterburg: Izd. A. S. Suvorina, 1902-1903.
   T. 1: 1800–1850. S priloženiem sinchronističeskoj tablicy, chronologičeskago ukazatelja pisatelej i polnoj bibliografii. 1902. 621 s.
   T. 2: 1850–1900. S priloženiem sinchronističeskoj tablicy, chronologii pisatelej, polnoj bibliografii i alfavitnago ukazatelja k oboim tomam. 1903. 570 s.

Ėrdė (pseud.)

Maksim Gor'kij i intelligencija. Moskva: Izd. Devjatoe janvarja, Tranposekcija, 1923. 32 s. (3.000)

Ėrenburg, Il'ja Grigor'evič

A vse-taki ona vertitsja. Moskva-Berlin: Knigoizd. Gelikon, 1922. 139 s., 22: ill.

Bubnovyj valet i Kᵒ: rasskazy. Moskva-Leningrad: Izd. Petrograd, 1925. 62 s.
   Veselyj finiš — Bubnovyj valet — Begun — V rozovom domike

Den' vtoroj: roman. 2-e izd. Moskva: Gos. izd. Chudožestvennaja literatura, 1934. 254 s. (25.000)

Edinyj front: roman. Berlin: Petropolis, 1930. 294 s.

Fabrika snov: chronika našego vremeni. Berlin: Petropolis, 1931. 243 s.

Lik vojny (vo Francii). Sofija: Rossijsko-Bolgarskoe Knigozd., 1920. 107 s.

Moskva slezam ne verit: roman. Moskva: Sovetskaja literatura, 1933. 192 s.

Neobyčajnyja pochoždenija Chulio Churenito i ego učenikov. Moskva-Berlin: Knigoizd. Gelikon, 1922. 353 s.

Nepravdopodobnyja istorii. Berlin: Izd. S. Efron, 1922. 137 s.
   Vmesto predislovija —Bubnovyj valet — V rozovom domike — "Veselyj finiš" — Begun — Ljubopytnoe proisšestvie — Uskomčel

Rasskazy. Leningrad: Priboj, 1928. 81 s.
   Veselyj Paolo — Dva druga — Noč' v Bratislave — Staryj skornjak — Loterejnyj bilet

Rvač: roman. Pariž: V tipogr. de Navarre, 1925. 448 s.

V protočnom pereulke: roman. Pariž: Gelikon, 1927. 224 s. (1.000)

Viza vremeni. Berlin: Petropolis, 1930. 370 s.

Žizn' i gibel' Nikolaja Kurbova. Berlin: Gelikon, 1923. 259 s.

Zolotoe serdce: misterija — Veter: tragedija. Moskva-Berlin: Gelikon, 1922. 194 s.

Eršov, Petr Pavlovič

Konek-gorbunok: russkaja skazka. Risunki A. F. Afanas'eva. Moskva: Gos. izd., 1920. 103 s.: ill. (Literaturnaja Komissija pri Pedagogičeskom Učreždenii Naš dom)
   Portr. of P. P. Eršov

Konek-gorbunok: russkaja skazka. S portretom i ill. Stokgol'm: Izd. Novaja Rus', 1921. 117 s.

Ėvarnickij, Dmitrij Ivanovič

Po sledam zaporožcev. S.-Peterburg: Tipo-litogr. P. I. Babkina, 1898. 324 s.

Zaporoz'e v ostatkach stariny i predanijach naroda. Č. 1-2. S.-Peterburg: Izd. L. F. Panteleeva, 1888. 294, 257 s.: ill.

Evgen'ev-Maksimov, Vladislav Evgen'evič

Očerk istorii novejšej russkoj literatury. Izd. 4-e. Leningrad: Gos. izd., 1927. 333 s.

Fadeev, Aleksandr Aleksandrovič

Razgrom: roman. Moskva: Gos izd. chudožestvennoj literatury, 1932. 255 s.: ill.

Fakely

Kn. 1. Redaktor izdatel' G. I. Čulkov. S.-Peterburg: Tipogr. Montvida, 1906. 211 s.
    V. Ivanov — F. Sologub — G. Čulkov —V. Brjusov — Konst. Ėrberg —A. Blok — A. Belyj — S. Gorodeckij — P. Solov'ev —I. Bunin —S. Rafalovič —L. Andreev — S. Sergeev-Censkij —O. Dymov — A. Remizov — L. Zinov'eva-Annibal'
    Kn. 2. S.-Peterburg: Izd. D. K. Tichomirova, 1907. 238 s. G. Čulkov — I. Davydov — A. Mejer — Lev Šestov — A. Vetrov — S. Gorodeckij — Vjač. Ivanov
    Kn. 3. S.-Peterburg: K-vo D. K. Tichomirova, 1908. 184 s.
    A. Blok — B. Zajcev — A. Remizov

— G. Čulkov — F. Sologub — S. Auslender — Vjač. Ivanov

Fedin, Konstantin Aleksandrovič

Brat'ja: roman. Berlin: Petropolis, 1928. 420 s

Goroda i gody: roman. 2 izd. Moskva-Leningrad: Gos. izd., 1926. 381 s. (5.000)

Pochiščenie Evropy: roman. Pariž: Izd. Zvezda, 1934. 255 s.

Feliče, Ar. —> Altaev, Al. & Feliče, Ar.

Fet, Afanasij (A. A. Šenšin)

Polnoe sobranie stichotvorenij A. A. Feta. Pod red. B. V. Nikol'skago. 1-3. S.-Peterburg: Izd. A. F. Marksa, 1901. cxii, 496, 654, 486 s.
    Chronologičeskij i alfavitnyj ukazateli stichotvorenij

Filippov, Michail Michajlovič

M. D. Skobelev, ego žizn' i voennaja dejatel'nost': biografičeskij očerk M. M. Filippova. S portretom Skobeleva, gravirovannym v Peterburge K. Adtom. S.-Peterburg: Tipogr. T-va Obščestvennaja pol'za, 1894. 96 s. (Žizn' zamečatel'nych ljudej)

Filosofov, Dmitrij Vladimirovič

Slova i Žizn': literaturnye spory novejšego vremeni (1901–1908 gg.). S.-Peterburg: Tipogr. Akc. Obšč. Tip. Dela, 1909. 324 s.

Fofanov, Konstantin Michajlovič

Stichotvorenija K. M. Fofanova. Čast' 1-5. S.-Peterburg: Izd. A. S. Suvorina, 1896. 96, 68, 96, 96, 173 s.

Fonvizin, Denis Ivanovič

Nedorosl': komedija v 5 dejstvijach, soč. Fonvizina. S.-Peterburg, 1901. 324 s.: ill. [folio] (P'esy chudožestvennago repertuara i postanovka ich na scene. Posobie dlja režisserov, teatral'nych direkcij, dramatičeskich artistov, dramatičeskich škol, ljubitelej dramatičeskogo iskusstva). Izdanie D. M. Musinoj pod red. Ju. Ė. Ozarovskago, artista Imperatorskich SPB-teatrov, prepodavatelja dramatičeskago iskusstva v Imperatorskom SPB. teatral'nom učilišče, vyp. l)

Polnoe sobranie sočinenij DI. Fon Vizina. Č. 1-4. Moskva: V tipogr. Semena Selivanskago, 1830. 263, 238, 162, 128 s. Portr.

—> Briliant, S. M.: Fon-Vizin... —> Vjazemskij, P. A.: Polnoe sobr. soč. T. 5: Fon-Vizin

Francev, Vladimir Andreevič

A. V. Kol'cov v češskoj literature: jubilejnaja zametka. Varšava: Tipogr. Varšavskago Učebnago Okruga, 1909. 13 s. (Otdel'nyj ottisk iz R. F. V. 1909; Russkij Filosofskij Vestnik)

Deržavin u slavjan: iz istorii russko-slavjanskich literaturnych vzaimootnošenij v XIX st. Praga: Plamja, 1924. 80 s.

Frug, Semen Grigor'evič

Stichotvorenija. 1-3. 3 izd. S.-Peterburg: Tipogr. Isidora Gol'dberga, 1897. 318, 288, 254 s.

Fülöp-Miller, René

Geist und Geschicht des Bolschewismus: Darstellung und Kritik des kulturellen Lebens in Sowjet-Russland. Mit 500 Abbildungen. Zürich-Leipzig-Wien: Amalthea-Verlag, 1926. 490 s.: ill.

Gallereja russkich pisatelej. Tekst redaktiroval I. Ignatov. Izd. S. Skirmunta. Moskva: Tipo-litogr. T-va I. N. Kušnerev, 1901. 589 s.: ill.

Cinkografičeskija klišė portretov ispolneny v chudožestvennoj masterskoj Otto Renara

Gangeblov, Aleksandr Semenovič

Vospominanija dekabrista Aleksandra Semenoviča Gangeblova. Moskva: Universitetskaja tipogr., 1888. 282 s.

Garin, N. (N. G. Michajlovskij)

Derevenskija panoramy. 2 izd. S.-Peterburg: Red. žurnala "Russkoe bogatstvo", 1899. 292 s.

Detstvo Temy (iz semejnoj chroniki) i Neskol'ko let v derevne. 3 izd. S.-Peterburg: Red. žurnala Russkoe bogatstvo, 1899. 432 s.

Gimnazisty: (iz semejnoj chroniki). 2 izd. S.-Peterburg: Red. žurnala Russkoe bogatstvo, 1898. 452 s.

Garšin, Vsevolod Michajlovič

Pervaja knižka razskazov. Izd. 2-e. S.-Peterburg: Tipogr. I. N. Skorochodova, 1888. 218 s.

Četyre dnja — Proissšestvie — Trus — Vstreča — Chudožniki — Noč' — Attalea princeps — To, čego ne bylo
+ izd. 4-e

Vtoraja knižka razskazov. S.-Peterburg: Tipogr. M. M. Stasjuleviča, 1899. 302 s. (Izd. Komiteta Obščestva dlja posobija nuždajuščimsja literatoram i učenym)
Denščik i oficer — Iz vospominanij rjadovogo – Krasnyj cvetok — Medved' — Skazka o žabe i roze — Nadežda Nikolaevna.
+ izd. 7-e

Gedeonov, Stepan Aleksandrovič

Otryvki iz izsledovanij o varjažskom voprose. Priloženie k 1-mu tomu Zapisok Imp. Akademii Nauk № 3. Sanktpeterburg, 1862. 239 s.

Varjagi i Rus': istoričeskoe izsledovanie. Č. 1. Sanktpeterburg: Tipogr. Imperatorskoj Akademii Nauk, 1876. xix, 569, cxiii s.

Gennadi, Grigorij Nikolaevič

Spravočnyj slovar' o russkich pisateljach i učenych umeršich v XVIII i XIX stoletijach i spisok russkich knig s 1725 po 1825 g. sostavil Grigorij Gennadi. Berlin: V tipogr. Rozentalja

T. 1: A-E. 1876. 351 s.
T. 2: Ž-M. 1880. S dobavlenijami Nikolaja Sobko. 433 s.

Geno, Aleksandr —> Pavel I: Sobranie anekdotov...

Gerbel', Nikolaj Vasil'evič

Polnoe sobranie stichotvorenij Nikolaja Gerbelja. T. 1-2. Sanktpeterburg: Tipogr. V. Bezobrazova, 1882. 414, 341 s.

Russkie poėty v biografijach i obrazcach. Izd. 3, ispr. i dopoln. pod red. P. Polevogo. Sanktpeterburg: Tipogr. M. Stasjuleviča, 1888. 581 s.

Gercen, Aleksandr Ivanovič

"Kolokol": izbrannyja stat'i A. I. Gercena (1857–1869). Ženeva: Vol'naja Russkaja Tipogr., 1887. 731 s. (Biblioteka social'nych znanij, Ser. 1, T. 1)

Sbornik posmertnych statej Aleksandra Ivanoviča Gercena (s portretom avtora). Izd. detej pokojnago. Ženeva: V tipogr. L. Černeckago, 1870. 292 s. Portr.
+ izd. 2-e. Genève-Bâle-Lyon: H. Georg, 1874. 312 s.

Sočinenija A. I. Gercena s predisloviem. T. 1-10. Genève-Bâle-Lyon: H. Georg, Libraire-éditeur, 1875–1879.
T. 1: Dnevnik — Dilettantizm v nauke. 1875. 383 s.
T. 2: Rannija proizvedenija (1834-1840) — Žurnal'nyja stat'i (1840-1845). 1876. 338 s.
T. 3: Kto vinovat? — Moskva i Peterburg — Novgorod-Velikij i Vladimir na Kljaz'me — Soroka-vorovka — Doktor Krupov — Mimoezdom (otryvok). 1878. 368 s.
T. 4: Dolg prežde vsego — Povreždennyj — Pis'ma iz Francii i Italii.

1878. 393 s.

T. 5: S togo berega — Russkij narod i socializm — Kreščenaja sobstvennost' — Staryj mir i Rossija — Vol'noe russkoe knigopečatanie v Londone — Jur'ev den'! Jur'ev den'! — Poljaki proščajut nas! — Vol'naja russkaja obščina v Londone — XXIII godovščina pol'skago vozstanija v Londone — Narodnyj schod v pamjat' fevral'skoj revoljucii. 1878. 351 s.

T. 6. Byloe i dumy: 1812-1838. 1878. 377 s.

T. 7. Byloe i dumy: 1838–1847. 1879. 381 s.

T. 8. Byloe i dumy: 1847–1850. 1879. 395 s.

T. 9. Byloe i dumy: 1850–1864. 1879. 427 s.

T. 10. Byloe i dumy: 1867–1868 — Raznyja stat'i. 1879. 437 s

—> Smirnov, V. D.: A.I. Gercen... —> Vetrinskij, Č.: Gercen...

Geršenzon, Michail Osipovič

Perepiska iz dvuch uglov — M. O. Geršenzon i V.I. Ivanov. Moskva-Berlin: Izd. Ogon'ki, 1922. 71 s.

[Pereizd. bez izmenenija s peterburgskogo izd. 1921]

Gippius, Zinaida Nikolaevna

Nebesnyja slova i drugie razskazy. Pariž: 1921. 342 s.

Nebesnyja slova — Vce k chudu — Kaban — Kometa — Vljublennye — Stranniček — Niniš — Večnaja ženskost' — Sud'ba — Tvar' — Svjataja plot'

Novye ljudi: razskazy. S.-Peterburg: Tipogr. M. Merkuševa, 1896. 451 s.

Jabloni cvetut — Bliže k prirode — Boginja — Prostaja žizn' — Goluboe nebo — Smirenie — Stichotvorenija — Mest' — Legenda — Cyganka — Vremja — Sovest' — Odinokij — Miss Maj

Sijanija. Pariž, [1939]. 46 s. Serija: Russkie poėty. Vyp. vtoroj (200)

Sobranie stichov: 1889–1903. Moskva: Knigoizd. Skorpion, 1904. 174 s.

Tret'ja kniga razskazov: Sumerki ducha —Kaban—Kometa—Sliškom rannie — Svjataja plot' — Svjataja krov'. S.-Peterburg: Izd. A. E. Kolpinskago, 1902. 466 s.

Zerkala: vtoraja kniga razskazov: Zerkala — Ved'ma — Živye i mertvye — Rodina — Utro dnej — Luna — Stichotvorenija — Zlatocvet. S.-Peterburg: Izd. N. M. Gerenštejna, 1898. 504 s.

Živyja lica. 1-2. Praha: Plamja, 1925.

Vyp. 1. 186 s. (Blok — Brjusov — Vyrubova)

Vyp. 2. 170 s. (Rozanov — Sologub — O mnogich)

Glinka, M.I. —> Bazunov, S. A.: M.I. Glinka

Glinskij, Boris Borisovič

Očerki russkago progressa: stat'i istoričeskija, po obščestvennym voprosam i kritiko-biografičeskija. S portretami i ill. S.-Peterburg: T-vo Chudožestvennoj Pečati, 1900. 578 s.

Gnedič, Petr Petrovič

Antipod i drugie razskazy. S.-Peterburg: Izd. A. S. Suvorina, 1902. 575 s.

Kavkazskie razskazy: Pustynja — Otec — Belye mal'čiki Asana — Sčastlivyj den'. S 71 risunkami M. M. Dal'keviča. S.-Peterburg: Tipogr. T-va Obščestvennaja pol'za, 1894. 173 s.

Novye razskazy. T. 1-2. S.-Peterburg: Tipogr. N. A. Lebedeva, 1890. 312, 303 s.

Gofman, Modest Ljudvigovič

Puškin: pervaja glava nauki o Puškine. Peterburg: Izd. Atenej, 1922. 156 s. (2.000)

Puškin — Don Žuan. Pariž: Izd. Sergeja Lifara, 1935. 110 s.

Gogol', Nikolaj Vasil'evič

Pochoždenija Čičikova ili Mertvyja duši: poèma. Tekst po poslednej redakcii akademika N.S. Tichonravova, s portretom N. V. Gogolja, gravirovannym na stali, 10 geliogravjurami i 355 ill. chudožnikov: V.A. Andreeva, A.F. Afanas'eva, N. N. Bažina, V. I. Bystrenina, M. M. Dal'keviča, F. S. Kozačinskago, I. K. Man'kovskago, N.V. Pirogova, E.P. Samokiš-Sudkovskoj, S. S. Solomko i N.N. Chochrjakova. Bukvy i vin'etki raboty N.S. Samokiša. Chudožestvennyj otdel vypolnen pod nabljudeniem P.P. Gnediča i M.M. Dal'keviča. S.-Peterburg: Izd. A.F. Marksa, 1900. 571 s. : ill. [folio]

Polnoe sobranie sočinenij N.V. Gogolja. 4 izd. ego naslednikov. 1-4. Moskva: Tipogr. T. I. Gagen, 1880. Portr.

T. 1: Večera na chutore bliz Dikan'ki — Mirgorod. 475 s.
T. 2: Povesti – Dramatičeskija sočinenija. 490 s.
T. 3: Pochoždenie Čičikova ili Mertvye duši. 312 s.
T. 4: Arabeski — Žurnal'nyja stat'i – Taras Bul'ba – Ostranica — Načal'nyja povesti — Pochoždenie Čičikova ili Mertvyja duši, t. 2 (v pervonačal'nom vide) — Vybrannyja mesta iz perepiski s druz'jami — Avtorskaja ispoved'. 826 s.

Sočinenija N. V. Gogolja. Red. N. S. Tichonravova i V. I. Šenroka. S portretom N. V. Gogolja i s biografičeskim očerkom, sostavlennym V. I. Šenrokom. 17 izd. v odnom tome. S.-Peterburg: Izd. A. F. Marksa, 1901. 1686 s.

Taras Bul'ba: povest'. Illjustrirovannoe izd. S risunkami M. Ziči, R. Štejna, I. Chrabrova, A. Kotljarevskago i dr. 4 izd. S.-Peterburg: Izd. A. F. Marksa, 1897. 170 s.: ill.

Taras Bul'ba. Peterburg: Gos. izd., 1920. 154 s. (Narodnaja biblioteka)

—> Annenskaja, A. N.: N. V. Gogol', ego žizn'... —> Mandel'štam, I. E.: O charaktere Gogolevskago stilja... —> Merežkovskij, D.: Gogol': tvorčestvo i žizn'... —> Merežkovskij, D.: Gogol' i čert... —> Russkaja biblioteka. 3: N. V. Gogol'... —> Vladimirov, P.V.: Iz učeničeskich let Gogolja...

Gol'dberg, G.A. —> Al'manach russkich dejatelej ...

Goleniščev-Kutuzov, Arsenij Arkad'evič

Sočinenija grafa A. Goleniščeva-Kutuzova. T. 1-2. S.-Peterburg: Tipogr. A. S. Suvorina, 1894. 218, 206 s.

Stichotvorenija grafa A. Goleniščeva-Kutuzova (1894–1901 g.). S.-Peterburg: Tipogr. M. M. Stasjuleviča, 1901. 94 s.

Golicyn, Dmitrij Petrovič

Vavilonjane: roman. S.-Peterburg: Izd. A. S. Suvorina, 1901. 343 s.

Golosa protiv: kritičeskij al'manach. Leningrad: Izd. Pisatelej, 1928. 172 s. (3.000)

    Predislovie — G. Gorbačev: Literaturnoe "zatiš'e" i ego pričiny — E. Mustangova: Est' li u nas kritika — G. Efimov: O tom, čego net v proletliterature — Zel. Štejnman: Pobediteli, kotorych sudjat — M. Majzel': Pornografija i patologija v sovremennoj literature

Golovačeva-Panaeva, Avdot'ja Jakovlevna

Russkie pisateli i artisty 1824 –1870. S.-Peterburg: Izd. V. I. Gubinskago, 1890. vii, 429 s. (Vospominanija A. Ja. Golovačevoj-Panaevoj)

    Pisateli: Aksakov – Annenkov — Bakunin — Belinskij — Gogol' — Granovskij — Gercen — Gončarov — Gerbel' — Glinka — Dobroljubov — Dostoevskij — Katkov — Kostomarov — Kavelin — Korš — Lažečnikov — Lermontov — Markevič — Michajlov — Nekrasov — Ogarev — Odoevskij — Ostrovskij — Panaev — Petraševskij — Pisemskij — Rešetnikov — Saltykov-Ščedrin — Turgenev — gr. L. N. Tolstoj — Černyševskij — Jazykov i dr.

    Artisty: Brjanskie — Martynov —

Maksimov — Karatyginy — Samojlovy — Petrov — Šumskij — Ščepkin — Semenova — Istomina i dr.

Golovin, Ivan Gavrilovič

Russland unter Alexander II. Original Ausg. Leipzig: Verlag von Paul Frohberg, 1870. 298 s.

Types et caractères russes. T. 1. Paris: Capelle, 1847. 391 s.

Golovin, Konstantin Fedorovič

Russkij roman i russkoe obščestvo. S.-Peterburg: Izd. tipogr. A. A. Porochovščikova, 1897. 472 s.

Gončarov, Ivan Aleksandrovič

Polnoe sobranie sočinenij I. A. Gončarova. S portretom avtora, gravirovannym akademikom I. P. Požalostinym i faksimile. Izd. vtoroe. T. 1-9. Sanktpeterburg: V tipogr. Glazunova, 1886–89.

    T. 1. Obyknovennaja istorija: roman v dvuch častjach. 1886. 184, 220 s.

    T. 2-3. Oblomov: roman v četyrech častjach. 1887. 196. 183, 116, 161 s.

    T. 4-5. Obryv: roman v pjati častjach. 1886. 461, 545 s.

    T. 6-7. Fregat Pallada: očerki putešestvija v dvuch tomach. 1886. xii, 392, 560 s.

    T. 8. Četyre očerka: Literaturnyj večer — Mil'on terzanij — Zametki o ličnosti Belinskago — Lučše pozdno čem nikogda. 1886. 265 s.

    T. 9. Vospominanija — Slugi starago veka. 1889. 264 s.

—> Slovar' literaturnych tipov: Gončarov…

—> Solov'ev, E. A.: I. A. Gončarov...

Gorbačev, Georgij Efimovič

Očerki sovremennoj russkoj literatury. 3 izd. Leningrad: Gos. izd. 1925. 203 s.

Gorelik, A. Z. —> Ležnev, A. (pseud.)

Gor'kij, Maksim
(Aleksej Maksimovič Peškov)

Chan i ego syn – Starucha Izergil'. Peterburg: Gos. izd., 1920. 39 s.

Chozjain: povest'. Berlin: J. Ladyschnikow, 1913. 126 s.

Čudaki.: sceny. Berlin: J. Ladyschnikow, 1910. 75 s.

Dačniki: sceny: četyre akta. Berlin: Verlag Snanije, 1905. 194 s.

Delo Artamonovych. Berlin: Verlag Kniga, 1925. 258 s.

Deti: komedija v odnom dejstvii. Berlin: J. Ladyschnikow, 1910. 63 s.

Deti solnca: drama v 4-ch dejstvijach. Stuttgart: Verlag von J. H. W. Dietz Nachfolger, 1905. 226 s.

Detstvo. Berlin: J. Ladyschnikow, 1914. 254 s.

9-oe janvarja: očerk. Peterburg: Gos. izd. 1920. 32 s.

9-e janvarja: očerk. Izd. tret'e, s ill. chud. V. D. Zamirajlo. Leningrad: Gos. izd. 1925. 30 s.: ill.

Dvadcat' šest' i odna: poėma. Petro-grad: Izd. Petrogradskago Soveta Rabočich i Krasn. Deputatov, 1919. 20 s.

Gorodok: zametki iz dnevnika; Vospominanija. Izd. 2-e. Moskva-Leningrad: Gos. izd., 1927. 59 s. (Universal'naja biblioteka, 25; 15.000)
    Gorodok – Znacharka – Pauk — A. N. Šmidt

Gorodok Okurov: chronika. Berlin: J. Ladyschnikov, 1910. 192 s.

Ispoved': povest'. Berlin: J. Ladyschnikow, 1908. 196 s.

Leto: povest'. Berlin: J. Ladyschnikow, 1909. 199 s.

Makar Čudra i dr. rasskazy. Izd. 11-oe. Tom 1. Moskva: Gos. izd., 1920. 296 s.
    Makar Čudra — O Čiže, kotoryj lgal, i o Djatle-ljubitele istiny — Emel'jan Piljaj — Ded Archip i Len'ka — Čelkaš — Starucha Izergil' — Odnaždy osen'ju — Ošibka — Moj sputnik — Delo s zastežkami — Pesnja o sokole

Mat': roman v dvuch častjach. Berlin: J. Ladyschnikow, 1908. 411 s.

Mat': kniga pervaja. Moskva-Petrograd: Knigoizd. Kommunist, 1919. 235 s. (Sobranie sočinenij Maksima Gor'kogo. T. 22)

Matvej Kožemjakin: povest'. Čast' 1-4. Berlin: J. Ladyschnikow, 1910–1911.
    Č. 1. 1910. 180 s.
    Č. 2. 1911. 137 s.
    Č. 3. 1911. 136 s.
    Č. 4. 1911. 197 s.

Moi universitety — Storož — Vremja Korolenko — O vrede filosofii — O pervoj ljubvi — V. G. Korolenko. Berlin:

Verlag Kniga, 1923. 234 s.

Mordovka: razskaz. Berlin: J. Ladysch-nikow, 1911. 62 s.

Na plotach. Petrograd: Izd. Petrograd-skago Soveta Rabočich i Krasn. Depu-tatov, 1918. 20 s.

O evrejach. Petrograd: Izd. Petrograd-skogo Soveta Rabočich i Krasn. Depu-tatov, 1919. 24 s.

O pervoj ljubvi: rasskazy. Izd. 2-e. Moskva-Leningrad: Gos. izd. 1927. 61 s. (Universal'naja biblioteka, 14; 15.000)
    O pervoj ljubvi — Pastuch

O russkom krest'janstve. Berlin: Izd. I. P. Ladyžnikova, 1922. 44 s.

O tarakanach. Moskva-Leningrad: Gos. izd. 1927. 91 s. (Universal'naja biblio-teka, 186-187; 15.000)

Po Rusi. Moskva-Leningrad: Gos. izd., 1928. 383 s. (10.000)

Požary: zametki iz dnevnika; Vospo-minanija. Moskva-Leningrad: Gos. izd., 1926. 64 s. (Universal'naja biblioteka, 3; 15.000)

Prochodimec. Petrograd: Izd. Petrograd-skago Soveta Rabočich i Krasn. Depu-tatov, 1919. 48 s.

Rasskaz o bezotvetnoj ljubvi. Izd. vto-roe. Moskva-Leningrad: Gos. izd., 1927. 89 s. (Universal'naja biblioteka, 50-51; 15.000)

Rasskazy. So vstupitel'noj stat'ej V. V. Vorovskogo. Moskva: Kooperativnoe Izd. Pisatelej Nikitinskie Subbotniki, 1927. 190 s. (7.000)

V. V. Vorovskij: Žizn' i tvorčestvo M. Gor'kogo — M. Gor'kij: biografija — Pes-nja o burevestnike — Čelkaš — Foma Gordeev (vyderžki iz romana) — Mat' (vyderžki iz romana) — 9-oe janvarja

Razskazy. 1-6. S.-Peterburg: Izd. T-va Znanie, 1901-1903.
    T. 1. 3 izd. 1901. 331 s.
    T. 2. 3 izd. 1901. 394 s.
    T. 3. 3 izd. 1901. 318 s.
    T. 4. 3 izd. 1901. 402 s.
    T. 5. 6 izd. 1903. 386 s.
    T. 6. P'esy: Meščane — Na dne. 1903. 286 s.

Revoljucionnyja pesni i ballady. S pre-disloviem M. Sukennikova. Berlin: Izd. Ioanna Pěde, 1903. 48 s.

Romantik: razskaz. Berlin: Bühnen- und Buch-Verlag russischer Autoren J. Ladyschnikow, [n.d.]. 43 s.

Russkija skazki. Berlin: J. Ladyschni-kow, 1912. 48 s.

Russkija skazki. Petrograd: Izd. Parus, 1918. 79 s.

Skazki. Berlin: J. Ladyschnikow, 1912. 152 s.

Skazki. S risunkami chudož. A. Ma-kovskogo. Peterburg: Gos. izd., 1920. 32 s.: ill. (Biblioteka detskogo žurnala Severnye skazki, 1)
    Stačka — Cvetok — Tonnel' — Pepe

Slučaj iz žizni Makara — Roždenie če-loveka: dva razskaza. Berlin: J. La-dyschnikow, 1912. 58 s.

Sobranie sočinenij. 1-13, 14-22. Izd. vtoroe. Moskva-Leningrad: Gos. izd. 1927-1929. (10.000)

T. 1. Rasskazy: Makar Čudra — O Čiže, kotoryj lgal, i o Djatle, ljubitele istiny — Emel'jan Piljaj — Ded Archip i Len'ka — Čelkaš — Starucha Izergil' — Odnaždy osen'ju — Ošibka — Moj sputnik — Delo s zastežkami — Pesnja o sokole — Na plotach — Boles' — Toska — Konovalov — Chan i ego syn — Vyvod — Suprugi Orlovy. 1927. 354 s.

T. 2. Rasskazy: Byvšie ljudi — Ozornik — Varen'ka Olesova — Tovarišči — V stepi — Mal'va — Jarmarka v Goltve — Zazubrina — Skuki radi — Družki — Prochodimec. 1927. 327 s.

T. 3. Rasskazy: Čitatel' — Kirilka — O čerte — Ešče o čerte — Vas'ka krasnyj — Dvadcat' šest' i odna — Pesn' o burevestnike — 9-oe janvarja — Soldaty — Tri dnja — Tjur'ma — Bukoemov — Tovarišč! — Rasskaz Filippa Vasil'eviča — Kain i Artem — Čelovek — Slučaj iz žizni Makara. 1927. 350 s.

T. 4: Foma Gordeev. 1927. 265 s.

T. 5: Troe. 1927. 274 s.

T. 6: Ispoved' — Leto. 1927. 288 s.

T. 7: Mat'. 1927. 313 s.

T. 8: Žizn' nenužnogo čeloveka — Gorodok Okurov. 1927. 316 s.

T. 9: Žizn' Matveja Kožemjakina. 1927. 499 s.

T. 10: Detstvo. 1927. 193 s.

T. 11: V ljudjach — Chozjain. 1927. 395 s.

T. 12: Po Rusi: Roždenie čeloveka — Ledochod — Gubun — Niluška — Kladbišče — Na parochode — Ženščina — V uščel'e — Kalinin — Edut — Pokojnik — Eralaš — Večer u Šamova — Večer u Panaškina — Večer u Suchomjatkina — Svetlo-seroe s golubym — Kniga — Kak složili pesnju — Ptičij grech — Grivennik — Sčast'e — Geroj — Kloun — Zriteli — Timka — Legkij čelovek — Strasti-Mordasti — Na Čangule — Vesel'čak — Devuška i Smert'

— Ballada o grafine Ėllen de Kursi. 1927. 396 s.

T. 13. Rasskazy i očerki: Romantik — Mordovka — Devočka — Požar — Kraža — Zlodej — V Amerike — Interv'ju — Skazki ob Italii — Russkie skazki — Žaloby — Rasskazy. 1927. 470 s.

T. 15. P'esy: Varvary; Vragi — Čudaki — Zykovy — Deti — Starik. 1927. 387 s.

T. 16: Moi universitety — Vospominanija. 1927. 381 s.

T. 17: Zametki iz dnevnika. 212 s.

T. 18. Rasskazy 1922-1924 gg.: Otšel'nik — Rasskaz o bezotvetnoj ljubvi — Rasskaz o geroe — Rasskaz ob odnom romane — Karamora — Anekdot — Repeticija — Golubaja žizn' — Rasskaz o neobyknovennom. 1927. 307 s.

T. 19: Delo Artamonovych. 1927. 258 s.

T. 20: Vospominanija — Rasskazy — Zametki: V. I. Lenin — O S.A. Tolstoj — Leonid Krasin — Sergej Esenin — N. F. Annenskij — O Garine-Michajlovskom — Provodnik — Mamaša Kemskich — Ubijcy — Ėmblema — O tarakanach — Fal'šivaja moneta — Zametki čitatelja. [1 izd.] 1928. 216 s.

T. 21-22: Žizn' Klima Samgina (sorok let): povest'. 1929. 501, 605 s.

Starik: p'esa. Berlin: Ladyschnikow, 1918. 71 s.

Storož: rasskazy. Moskva-Leningrad: Gos. izd., 1926. 124 s. (Universal'naja biblioteka, 79-80; 15.000)
Storož — N.A. Bugrov — Strasti-Mordasti

Strasti-Mordasti: vospominanija. Berlin: J. Ladyschnikow, 1918. 173 s.
Strasti-Mordasti — Eralaš — Večer u Šamova — Večer u Suchomjatkina

— Svetlo-seroe s golubym — Kniga — Kak složili pesnju — Ptičij grech — Sčasťe — Geroj — Timka — Legkij čelovek — Na Čangule

Tri dnja: razskaz. Berlin: J. Ladyschnikow, 1912. 97 s.

U russkogo carja. Moskva-Leningrad: Gos. izd., 1926. 29 s. (35.000)

V Amerike: očerki. Berlin: J. Ladyschnikow, [n.d.]. 86 s.

V ljudjach. Berlin: J. Ladyschnikow, 1916. 388 s.

V ljudjach. Petrograd: Izd. Parus, 1918. 333 s.

Varvary: drama v 4-ch dejstvijach. Stuttgart: Verlag von J. H. W. Dietz Nachfolger, 1906. 204 s.

Vaśka Krasnyj. Petrograd: Izd. Petrogradskogo Soveta Rabočich i Krasn. Deputatov: 1919. 24 s.

Veseľčak: vospominanija. Berlin: Izd. I. P. Ladyžnikova, 1918. 77 s.
   Veseľčak — Kloun — Nesoglasnyj — Grivennik — Večer u Panaškina — Edut — Zriteli

Žaloby: razskaz. Berlin: J. Ladyschnikow, 1911.
   Razskaz pervyj — Razskaz vtoroj — Razskaz tretij — Razskaz četvertyj

Zapiski prochodjaščago: očerki. Č. 1-2. Berlin: J. Ladyschnikow, 1913. 160, 95 s.

Žizn' Klima Samgina: povesť. Moskva-Leningrad: Gos. izd., 1928. 619 s. (20.000)

Žizn' nenužnago čeloveka: roman. Berlin: J. Ladyschnikow, 1908. 272 s.

Zykovy: sceny. Berlin: J. Ladyschnikow, 1913. 81 s.

—> Čukovskij, K. I.: Dve duši M. Gor'kogo... —> Èfros, N.: "Na dne"... —> Èrdè: Maksim Gor'kij... —> Grigor'ev, R.: M. Gor'kij... —> Gruzdev, I. A.: Žizn' i priključenija Maksima Gor'kogo... —> Kritičeskija staťi o proizvedenijach Maksima Gor'kago... —> M. Gor'kij: materialy i issledovanija... —> M. Gor'kij v portretach... —> M. Gor'kij 1868-1928: katalog knig... —> Maksim Gor'kij, Moskva: Nikitinskie Subbotniki... —> Polonskij, V. P.: Maksim Gor'kij: očerk... —> Porickij, I. E.: Maksim Gor'kij i ego proizvedenija... —> Rusakov, V.: Maksim Gor'kij v karrikaturach... —> Šklovskij, V. B.: Udači i poraženija Maksima Gor'kogo... —> Solov'ev, E. A.: Kniga o Maksime Gor'kom... —> Speranskij, V.: Istoriko-kritičeskie materialy... —> Stroev, V. A.: M. Gor'kij...

Gor'kij, M. —> Ščit... —> Sbornik armjanskoj literatury...

Gosplan Literatury: sbornik Literaturnogo Centra Konstruktivistov (LCK) pod red. Kornelja Zelinskogo i Iľi Seľvinskogo. Moskva-Leningrad: Krug, 1925. 143 s.
   Deklaracija LCK: Osnovnye položenija konstruktivizma, staťi Borisa Agapova, I. A. Aksenova, K. Zelinskogo, V. Inber, I. Seľvinskogo, D. Tumannogo, a takže priloženija: Izvestija LCK, Avgust 1925 i Karta stroiteľstva socializma

Graf Lev Tolstoj: velikij pisateľ zemli russkoj v portretach, gravjurach, medaljach, živopisi, skuľpture, karrikaturach i t.d. SPB: Izd. T-va M. O. Voľf, 1903. 98, 6 s.: ill. [folio]

Grebenka, Evgenij Pavlovič

Čajkovskij: roman. S portretom avtora i biografiej. S.-Peterburg: Izd. A. S. Suvorina, 1900. 209 s. (Deševaja biblioteka, 319)

Greč, Nikolaj Ivanovič

Zapiski moej žizni N. I. Greča. S.-Peterburg: Izd. A. S. Suvorina, 1886. 504, xlvii, 26 s. Portr.

Griboedov, Aleksandr Sergeevič

Gore ot uma: komedija v četyrech dejstvijach. Red., vstup. stať ja i primečanija E. A. Ljackago. Stokchoľm: Severnye ogni, 1920. 139 s.

Polnoe sobranie sočinenij A.S. Griboedova. Pod red. I.A. Šljapkina. (S priloženiem dvuch portretov A. S. Griboedova i faksimile ego počerka). 1-2. S.-Peterburg: Izd. I. P. Vargunina, 1889.
    T. 1: Prozaičeskija stať i perepiska. 472 s.
    T. 2: Poèzija. 536 s.

Polnoe sobranie sočinenij A. S. Griboedova. Pod red. Ars. I. Vvedenskago. S biografičeskim očerkom i portretom A. S. Griboedova, gravirovannym na stali F. A. Brokgauzom v Lejpcige. S.-Peterburg: Izd. A. F. Marksa, 1892. 392 s.

—> Russkaja biblioteka, 5: A.S. Griboedov

—> Skabičevskij, A. M.: A. S. Griboedov... —> Slovar' literaturnych tipov, t. 5

Grigor'ev, Rafail

M. Gor'kij. Moskva: Gos. izd., 1925. 146 s. (Kritiko-bibliografičeskaja serija; 5.000)

Grigorovič, Dmitrij Vasiľevič

Anton–Goremyka: povesť. Petrograd: Literaturno-izdateľskij Otdel Narodnogo Komissariata po Prosveščeniju, 1919. 142 s. (Narodnaja biblioteka)

Četyre vremeni goda: povesť iz narodnago byta. S.-Peterburg: Izd. N. G. Martynova, 1897. 64 s.

Polnoe sobranie sočinenij D. V. Grigoroviča v 12 tomach. 3-e, vnov' peresm. i ispravl. avtorom izd. S.-Peterburg: Tipogr. A. F. Marksa, 1896.
    T. 1: Peterburgskie šarmanščiki — Sosedka — Loterejnyj bal — Derevnja — Anton-Goremyka — Bobyľ — Kapeľmejster Suslikov — Četyre vremeni goda. 372 s.
    T. 2: Pochoždenija Nakatova, ili Nedolgoe bogatstvo — Neudavšajasja žizn' — Svetloe Christovo Voskresen'e — Svistuľkin — Mať i doč'. 391 s.
    T. 3-4: Proseločnyja dorogi. Č. 1-2. 387, 340 s.
    T. 5: Smedovskaja dolina — Zimnij večer — Rybaki. 457 s.
    T. 6: Pereselency: roman iz narodnago byta. 454 s.
    T. 7: Prochožij — Stoličnye rodstvenniki — Pachar' — Škola gosteprimstva. 320 s.
    T. 8: Skučnye ljudi — Očerki sovremennych nravov — V ožidani paroma

—Počtennye ljudi, obremennenye mno-
gočislennym semejstvom — Koška i
myška —Pachatnik i barchatnik. 304 s.

T. 9: Korabl' "Retvizan". 363 s.

T. 10: Dva generala — Stoličnyj voz-
duch — Guttaperčevyj mal'čik — Ne-
dolgoe sčast'e — Kar'erist. 350 s.

T. 11: Akrobaty blagotvoritel'nosti
— Son Karelina — Ne po chorošu mil –
po milu choroš — Kartiny anglijskich
živopiscev na vystavkach 1862 goda v
Londone — Chudožestvennoe obrazo-
vanie v priloženii k promyšlennosti na
vsemirnoj Parižskoj vystavke 1867
goda. 384 s.

T. 12: Roždestvenskaja noč' — Moj
djadja Bandurin — Zamševye ljudi —
Gorod i derevnja — Literaturnyja vospominanija — Porfirij Petrovič Kukuš-
kin. 406 s.

Grjunberg, Julij Osipovič —> Vasil'ki…

Grossman, Leonid Petrovič

Dostoevskij na žiznennom puti. Vyp. I:
Molodost' Dostoevskogo 1821–1850.
Moskva: Nikitinskie Subbotniki, 1928.
223 s. (3.000)

Ėtjudy o Puškine. Moskva-Petrograd:
Izd. L. D. Frenkel, 1923. 117 s. (2.000)

Grot, Jakov Karlovič

Ekaterina II v perepiske s Grimmom.
Priloženie k XXXIV-mu tomu Zapisok
Imp. Akademii Nauk, 1. Sanktpeter-
burg: 1879. 130 s.

Trudy Ja. K. Grota. 1-5. Izdany pod red.
prof. K. Ja. Grota. S.-Peterburg 1898-
1903.

T. 1: Iz skandinavskago i finskago
mira (1839–1881): očerki i perevody.
1898. 1071 s.

T. 2: Filologičeskija razyskanija
(1852–1892). 1899. 939 s.

T. 3: Očerki iz istorii russkoj literatury (1848–1893). Biografija, charakteristiki i kritiko-bibliografičeskija zametki. 1901. 510, 329 s.

T. 4: Iz russkoj istorii: izsledovanija,
očerki, kritičeskija zametki i materialy
(1845–1890). 1901. 768 s.

T. 5: Dejatel'nost' literaturnaja, pedagogičeskaja i obščestvennaja: stat'i,
putevye vpečatlenija, zametki, stichi i
detskoe čtenie. S priloženiem portreta-
oforta raboty chudožnika V. I. Bystrenina. 1903. viii, 628 s.

Žizn' Deržavina po ego sočinenijam i
pis'mam i po istoričeskim dokumentam opisannaja Ja. Grotom. 1-2. S.-
Peterburg: Izd. Imperatorskoj Akademii
Nauk, 1880–1883.

T. 1. 1880. viii, 1043 s. Portr.

T. 2. So snimkami portretov, nota-
mi i ukazatelem k oboim tomam biografii. Dopoln. primečanija i raznogo
roda priloženija. 1883. x, 661 s.

Gruševskij, Michajlo

Iljustrovana istorija Ukraini. Kiiv-L'viv,
1911. 554 s.: ill.

> Ded.: Vysokouvažaemomy D^{ru} Al'-
> fredu Ensenu s privetom ot avtora

Istorija ukrainskoi kozaččini. T. 2:
1626–1638. Kiiv-L'viv, 1913. 315 s.

Kul'turno-nacional'nij ruch na Ukraini
v XVI-XVII vici. Kiiv-L'viv, 1912. 248 s.:
ill.

> Ded.: Al'fredu Ensenu ot avtora

Očerk istorii ukrainskago naroda. Izd. vtoroe, dopoln. S.-Peterburg: Tipogr. T-va Obščestvennaja poľza, 1906. 315 s.

Ded.: Vysokouvažaemomu D^{ru} Aľfredu Enzenu — avtor

Osvoboždenie Rossii i ukrainskij vopros: staťi i zametki. S.-Peterburg: Tipogr. T-va Obščestvennaja poľza, 1907. 291 s.

Gruzdev, Iľja Aleksandrovič

Žizn' i priključenija Maksima Gor'kogo (po ego rasskazam). Sostavil Iľja Gruzdev. Risunki N. Tyrsy. Izd. vtoroe, dopoln. novymi risunkami. Moskva-Leningrad: Gos. izd. 1927. 173 s.: ill. (Dlja detej srednego i staršego vozrasta)

Gruzinskij, A. —> Aľferov, A., Gruzinskij, A.: Sbornik...

Gusin, V. P. —> Polonskij, V. P.

Ignatov, I. —> Gallereja russkich pisatelej...

Ikonnikov, Vladimir Stepanovič

Opyt russkoj istoriografii. T. 1: 1-2. Kiev: Tipogr. Imperatorskago Universiteta sv. Vladimira, 1891–1892. 1539, ccclxxi, 149 s.

Ilovajskij, Dmitrij Ivanovič

Istorija Rossii. Č. 1-4. Moskva: Tipogr.

Gračeva 1876–1899.
   Č. 1: Kievskij period. 1876. 333 s.
   Č. 2: Vladimirskij period. 1880. 578 s.
   Č. 3: Moskovsko-carskij period: pervaja polovina ili XVI vek. 1890. 717 s.
   Č. 4: Êpocha Michaila Fedoroviča Romanova. Vyp. 2-j. 1899. 375 s.

Razyskanija o načale Rusi. 2-e izd. s prisoedineniem dopoln. polemiki po voprosam varjago-russkomu i bolgaro-gunskomu. Moskva 1882–1886. 557 s.

Smutnoe vremja Moskovskago gosudarstva [1603–1613 gody]. Soč. D. Ilovajskago. Okončanie istorii Rossii pri pervoj dinastii. Moskva: Tipogr. M. G. Volčaninova, 1894. 343 s.

Sočinenija D. I. Ilovajskago: Istorija Rjazanskago knjažestva — Ekaterina Romanovna Daškova — Graf Jakov Sivers. Moskva: Izd. knigoprodavca A. L. Vaspľeva, 1884. 596 s.

Iskra za dva goda [1905–1906]: sbornik statej iz ʺIskryʺ: P. Akseľroda, M. B-va, F. Dana, V. Zasulič, Koľcova, L. Martova, Martynova, N. Negoreva, Parvusa, G. Plechanova, Starovera, P. Streľskago, N. Trockago. Izd. S. N. Saltykova. 688 s.

Istrin, Vasilij Michajlovič

Očerk istorii drevnerusskoj literatury domoskovskogo perioda (11–13 vv.) Petrograd: Nauka i Škola, 1922. 248 s.

Ivan Groznyj —> Solov'ev, E. A.: Ioann Groznyj...

Ivanov, A. A. —> Comakion, A. I.: A.A. Ivanov, ego žizn'...

Ivanov, Ivan Ivanovič

Istorija russkoj kritiki. Č. 1-4. S.-Peterburg: Izd. žurnala Mir Božij, 1898-1900.
    Č. 1-2. 1898. x, 509 s.
    Č. 2-3. 1900. 716 s.

Iz zapadnoj kultury: stat'i po voprosam literatury, filosofii, politiki, iskusstva i obščestvennoj žizni Zapadnoj Evropy novago vremeni. Izd. žurnala Mir Božij. T. 1-2. S.-Peterburg: Tipogr. I. N. Skorochodova, 1899. 460, 165 s.

Novaja kul'turnaja sila: russkie pisateli XIX-go veka: Puškin, Lermontov, Belinskij, Turgenev, Nekrasov, Ševčenko, Žadovskaja, Nikitin, Griboedov. S.-Peterburg: Izd. žurnala Mir Božij, 1901. xxxii, 364 s.

Ivanov, I. M.

Petr Velikij, ego žizn' i gosudarstvennaja dejatel'nost': biografičeskij očerk I. M. Ivanova. S portretom Petra Velikago, gravirovannym v Lejpcige Gedanom. S.-Peterburg: Tipogr. Obščestvennaja pol'za, 1898. 95 s. (Žizn' zamečatel'nych ljudej)

Ivanov, Vjačeslav Ivanovič —> Geršenzon, M. O.: Perepiska...

Ivanov, Vsevolod Vjačeslavovič

Cvetnye vetra: povest'. Peterburg: Ėpocha, 1922. 185 s.

Ivanov-Klassik, Aleksej Fedorovič

Stichotvorenija A. F. Ivanova-Klassika. S.-Peterburg: Izd. D. D. Fedorova, 1891. 186 s.

Ivanovskij, Nikolaj Ivanovič

Rukovodstvo po istorii i obličeniju staroobrjadčeskago raskola s prisovokupleniem svedenij o sektach racionalističeskich i mističeskich. Sost. N. Ivanovskij. Č. 2-ja. 5-e izd. Kazan': Tipo-litografija Imperatorskago Universiteta, 1899. 245 s.

Iz ėpochi "Zvezdy" i "Pravdy" (1911-1914 gg.). Moskva: Gos. izd., 1921. 191 s. (Komissija dlja sobiranija i obrabotki materialov po istorii Oktjabr'skoj Revoljucii i R.K.P (b-kov); 40.000)
    M. Ol'minskij: O memuarach; Obščij očerk ėpochi — A. Vinokurov: Rabočee strachovoe dviženie — Priloženija: Postanovlenie Soveta Narodnych Komissarov — Plan rabot Istparta — N. Baturin: Konspekt-minimum dlja vospominanij — A. Bubnov: Proekt plana rabot za 1917–1920 gg. — Instrukcija dlja mestnych bjuro Istparta — Iz otčeta Istparta

Izmajlov, Aleksandr Alekseevič

Pomračenie božkov i novye kumiry: kniga o novych vlijanijach v literature: Leonid Andreev, Arcybašev, Bal'mont, Brjusov, Blok, Gorodeckij, Vjačeslav Ivanov, Gippius, Merežkovskij, Fedor Sologub, Kamenskij, Minskij, Andrej Belyj, Osip Dymov, Kuzmin, Sergeev-Censkij, Auslender. Moskva: Tipogr. T-va I. D. Sytina, 1910. 251 s.

Uragan: roman. Razskazy: Ržavčina — Appartamento — Kapitan Nemo — Kto on? — Propavšaja gramota — Avgury. Moskva: Tipogr. T-va I. D. Sytina, 1909. 257 s.

Jakobson, Roman Osipovič

Novejšaja russkaja poèzija. Nabrosok pervyj [V. V. Chlebnikov]. Praga: Tipogr. Politika, 1921. 68 s.

Jakovenko, V. I.

Bogdan Chmel'nickij, ego žizn' i obščestvennaja dejatel'nost': biografičeskij očerk V. I. Jakovenko. S portretom Bogdana, gravirovannym v Lejpcige Gedanom. S.-Peterburg: Tipogr. T-va Obščestvennaja pol'za, 1894. 160 s. (Žizn' zamečatel'nych ljudej)

T. G. Ševčenko, ego žizn' i literaturnaja dejatel'nost': biografičeskij očerk V. I. Jakovenko. S portretom T. G. Ševčenko, gravirovannym v Peterburge K. Adtom. S.-Peterburg: Tipogr. T-va Obščestvennaja pol'za, 1894. 95 s. (Žizn' zamečatel'nych ljudej)

Jakovlev, Vladimir Alekseevič

Domostroj. 2., ispr. izd. Odessa: Tipogr. A. Šulce, 1887. 145 s.

Jakubovič, Petr Filippovič

Stichotvorenija. 5 izd. 1-2. S.-Peterburg: Red. žurnala Russkoe bogatstvo, 1902.
    T. 1: 1878–1897. 282 s.
    T. 2: 1898–1902. 295 s.

V mire otveržennych: zapiski byvšago katoržnika L. Mel'šina. 3 izd. 1-2. S.-Peterburg: Red. žurnala Russkoe bogatstvo, 1903.
    T. 1: V preddverii — Šelaevskij rudnik — Ferganskij orlenok — Odinočestvo. 386 s.
    T. 2: S tovariščami — Kobylka v puti — Sredi sopok — Èpilog — Ot avtora. 400 s.

Jamščikova, L. A. & M. V. —> Altaev, Al. & Feliče, Ar.

Jarcev, Aleksej Alekseevič

F. G. Volkov (osnovatel' russkago teatra), ego žizn' v svjazi s istoriej teatral'noj stariny: biografičeskij očerk A. A. Jarceva. S portretami F. G. Volkova, Dmitrevskago, Jakovleva, Plavil'ščikova i Semenovoj. S.-Peterburg: Tipogr. T-va Obščestvennaja pol'za, 1891. 94 s. (Žizn' zamečatel'nych ljudej)

M. S. Ščepkin, ego žizn' i sceničeskaja dejatel'nost' v svjazi s istoriej sovremennago emu teatra: biografičeskij očerk A. A. Jarceva. S portretom Ščepkina, gravirovannym Konstantinom Adtom. S.-Peterburg: Tipogr. T-va Obščestvennaja pol'za, 1893. 96 s. (Žizn' zamečatel'nych ljudej)

Jazykov, Nikolaj Michajlovič

Stichotvorenija N. M. Jazykova. S portretom i biografiej. T. 1-2. S.-Peterburg: Izd. A. S. Suvorina, 1898. 376, 166. (Deševaja biblioteka, 203-204)

Juškevič, Semon Solomonovič

Razskazy. 2 izd. 1-2. S.-Peterburg: Izd. T-va Znanie, 1904–1905. 355, 302 s.

Južakov, Sergej Nikolaevič

M.M. Speranskij, ego žizn' i obščestvennaja dejatel'nost': biografičeskij očerk S.N. Južakova. S portretom M.M. Speranskago, gravirovannym v Lejpcige Gedanom. S.-Peterburg: Tipogr.T-va Obščestvennaja pol'za, 1892. 88 s. (Žizn' zamečatel'nych ljudej)

K novym daljam: lirika nežnych sozvučij. Izd. 2-e. Stokchol'm: Izd. Severnye ogni pod občej red. I. A. Lundelja i E.A. Ljackago, 1921. 119 s. [orig. izd., S.-Peterburg: Ogni, 1909]

Kak my pišem. Leningrad: Izd. Pisatelej, 1930. 216 s.

A. Belyj, M. Gor'kij, Evg. Zamjatin, Mich. Zoščenko, V. Kaverin, B. Lavrenev, Ju. Libedinskij, Nik. Nikitin, B. Pil'njak, M. Slonimskij, Nik. Tichonov, A. Tolstoj, Ju. Tynjanov, Konst. Fedin, Ol'ga Forš, A. Čapygin, Vjač. Šiškov, V. Šklovskij

Kankrin, E.F. —> Sementkovskij, R.I.: E.F. Kankrin...

Kannegiser, Leonid Ioakimovič

Iz posmertnych stichov Leonida Kannegisera. Stat'i Georgija Adamoviča, M.A. Aldanova, Georgija Ivanova. Pariž, 1928. 88 s.

Kantemir, Antioch Dmitrievič

Izbrannyja satiry. Satiry I, II i IX s primečanijami. Ob"jasnitel'nyja stat'i. S.-Peterburg: Izd. I. Glazunova, 1892. 95 s. Portr. (Russkaja klassnaja biblioteka izd. pod red. A.N. Čudinova. Posobie pri izučenii russkoj literatury, vyp. XII)

S. 63-95: A.D. Galachov: Satiry Kantemira (Materialy dlja izučenija Kantemira)

Reljacii Kn. A.D. Kantemira iz Londona (1732-1733). T. 1, s vvedeniem i primečanijami V.N. Aleksandrenko, professora Varšavskogo Universiteta. Moskva: Universitetskaja tipogr., 1892. viii, 262 s.

Sočinenija, pišma i izbrannye perevody knjazja Antiocha Dmitrieviča Kantemira. S portretom avtora, so stat'eju o Kantemire i s primečanijami V. Ja. Stojunina. Red. izd. P. A. Efremova. T. 1-2. S.-Peterburg: Izd. Ivana Il'iča Glazunova, 1867–1868. (Russkie pisateli XVIII i XIX st.)

T. 1. Satiry — Melkija stichotvorenija i perevody v stichach. 1867. 559, 50 s.

T. 2. Sočinenija i perevody v proze, političeskija depeši i pis'ma. 1868. 462 s.

—> Sementkovskij, R. I.: A. D. Kantemir...

Karamzin, Nikolaj Michajlovič

Izbrannyja sočinenija. Č. 1-2. S.-Peterburg: Izd. I. Glazunova. 1892. Portr.

Č. 1: Povesti — Razsuždenija — Stichotvorenija. 199 s.

Č. 2: Pis'ma russkago putešestvennika, s primečanijami. 272 s.

Geschichte des russischen Reiches. Von Karamsin. Nach der zweiten Original Ausg. übersetzt. Bd. 1-11. Riga & Leipzig 1820–33.

—> Solov'ev, E. A.: N. M. Karamzin...

Karazin, V.N. —> Abramov, Ja.V.: V.N. Karazin...

Karonin (pseud.) —> Petropavlovskij, N. E.

Karpinskij, Vjačeslav Alekseevič

My i oni: narodnaja drama v 2-ch dejstvijach. Moskva: Gos. izd., 1920. 32 s. (Krasnaja knižka, 21)

Karpov, Pimen

Trubnyj golos: rasskazy. Moskva: Gos. izd. 1920. 40 s.

Karpova-Mongird, Vera Aleksandrovna (pseud.: Sergej Romias)

Ars longa, vita brevis: razskazy. Moskva: Tipogr. G. Lissnera, 1904. 335 s. 8-j tom proizvedenij V. A. Karpovoj-Mongird, pisavšej pod psevd. Sergej Romias

Derevnja našego vremeni: očerki. Moskva: Tipogr. T-va I. N. Kušnerev, 1897. 281 s.

Ljubov' li? Moskva: Tipogr. T-va I. N. Kušnerev, 1900. 280 s.

Moej rodine. Moskva: Tipogr. G. Lissnera, 1908. 384 s.

Neveselaja kniga (kniga žizni-krest'janskaja) i priloženie. Moskva: Tipogr. G.

Lissnera, 1905. 273 s.

Obliki. Moskva: Tipogr. G. Lissnera, 1910. 301 s.

Poėmy bez slov i razskazy. Moskva: Izd. avtora, 1902. 259 s.

Sem'ja Nikitinych: roman-chronika. Moskva: Tipogr. I. N. Kušnerev, 1899. 566 s.

Važnaja kniga. Moskva: Tipogr. G. Lissnera, 1912. 193 s.

Ženščiny: razskazy. T. 1-2. S dvumja portretami avtora. Moskva: Tipogr. G. Lissnera, 1901. 315, 236 s.

Karuzin, P. I.

Rukovodstvo po plastičeskoj anatomii. Vyp. I: O razmerach, roste i proporcijach čelovečeskogo tela. Moskva: Gos. izd., 1921. 86, s., x tabl.

Kasatkin, Ivan Michajlovič

Na barkach: rasskaz. Moskva: Gos. izd., 1920. 48 s.: ill. (Krasnaja knižka, 14)

Petrun'kina žizn'. Moskva: Gos. izd., 1920. 32 s.: ill. (Krasnaja knižka, 6)

Put'-doroga: rasskaz. Moskva: Gos. izd., 1920. 31 s.: ill. (Krasnaja knižka, 9)

Kataev, Ivan Ivanovič

Serdce: povesti. Izd. tret'e, Moskva: Izd. Federacija, 1931. 254 s.
  Serdce — Poėt — Žena

Kataev, Valentin Petrovič

Vremja, vpered! Risunki V. Roskina. Moskva: Federacija, 1932. 429 s.: ill.

Katalog knižnago magazina Novogo vremeni A. S. Suvorina. Vyp. pervyj: Bogoslovie; Filosofija, psichologija i logika; Estestvoznanije; Slovesnosť'. S.-Peterburg: Tipogr. A. S. Suvorina, 1899. 696 s.

Katarina II —> Ekaterina II

Katenin, P.

Očerki russkich političeskich tečenij: socialdemokraty, socialisty-revoljucionery, osvoboždency, anarchisty. S priloženiem polnych partijnych programm. Berlin: Izd. F. Gottgejnera/Fried. Gottheiner's, 1906. 101 s.

Kavelin, Konstantin Dmitrievič

Sobranie sočinenij K. D. Kavelina. S.-Peterburg: Tipogr. M. M. Stasjuleviča, 1897–1900.
　　T. 1: Monografii po russkoj istorii. S portretom avtora, biografičeskim očerkom i primečanijami D. A. Korsakova. 1897. xxxii, 1051, iii stb.
　　T. 2: Publicistika. S portretom avtora, vstupiteľnoju staťeju V. D. Spasoviča i primečanijami D. A. Korsakova. 1898. xxxi, 1258 stb.
　　T. 3: Nauka, filosofija i literatura. S portretom avtora, vstupiteľnoju staťeju A. F. Koni i primečanijami D. A. Korsakova. 1899. xx, 1256 stb.
　　T. 4: Ètnografija i pravovedenie. S primečanijami D. A. Korsakova. 1900. 1347 stb.

Kazanovič, Evlampija Pavlovna

D. I. Pisarev (1840–1856). Petrograd: Nauka i Škola, 1922. 200 s. (2.500)

Kedrov, M. N.

Kommunistka: dramatičeskij ètjud v odnom dejstvii iz èpochi graždanskoj vojny. Moskva: Gos. izd., 1921. 31 s. (Krasnaja knižka, 45; 100.000)

Kireevskij, P. V. —> Pesni sobrannyja P. V. Kireevskim... —> Pesni sobrannyja P. V. Kireevskim. Novaja serija...

Keržencev, P. M.
(Platon Michajlovič Lebedev)

Tvorčeskij teatr. Peterburg: Gos. izd., 1920. 155 s.: ill.

Keržencev, V.
(Platon Michajlovič Lebedev)

Biblioteka kommunista: sistematičeskij ukazateľ socialističeskoj literatury. 4-oe dopoln. izd. Moskva: Gos. izd., 1919. 96 s.

Kirillov, Vladimir Timofeevič

Zori grjaduščego: stichi. Izd. treť'e. Peterburg: Biblioteka Proletkuľta, 1919. 62 s.
　　Zori grjaduščego — Liričeskie stichi

Kirsanov, Semen Isaakovič

Pjatiletka: poèma. Moskva-Leningrad: Gos. izd. chudožestvennoj literatury, 1931. 173 s.: ill.

Kjustin, de —> Custine, A.-L.-L. de

Klejnbort, Lev Maksimovič

Russkij čitatel'-rabočij. Po materialam, sobrannym avtorom. Leningrad: Izd. Leningradskogo Gubernskogo Soveta Professional'nych Sojuzov, 1925. 258 s. (10.000)

Ključevskij, Vasilij Osipovič

Kurs russkoj istorii. Č. 1. Peterburg: Gos. izd. 1920. 464 s.

Kniga bylin—> Avenarius, V.P.: Kniga bylin

Kniga o Leonide Andreeve: vospominanija M. Gor'kogo, K. Čukovskogo, A. Bloka, G. Čulkova, B. Zajceva, N. Telešova, E. Zamjatina. Peterburg-Berlin: Izd. Z. I. Gržebina, 1922. 109 s.

Kniga razdumij: K. D. Bal'mont. Valerij Brjusov. Modest Durnov. Iv. Konevskoj. S.-Peterburg-Varšava-Vitebsk: S.-Peterburgskij knižnyj sklad M. Zalšupina, 1899. 82 s.
    K. D. Bal'mont: Lirika myslej i Simvolika nastroenij — M. Durnov: Krasočnye sny — V. Brjusov: Razdum'ja — Iv. Konevskoj: Ot solnca k solncu

Kniga razskazov i stichotvorenij. Moskva: Izd. knižnago magazina Torgovago Doma S. Kurnin, 1902. 358 s.

Knjazev, Evgenij

Razskazy iz kavkazskoj žizni. Vil'na: Tipogr. Štaba Vilenskago voennago okruga, 1901. 160 s.

Knjazev, Vasilij Vasil'evič

Pervaja kniga stichov (1905–1916). Peterburg: Gos. izd., 1919. 415 s.

Pesni krasnogo zvonarja. Petrograd: Izd. Petrogradskogo Soveta Rabočich i Krasn. Deputatov, 1919. 118 s.

Sovremennye častuški: 1917–1922. Moskva-Petrograd: Gos. izd., 1924. 76 s.

Kogan, Petr Semenovič

Literatura ětich let: 1917–1923. Ivanovo-Voznesensk: Knigoizd. T-vo Osnova, 1924. 146 s. (3.000)

Očerki po istorii novejšej russkoj literatury. T. 1. Vyp. I. Izd. vtoroe. Moskva: Tipogr. T-va I. D. Sytina, 1910. 257 s.

Kogen, A.

Stichotvorenija. Kiev: Tipogr. S. V. Kul'ženko, 1893. 153 s.

Kol'cov, Aleksej Vasil'evič

Stichotvorenija A. V. Kol'cova pod red. P. V. Bykova. Izd. vtoroe, ispr. i dopoln. S biografičeskim očerkom, kritičeskimi stat'jami, primečanijami, portretom, snimkom počerka i 39-ju risunkami i vin'etkami, ispolnennymi členami Tovariščestva Russkich Illjustratorov. S.-Peterburg: Knigoizd. German Goppe, 1895. 148 s.: ill.

Stichotvorenija i pis'ma A. V. Kol'cova. Polnoe sobranie. Vnov' ispr. i značitel'no dopoln. izd. pod red. Ars. I. Vvedenskago. S kritiko-biografičeskim očerkom i portretom A. V. Kol'cova, gravirovannym na stali F. A. Brokgauzom v Lejpcige. S.-Peterburg: Izd. A. F. Marksa, 1895. xx, 327 s.

—> Francev, V. A.: A. V. Kol'cov v češskoj literature... —> Ogarkov, V. V.: A.V. Kol'cov, ego žizn'...

Kol'tonovskij, Andrej Pavlovič

Stichotvorenija. S.-Peterburg: Izd. B. N. Zvonareva, 1901. 184 s.

Kondakov, N.P. —> Nikodim Pavlovič Kondakov... —> Russkija drevnosti...

Konopnickaja, Marija

Staryj perepletčik i ego vnuk (Mendel Gdanski): rasskaz s pol'skogo. Moskva: Gos. izd., 1920. 32 s. (Krasnaja knižka, 5)

Konradi, Evgenija Ivanovna

Sočinenija E. I. Konradi v dvuch tomach. Pod red. M. A. Antonoviča. T. 1-2. S.-Peterburg: Izd. V. A. Balandinoj, 1899–1900.
    T. 1: Ispoved' materi. 1899. xxxiv, 535 s. Portr.
    T. 2: Stat'i publicističeskija, literaturno-kritičeskija, pedagogičeskija i dr. 1900. 581 s.

Korf, N. A.—> Peskovskij, M. L.: Baron N.A. Korf...

Korinfskij, Apollon Apollonovič

"Byval'ščiny" i "Kartiny Povolž'ja". 2 izd. S.-Peterburg: Tipogr. E. Evdokimova, 1899. 307 s.

Černyja rozy: stichotvorenija 1893-1895 gg. S.-Peterburg: Tipogr. M. Merkuševa, 1896.
    Černyja rozy — Byval'ščiny — Otgoloski

Imja krasot i drugija novyja stichotvorenija. S.-Peterburg: Tipogr. Ja. I. Libermana, 1899. 315 s.

Narodnaja Rus': kruglyj god skazanij, poverij, obyčaev i poslovic russkago naroda. Moskva: Izd. knigoprodavca M.V. Kljukina, 1901. 724 s.

Teni žizni: stichotvorenija 1895–1896 gg. S.-Peterburg: Tipogr. Nadežda, 1897. 263 s.

Vol'naja ptica i drugie razskazy. S.-Peterburg: Tipogr. Nadežda, 1897. 327 s.

Korolenko, Vladimir Galaktionovič

Bez jazyka: razskaz. 2 izd. S.-Peterburg: Red. žurnala Russkoe bogatstvo, 1903. 218 s.

Istorija moego sovremennika. Č. 1: Rannee detstvo i Gody učenija. S.-Peterburg: Tipogr. Pervoj Spb. Trudovoj Arteli, 1909. 469 s.
    Ded.: D^ru Al'fredu Iensenu ot uvažajuščago avtora na pamjat' o svidanii v 1909 godu — V. Korolenko

Očerki i razskazy. 1-3. Moskva: 1887-1903.
    Kn. 1. Moskva: Izd. žurnala Rus-

skaja mysl', 1887. 401 s.

V durnom obščestve — Son Makara — Les šumit — V noč' pod svetlyj prazdnik — V posledstvennom otdelenii — Staryj zvonar' — Očerki sibirskago turista — Sokolincev

Kn. 2. Moskva: Izd. žurnala Russkaja mysl', 1896. 3 izd. 408 s.

Reka igraet — Na zatmenii — At-Davan — Čerkes — Sudnyj den' (Iom-kipur)

Kn. 3. S.-Peterburg: Izd. žurnala Russkoe bogatstvo, 1903. 2 izd. 349 s.

Ogon'ki — Skazanie o Flore, Agrippe i Menacheme — "Gosudarevy jamščiki" — Moroz — Poslednij luč — Marusina zaimka — Mgnovenie — V oblačnyj den'

Slepoj muzykant: ėtjud. 7 izd. S.-Peterburg: Izd. žurnala Russkoe bogatstvo, 1899. 201 s.

Soročinskaja tragedija (po dannym sudebnago razsledovanija). S.-Peterburg: Izd. redakcii žurnala Russkoe bogatstvo, 1907. 82 s.

> *Ded.:* D^{ru} Al'fredu Iensenu na pamjat' o Poltave — Vl. Korolenko. 1909

Sudnyj den' (Iom-Kipur): malorusskaja skazka. Petrograd: Izd. Petrogradskogo Soveta Rabočich i Krasnoarmejskich Deputatov, 1919. 61 s.

V golodnyj god: nabljudenija, razmyšlenija i zametki. 3 izd. S.-Peterburg: Izd. red. žurnala Russkoe bogatstvo, 1897. 362 s.

Koškarov, Sergej Nikolaevič
(pseud.: S. Zarevoj)

Pulemet. Moskva: Gos. izd. 1919. 35 s.: ill.

Kostomarov, Nikolaj Ivanovič

Bogdan Chmel'nickij: istoričeskaja monografija Nikolaja Kostomarova. T. 1-3. Izd. 4-e, ispr. i dopoln. S.-Peterburg: Tipogr. M. M. Stasjuleviča, 1884. xii, 378, 445, 455 s. (Istoričeskija monografii i izsledovanija Nikolaja Kostomarova, 9)

Černigovka: byl' vtoroj poloviny XVII veka. S.-Peterburg: Tipogr. M. M. Stasjuleviča, 1890. 316 s.

Choluj: ėpizod iz istoričesko-bytovoj russkoj žizni pervoj poloviny XVIII stoletija N. I. Kostomarova. 2 izd. S.-Peterburg: Tipogr. M. M. Stasjuleviča, 1897. 297 s.

Kovalevskaja, S.V. —> Litvinova, E.F.: S.V. Kovalevskaja...

Kovalevskij, Pavel Ivanovič

Petr Velikij i ego genij. S.-Peterburg: Izd. Russk. Medicinsk. Vestnika, 1900. 248 s.

Kovalevsky, M. W. —> La Russie...

Kozlov, Ivan Ivanovič

Stichotvorenija I. I. Kozlova. Izd. ispravl. i znač. dopoln. Ars. I. Vvedenskim. S biografičeskim očerkom i s portretom Kozlova gravirovannym na stali F. A. Brokgauzom v Lejpcige. S.-Peterburg: Izd. A. F. Marksa, 1892. 344 s.

Kozlov, Pavel Alekseevič

Polnoe sobranie sočinenij. 4 izd. T. 1-4. Moskva: Izd. red. žurnala Russkaja mysl', 1897. 308, 497, 466, 384 s.

Kramskoj, I. N. —> Suvorin, A.: Ivan Niko-laevič Kramskoj...

Krašeninnikov, Nikolaj Aleksand-rovič

Devstvennost': zapiski strannago čelo-veka: roman v dvuch častjach. Mosk-va: Moskovskoe knigoizd., 1913. 404 s.

Dve žizni: povest'-skazka. Moskva: Ti-pogr. N. N. Kušnerev, 1909. 119 s.
> Ded.: V znak glubokago uvaženija
> Gospodinu Al'fredu Iensenu
> N. Krašeninnikov, Moskva,
> 1911, 11 sentjabrja

Iz vešnjago vremeni. S risunkami. Moskva: Izd. red. žurnalov Svetljačok i Putevodnyj ogonek, 1908. 120 s.: ill.

Mečty o žizni: razskazy. T. 1. Moskva: Moskovskoe knigoizd., 1911. 280 s.
> Ded.: Glubokouvažaemomu
> Gospodinu Al'fredu Iensenu v
> znak uvaženija N. Krašeninnikov

Nevozvratnoe. Moskva: Moskovskoe knigoizd., 1914. 209 s.

Ugasajuščaja Baškirija. Moskva: Tipo-litografija T-va I. N. Kušnerev, 1907. 134 s.,8 tabl.

Krasnaja knižka. Moskva: Gos. izd., 1920–1921.
—>
Barankevič, Iv.: Staryj Nil (2)
Belkina, O.: Dezertir (3)
Sivačev, M.: Proškino gore (4)
Konopnickaja, M.: Staryj perepletčik (5)
Kasatkin, I.: Petruškina žizn' (6)
Pod"jačev, S.: Prošenie (7)

Kasatkin, Iv.: Put' doroga (9)
Pod"jačev, S.: Doma (10)
Boreckaja, M.: V lesu dikosti (13)
Kasatkin, Iv.: Na barkach (14)
Zarevoj, S.: Velikaja nov' (15)
Boreckaja, M.: V železnom kruge (16)
Boreckaja, M.: Golodnye (17)
Mordvinkin, V.: Egoruškina žizn' (18)
Karpinskij, V. A.: My i oni (21)
Neverov, A.: Baby (23)
Derjabina, S.: Na zare novogo mira (25)
Šubin, N.: Strannik (26)
Velikij kommunar (27)
Čiževskij, D.M.: Ego veličestvo Trifon (29)
Brik, O.M.: Barin, pop i kulak (30)
Belov, A.A.: Kak tri mužika... (31)
Basov-Verchojancev, S.: Žadnyj mužik (32)
Bachmetev, E.: Sorok mesjacev...(36)
Boreckaja, M.: Plovučij majak (37)
Semenovskij, D.M.: Krasnyj uzor (38)
Dolinov, M.: Oktjabr' (40)
Kedrov, M.: Kommunistka (45)
Sbornik revoljucionnych stichov (46)

Krasnov, P. N.

Venok na mogilu neizvestnago soldata imperatorskoj rossijskoj armii. Varša-va: P. Szwede, 1924. 51 s.

Kravčinskij, S. M. —> Dejč, L.: S. M. Krav-činskij...

Kremnev, Ivan
(A. V. Čajanov = Botanin X)

Putešestvie moego brata Alekseja v stranu krest'janskoj utopii. Č. 1. S pre-disloviem P. Orlovskogo. Moskva: Gos. izd., 1920. 61 s.

Alfred Nobel, with his signature in Cyrillic characters. In
*Prazdnovanie dvadcatipjatiletija tovariščestva neftjanogo
proizvodstva Brat'ev Nobel'*, 1905.

Front cover of *Prazdnovanie dvadcatipjatiletija tovariščestva neftja-nogo proizvodstva Brat'ev Nobel'*, 1905.

Emanuel Nobel's residence and factory in St. Petersburg. The Headquarters of Nobel Brothers Petroleum Production Company. In *Na pamjat' o dne pjatidesjatiletija Ėmmanuila Ljudvigoviča Nobel'*, 1909.

Emanuel Nobel's school for workers' children in St. Petersburg. In *Na pamjat' o dne pjatidesjatiletija Ėmmanuila Ljudvigoviča Nobel'*, 1909.

Скандинаву Альфреду Іенсену,
отъ давнишняго почитателя
богатой сагами Скандинавіи.

К. Д. БАЛЬМОНТЪ.   К. Бальмонтъ

Просторы Сибирскіе ектон.
1916. Мартъ.

ЯСЕНЬ.

ВИДѢНІЕ ДРЕВА.

Konstantin Bal'mont: Dedication to Alfred Jensen in *Jasen'*, 1916.

Альфреду Іенсену

Въ знакъ уваженія

1907   Валерій Брюсовъ

ПУТИ И ПЕРЕПУТЬЯ

ТОМЪ I.

Valerij Brjusov: Dedication to Alfred Jensen in *Puti i pereput'ja*, t. I, 1908.

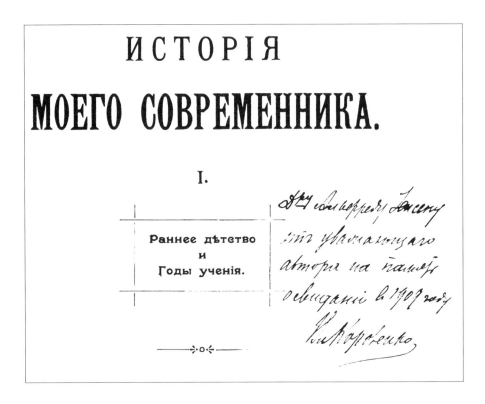

V. Korolenko: Dedication to Alfred Jensen in *Istorija moego sovremennika*, 1909.

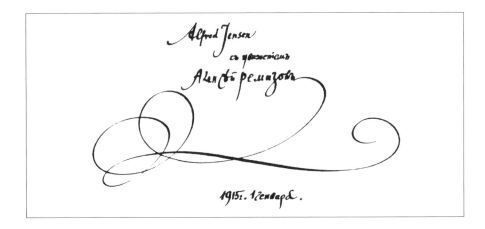

Aleksej Remizov: Dedication to Alfred Jensen in *Vesennee poroše*, 1915.

Памятникъ Горькому отъ босяковъ.
Каррикатура Овода.   *Стрекоза.*

Caricature of Maksim Gor'kij. In Viktor Rusakov, *Maksim Gor'kij v karrikaturach i anekdotach,* 1903.

No. 1967.

IJ.

Stockholm, den 20 juni 1921.

SVENSKA AKADEMIEN,

S t o c k h o l m

Enligt bifogande lista hava vi härmed
nöjet översända från Ryska Statsförlag erhållna
böcker.

Högaktningsfullt

För RYSKA HANDELSDELEGATIONEN I SVERIGE

N. Oschmiansky

A letter from the Russian Trade Delegation in Stockholm accompanying a book donation to
Nobel Library (1921).

Krestovskij, V.
(N. D. Zaiončkovskaja)

Sobranie sočinenij V. Krestovskago (psevdonim). T. 1-5. S portretom avtora. S.-Peterburg: Izd. A. S. Suvorina, 1892.

T. 1: Biografija — Anna Michajlovna — Provincija v starye gody — Dnevnik sel'skago učitelja — Iskušenie — Utrennij vizit. xviii, 471 s.

T. 2: Neskol'ko letnich dnej — U ženicha i u nevesty — Ispytanie — V doroge — Razgovor — Derevenskaja istorija — Dlja detskago teatra — Iz svjazki pisem, brošennoj v ogon' — Bariton — Dobroe delo — Staroe gore — Bratec — Nedopisannaja tetrad' — Pansionerka. 496 s.

T. 3: Vstreča — V ožidanii lučšago — Stojačaja voda — Za stenoju — Domašnee delo — Staryj portret, novyj original — Dva pamjatnye dnja — Pervaja bor'ba. 484 s.

T. 4: Nedavnee — Bol'šaja medvedica — Sčastlivye ljudi — Na večer — Vera. 458 s.

T. 5: Al'bom. Gruppy i portrety — Svidanie — Učitel'nica — Posle potopa — Zdorov'e — Proščanie — Objazannosti — Žit' kak ljudi živut — Byloe — Orleanskaja Deva. 449 s.

Krestovskij, Vsevolod Vladimirovič

Sobranie sočinenij Vsevoloda Vladimiroviča Krestovskago. T. 1-8. S biografiej V. V. Krestovskago i ego portretom, pod red. Ju. L. El'ca. S.-Peterburg: Izd. T-va Obščestvennaja pol'za, 1899-1900.

T. 1-2: Peterburgskija truščoby. Č. 1-6. 1899. 862 s.

T. 3: Krovavyj puf — Očerki: Pan Pšependovskij — Pod kaštanami Sak-

sonskago sada. 1899. 622 s.

T. 4: Dedy — Ne byt' po semu — Očerki kavalerijskoj žizni — Očerki i razskazy — Stichotvorenija. 1899. 288, 257 s.

T. 5: Dvadcat' mesjacev v dejstvujuščej armii — Razskaz o tom, kak my s Solomonom Solomonovičem echali iz Čauški — Bakšiš — Srednij soldat — Naša buduščaja vojna. 1899. 580 s.

T. 6: V dal'nich vodach i stranach. 1899. 505 s.

T. 7: V gostjach u émira Bucharskago — Vdol' Zakavkazskoj granicy — Vdol' Avstrijskoj granicy — Russkij gorod pod avstrijskoj markoj — Novyj put' v Central'nuju Aziju — Po povodu tolkov o putjach k Bosforu — Russkaja cerkov' na Japonskom more — Lovkij i sil'nyj udar angličan po Rossii — Sinto i Bukk'jo — Pos'et, Sujfun i Ol'ga — Belovežskaja pušča — Očerki kampanii 1829 goda v Evropejskoj Turcii — Tambovskie dvorjanskie vybory — Nespokojnyj dom — Stepnoe gnezdo — Mezonin v Revjakonoj ulice — Zmeinyj ded — Vne zakona. 1900. 724 s.

T. 8: T'ma egipetskaja — Tamara Bendavid — Toržestvo Vaala. 1900. 489 s.

Kritičeskija stat'i o proizvedenijach Maksima Gor'kago: Michajlovskij, Skabičevskij, Men'šikov, Minskij, Posse, Obolenskij, Bocjanovskij, Ignatov, Gekker, A.B., S.M. V S.-Peterburge 1901. 254 s.

Krivenko, Sergej Nikolaevič

M. E. Saltykov, ego žizn' i literaturnaja dejatel'nost'. S portretom M. E. Saltykova, gravirovannym v Lejpcige Gedanom. 2-e izd. S.-Peterburg: Tipogr. T-va Obščestvennaja pol'za, 1896. 88 s. (Žizn' zamečatel'nych ljudej)

Kruglov, Aleksandr Vasil'evič

Na čužom pole: očerki i razskazy. Moskva: Izd. 2-e dopoln. D. P. Efimova, 1895. 320 s. (Živyja duši. T. 2)

Ne geroi: očerki i razskazy. Moskva: Izd. 2-e dopoln. D. P. Efimova, 1895. 278 s. (Živyja duši. T. 1)

Stichotvorenija. Moskva: Tipogr. T-va I. N. Kušnerev, 1897. 324 s.

Krylov, Ivan Andreevič

Basni: polnoe sobranie. Red., vstupitel'naja stat'ja i primeč. E. A. Ljackago. Stokcholm: Severnye ogni, 1921. 248 s.

Basni Krylova: polnoe sobranie s biografiej i primečanijami (dva portreta, vidy pamjatnika, mogily Krylova i 15 risunkov). Izd. 2-e. S.-Peterburg: Izd. A. S. Suvorina, 1899. 300 s.: ill. (Deševaja biblioteka, 319)

—> Briliant, S. M.: I. A. Krylov...

Krylov, Viktor (Aleksandrov)

Dramatičeskija sočinenija. T. 1-6. S.-Peterburg: Tipogr. Šredera, 1885-1899.
    T. 1: K mirovomu — Po duchovnomu zaveščaniju — Na chlebach iz milosti. 2 izd. 1892. x, 472 s.
    T. 2: V osadnom položenii — Zemcy. 2 izd. 1885. 338 s.
    T. 3: Šalost' — Poėzija ljubvi — V duche vremeni. 1899. 447 s.

T. 4: Ot avtora — Gore-zlosčast'e — Sekretnoe predpisanie — My possorilis'. 1888. xiii, 386 s.
    T. 5: Sorvanec — Nadja Muranova — Medved' sosvatal. 1890. 372 s.
    T. 6: Sem'ja — Razlad — Dividend — Vnučka. 1892. 452 s.

Stichotvorenija. S.-Peterburg: Tipogr. Šredera, 1896. 215 s.

Kubikov, Ivan Nikolaevič
(I. N. Dement'ev)

Rabočij klass v russkoj literature. Izd. 3-e, vnov' pererabotannoe i dopoln. Ivanovo-Voznesensk: Osnova, 1926. 346 s.

Kudrin, N. E. —> Rusanov, N. S.

Kukol'nik, Nestor Vasil'evič

Dva Ivana, dva Stepanyča, dva Kostyl'kova: roman. T. 1-2. S.-Peterburg: Izd. A. S. Suvorina, [n.d.]. 383, 401 s. (Deševaja biblioteka, 205-206)

Kunik, Arist Aristovič

Sbornik materialov dlja istorii Imperatorskoj Akademii Nauk v XVIII veke. Izdal A. Kunik. Č. 1-2. S.-Peterburg, 1865. lvi, 530 s.

Kuprin, Aleksandr Ivanovič

Razskazy. T. 1. S.-Peterburg 1903

Sočinenija. T. 6, 7: 1. S.-Peterburg
    T. 6: Literaturnyja charakteristiki

— Šutki — Očerki — Belletristika. 1909.

    T. 7. Č. 1: V Krymu — Jama. 1910.

Kušnerev, Ivan Nikolaevič

Sočinenija I.N. Kušnereva. S portretom i faksimile avtora. Izd. 2-e., dopoln. očerkami i razskazami, napisannymi posle vychoda v svet pervago izd. Moskva: Tipo-lit. T-va I. N. Kušnerev, 1895.

    T. 1: Provincial'nye očerki. 273 s.

    T. 2: Belletristika. 256 s.

    T. 3: Očerki iz narodnago byta. 183 s.

Kutorga, Michail Semenovič

Sobranie sočinenij Michaila Semenoviča Kutorgi. S portretom avtora. Izd. pod red. Mich. Step. Kutorgi. T. 1-2. S.-Peterburg: Izd. L. F. Panteleeva, 1894-1896. 566, 700 s.

    S. 647-700: Ukazatel' ličnych, mifologičeskich, geografičeskich imen i vyraženij

Kuzmin, Michail Alekseevič

Voennye razskazy: Angel severnych vrat — Serenada Gretri — Pastyr' voinskij — Kirikova lodka — Pravaja lampočka — Dva brata — Tretij vtornik — Pjat' putešestvennikov. Petrograd: Tipogr. Sirius, 1915. 96 s.

L.N. Tolstoj — žizn' i tvorčestvo 1828-1908. Kritiko-biografičeskoe izd. N. G. Molostvova i P. A. Sergeenko pod red. A. L. Volynskago. S.-Peterburg: Izd. P.P. Sojkina, [n.d.]. 68 s.: ill.

Lacis, Martyn Ivanovič
(Jan Fridrichovič Sudrabs)

Črezvyčajnye Komissii po bor'be s kontr-revoljuciej. Moskva: Gos. izd.,1921. 62 s. (10.000)

Lamanskij, V. I. —> Rossija...

Lazarev, Nikolaj Artemovič
(pseud.: N. A. Temnyj)

Rasskazy. Pod red. I. A. Belousova. S biografičeskim očerkom, portretom avtora i snimkom s pamjatnika na ego mogile. Moskva: Gos. izd., 1920. 108 s.

    Nasledstvo — Sirotki — Obysk — Jubilej "Blochi" — Ne ubili — Dokladnaja zapiska — Sobač'ja dolja — Na golubom ozere

L'dov, K. —> Rozenbljum, V. K. N.

Lebedenko, Aleksandr Gervasevič

Tjaželyj divizion. Avtolitografii E. Kibrika. Izd. četvertoe. Leningrad: Izd. pisatelej, 1934. 603 s.: ill. (5.600)

Legendy, skazanija, mify narodov.
Pod red. Vladimira Astrova. 1-2. Berlin: Izd. S. Efron, 1923.

    T. 1: Indijskija skazanija. Perevod V. Astrova. 284 s.

    T. 2: Skazanija drevnego Vavilona. Perevod V. Bogrovoj i V. Astrova. 258 s.: ill.

Lejkin, Nikolaj Artemovič

Christova nevesta: roman. 4 izd. S.-Peterburg: Pečatnaja S. P. Jakovleva, 1901. 288 s.

Dačnye stradal'cy: pjat' jumorističeskich razskazov. 2 izd. S.-Peterburg: Pečatnaja S. P. Jakovleva, 1897. 244 s.
Dačnye stradal'cy — V dačnom poezde — Dačnyj ženich — Na uroke — Proščal'nyj večer — Dača po ob"javleniju

Gde apel'siny zrejut: jumorističeskoe opisanie putešestvija suprugov Nikolaja Ivanoviča i Glafiry Semenovny Ivanovych po Riv'ere i Italii. 9 izd. S.-Peterburg: Tipogr. S. P. Chudekova, 1896. 486 s.

Kum-požarnyj. Šutočnyja scenki v odnom dejstvii N. A. Lejkina. S.-Peterburg: Tipogr. R. Golike, 1888. 32 s.

Lipočka. Pustoj dom: razskazy doktora. S.-Peterburg: Pečatnaja S. P. Jakovleva, 1900. 260 s.

Medal': šutočnyja sceny v odnom dejstvii. 4 izd. S.-Peterburg: Tipogr. R. Golike, 1892. 23 s.

Na aristokratičeskij maner': šutka v 1 dejstviui N. A. Lejkina i V. V. Balibina. S.-Peterburg: Pečatnaja R. Golike, 1901. 28 s.

Na dačnom prozjabanii: 10 jumorističeskich razskazov. S.-Peterburg: Tipogr. R. Golike, 1900. 320 s.

Na pobyvke: roman iz byta piterščikov v derevne. S.-Peterburg: Pečatnaja S. P. Jakovleva, 1900. 375 s.

Na slučaj nesostojatel'nosti: šutočnyja sceny v odnom dejstvii. Izd. 3-e. S.-Peterburg: Pečatnaja S. P. Jakovleva, 1901. 25 s.

Na zarabotkach: roman iz žizni černorabočich ženščin. 3 izd. S.-Peterburg: Pečatnaja S. P. Jakovleva, 1902. 418 s.

Ne v mast': roman. 2 izd. S.-Peterburg: Tipogr. S. N. Chudekova, 1895. 239 s.

Po vsjudu: razskazy. 2 izd. S.-Peterburg: Pečatnaja S. P. Jakovleva, 1901. 332 s.

Pod južnym nebom: jumorističeskoe opisanie poezdki suprugov Nikolaja Ivanoviča i Glafiry Semenovny Ivanovych v Biaric i Madrid. 4 izd. S.-Peterburg: Pečatnaja S. P. Jakovleva, 1900. 555 s.

Radi potechi: jumorističeskija šalosti pera. 3 izd. S.-Peterburg: Tipogr. R. Golike, 1895. 384 s.

Rebjatiški: razskazy. 3 izd., dopoln. S.-Peterburg: Pečatnaja S. P. Jakovleva, 1898. 345 s.

Roždestvenskie razskazy. S.-Peterburg: Pečatnaja S. P. Jakovleva, 1901. 94 s.

Sčastlivec: roman. S.-Peterburg: Pečatnaja S. P. Jakovleva, 1901. 228 s.

Sredi pričta: roman. 2 izd. S.-Peterburg: Pečatnaja S. P. Jakovleva, 1898. 312 s.

Stukin i Chrustal'nikov: bankovaja èpopeja. S.-Peterburg: Tipogr. R. Golike, 1886. 342 s.

Susal'nyja zvezdy: roman. S.-Peterburg: Pečatnaja S. P. Jakovleva, 1898. 423 s.

Tščeslavie i Žadnost': dve povesti. S.-Peterburg: Tipogr. S. P. Chudekova, 1896. 377 s.

V carstve gliny i ognja: roman. S.-Peterburg: 1890. 210 s.

V gostjach u turok: jumorističeskoe opisanie putešestvija suprugov Nikolaja Ivanoviča i Glafiry Semenovny Ivanových čerez Slavjanskija zemli v Konstantinopol'. 7 izd. S.-Peterburg: Pečatnaja S. P. Jakovleva, 1900. 584 s.

V ožidanii nasledstva ili Stranica iz žizni Kosti Berežkova: roman. 2 izd. S.-Peterburg: Pečatnaja S. P. Jakovleva, 1901. 642 s.

Zaduševnyja pis'ma: jumorističeskie razskazy. S.-Peterburg: Tipogr. R. Golike, 1895. 274 s.

Leonov, Leonid Maksimovič

Barsuki. Gravjuri na dereve Alekseja Kravčenko. Moskva: Sovetskaja literatura, 1933. 487 s.: ill. (10.000)

Derevjannaja koroleva — Bubnovyj valet — Valina kukla. Gravjury na dereve Alekseja Kravčenko. Petrograd: Izd. M. i S. Sabašnikových, 1923. 68 s.: ill. (2.000).

Konec melkogo čeloveka. Moskva: Izd. Sabašnikových, 1924. 168 s. (2.000)

Skutarevskij. Moskva: Gos. izd. Chudožestvennaja literatura, 1935. 365 s. (15.000)

Sot': roman. Moskva: Gos. izd. Chudožestvennaja literatura, 1935. 327 s. (15.000)

Tuatamur. Moskva: Izd. M. i S. Sabašnikových, 1924. 72 s. (2.000)

Vor: roman v četyrech častjach. Moskva-Leningrad: Gos. izd., 1928. 539 s. (10.000)

Leont'ev, Konstantin Nikolaevič

O romanach gr. L. N. Tolstogo: analiz, stil, vejanie: (kritičeskij étjud). Pisano v Optinoj Pustyni v 1890 godu. Moskva 1911. Portr. of K. Leont'ev

Vostok, Rossija i slavjanstvo: sbornik stat'ej. T. 1-2. Moskva: Tipo-Litogr. I. N. Kušnerova, 1885—1886. 312, 420 s.

Lermontov, Michail Jur'evič

Demon. M. Ju. Lermontova. Ill. A. Ėberlinga. S.-Peterburg: Izd. T-va Golike i A. Vil'borg, 1910. 64 s.: ill. Faksimile rukopisi M. Ju. Lermontova. 20 s.

Geroj našego vremeni. S portretom i original'nym risunkom M.Ju. Lermontova. Red., vstupitel'naja stat'ja i primečanija E. A. Ljackago. Stokcholm: Severnye ogni, 1921. 236 s.

Knjažna Meri. Peterburg: Gos. izd., 1920. 102 s.: ill. Obložka i illjustracii chudožnika. V. Belkina. (Narodnaja biblioteka)

Polnoe sobranie sočinenij M. Ju. Lermontova. Pod red. Ars. I. Vvedenskago. V 4-ch tomach. S biografičeskim očerkom, faksimile i portretom Lermontova, gravirovannym na stali F. A. Brokgauzom v Lejpcige. 1-4. S.-Peterburg: Izd. A. F. Marksa, 1891.
    T. 1: Stichotvorenija. xiv, 282 s.

T. 2: Poėmy. 374 s.
T. 3: Proza. 272 s.
T. 4: Dramy. 320 s.

Sočinenija Lermontova. S portretom ego, dvumja snimkami s rukopisi i biografičeskim očerkom. 4 izd. vnov' sverennoe s rukopisjami, ispr. i dopoln. pod red. P. A. Efremova. T. 1-2. S.-Peterburg: Izd. Glazunova, 1880. xxxvi, 580,vii, 624 s.

Sočinenija M. Ju. Lermontova. S portretom ego i biografičeskim očerkom. S.-Peterburg Tipogr. Glazunova, 1891. 460 s. (Rublevoe izdanie v odnom tome)

—> Russkaja biblioteka. 2: M. Ju. Lermontov... —> Skabičevskij, A. M.: M. Ju. Lermontov... —> Slovar' literaturnych tipov: Lermontov...

Lerner, Nikolaj Osipovič

Belinskij. Berlin-Peterburg-Moskva: Izd. Z. I. Gržebina, 1922. 220 s. Portr.

Leskov, Nikolaj Semenovič

Polnoe sobranie sočinenij N. S. Leskova. Izd. vtoroe s kritiko-biografičeskim očerkom R. I. Sementkovskago, s priloženiem pjati portretov Leskova i snimka s ego rabočago kabineta, gravirovannych na stali F. A. Brokgauzom v Lejpcige. T. 1-12. S.-Peterburg: Izd. A. F. Marksa, 1897.
T. 1: Soborjane — Na kraju sveta — Zapečatlennyj angel. 526 s.
T. 2: Pravedniki. 519 s.
T. 3: Obojdennye — Ostrovitjane. 565 s.
T. 4: "Nekuda". 813 s.

T. 5: Smech i gore — Voitel'nica — Ledi Makbet Mcenskago uezda — Grabež—Antuka — Kolyvanskij muž—Rakušanskij melamed —Belyj orel — Čertogon —Plamennaja patriotka. 609 s.
T. 6: Zachudalyj rod — Razskazy i vospominanija — Starye gody v sele Plodomasov — Kotin doilec i Platonida — Tupejnyj chudožnik — Tomlen'e ducha. 515 s.
T. 7: Svjatočnye razskazy —Razskazy kstati. 575 s.
T. 8: Zagadočnyj čelovek — Na nožach: roman v šesti častjach. Č. 1-3. 575 s.
T. 9: Na nožach. Č. 4-6 i Épilog. 505 s.
T. 10: Gora — Legenda o sovestnom Danile — Povest' o bogougodnom drovokole — Prekrasnaja Aza — Skomoroch Panfalon — Lev starca Gerasima — Askalonskij zlodej — Skazanie o Fedore-christianine i druge ego Abrame-židovine — Pečerskie antiki — Čertovy kukly. 507 s.
T. 11: Čast' voli Božiej — Polunoščniki — Judol' — O kvakerejach — Improvizatory — Pustopljasy — Durаček — Nevinnyj Prudencij — Legendarnye charaktery. 469 s.
T. 12: Zimnij den' — Razskazy kstati — Produkt prirody — Sibirskija kartinki XVIII-go veka — Vdechnovlennye brodjagi — Nekreščennyj pop — Vladyčnyj sud — Jazvitel'nyj — Domašnjaja čeljad' — Sošestvie vo ad. 468 s.

Skazanie o Fedore-christianine i o druge ego Abrame-židovine. Petrograd: Gos. izd., 1919. 32 s.

Levitov, Aleksandr Ivanovič

Sobranie sočinenij A. I. Levitova. S portretom avtora, gravirovannym v Lejpcige, i stat'eju o žizni ego F.D. Nefedova. Izd. K. T. Soldatenkova. T. 1-2. Moskva: Moskovskaja Gorodskaja Tipogr., 1884. 736, 798 s.

Levitskij, Valerij

Gimnazičeskie rukopisnye žurnaly. Praga, 1925. 14 s. (Pedagogičeskoe Bjuro po delam srednej i nizšej russkoj školy zagranicej, 8)

Ležnev, A.
(Abram Zelikovič [Zacharovič] Gorelik)

Sovremenniki: literaturno-kritičeskie očerki. Moskva: Artel' pisatelej Krug, 1927. 179 s. (3.000)
    Delo o trude — Boris Pasternak — Leonid Leonov — Il'ja Sel'vinskij — Iosif Utkin — I. Babel' — Tri knigi [Klyčkov; V. Šklovskij; I. Evdokimov] — Pisatel' odnoj temy (o Georgie Nikiforove) — Dialogi o kritike i pisatele — "Razgrom" Fadeeva

Libedinskij, Jurij Nikolaevič

Nedelja. Gravjury na dereve Ja. Teliševskogo. Moskva: Federacija, 1932. 133 s.: ill.

Lichačev, Nikolaj Petrovič

Biblioteka i archiv Moskovskich Gosudarej v XVI stoletii. S.-Peterburg, 1894. 152, 81 (priloženija)

Likvidatoram negramotnosti: praktičeskoe rukovodstvo. (Kollektivnaja rabota kursantov Vserossijskich Kursov po Likvidacii Negramotnosti). Pod red. D. Él'kinoj. Moskva: Gos. izd., 1921. 151 s. (Vserossijskaja Črezvyčajnaja Komissija po Likvidacii Bezgramotnosti; 30.000)

Lipskerov, Konstantin Abramovič

Den' šestoj. Moskva-Petrograd: Tvorčestvo, 1922. 78 s. (1. 500)

Literatura fakta: pervyj sbornik materialov rabotnikov LEFa pod red. N. F. Čužaka. Avtory: O. M. Brik, T. S. Gric, P. V. Neznamov, V. O. Percov, V. V. Trenin, S. M. Tret'jakov, N. F. Čužak, V. B. Šklovskij. Moskva: Izd. Federacija, 1929. 268 s. (3.000)

Literaturno–chudožestvennyj al'manach izdatel'stva Šipovnik. Kn. 1-21. S.-Peterburg 1907–1913.
    Kn. 1. 1907. 290 s.: ill. A. Serafimovič: U obryva — A. Kuprin: Vred — S. Sergeev-Censkij: Lesnaja top' — N. Garin: Kogda-to — Bor. Zajcev: Polkovnik Rozov — V. Brjusov: Gorod; risunki: M. Dobužinskij, V. Bakst, N. Rerich — L. Andreev: Žizn' čeloveka
    Kn. 2. 1907. 283 s.: ill. V. Mužel': Poka — A. Kojranskij: Cholod — Iv. Bunin: U istoka dnej — B. Zajcev: Maj — Stichi: Iv. Bunin, S. Gorodeckij, Al. Blok — Aleksandr Benua: Smert' (6 ris.) — Saint-George de Vernay: Korol' bez venca
    Kn. 3. 1907. 305 s. L. Andreev: T'ma — Iv. Bunin: Astma — Bor. Zajcev: Sestra — A. Kuprin: Izumrud — A. Serafimovič: Peski — Stichi: A. Blok, G. Čulkov — F. Sologub: Tvorimaja legenda (pervaja č. romana Nav'i čary)
    Kn. 4. 1908. 273 s. Bor. Zajcev:

Agrafena: povest' — S. Juškevič: Pochoždenija Leona Drea (v dvuch častjach) — V. Brjusov: Ispolnennoe obeščanie: poèma — Al Blok: Kleopatra; Ty i ja: stichotvorenija — L. Andreev: Smert' čeloveka

Kn. 5. 1908. 240 s. Šolom Aš: Sabbataj Cevi — K. Bal'mont: Litva: stichotvorenija — S. Sergeev-Censkij: Beregovoe — L. Andreev: Razskaz o semi povešennych

Kn. 6. 1908. 261 s. M. Meterlink: Sinjaja ptica — K. Bal'mont: Krik v noči; Revnosť — A. Belyj: Golosa v poljach: stichi — N. Minskij: Videnie; Treugoľnik: stichi — L. Andreev: Moi zapiski

Kn. 7. 1908. 242 s. L. Andreev: Černyja maski — A. Frans: Iz knigi razskazov Žaka Turnebroš — P. Nilus: Na beregu morja — F. Sologub: Nav'i čary: roman (č. vtoraja: Kapli krovi)

Kn. 8. 1909. 266 s. L. Semenov: U poroga neizbežnosti; Listki — M. Rozenknop: Gorod — A. Čapygin: Prozrenie; Obraz — O. Mirtov: Kaštany — V. Jarova: Tri komnaty — S. Gorodeckij: Kroty; Jarmarka; Skala — Vl. Volkenštejn: Ioann Groznyj

Kn. 9. 1909. 252 s. S. Sergeev-Censkij: Pečaľ polej — Bor. Zajcev: Sny — L. Andreev: Syn čelovečeskij — Al. Blok: Pesnja suďby

Kn. 10. 1909. 278 s. M. Meterlink: Marija Magdalena — F. Sologub: Nav'i čary (č. treťja: Koroleva Ortruda) — A. Blok: Na Kulikovom pole: stichi

Kn. 11. 1909. 245 s. B. Zajcev: Vernosť — P. Giršbejn: Obručenie — Ju. Slovackij: Gelion-Éolion — L. Andreev: Anfisa

Kn. 12. 1910. 295 s. Bor. Zajcev: Zarja — G. Flober: Prostoe serdce (perevod B. Zajceva) — F. Sologub: Puť v Damask — Al. Tolstoj: Zavolž'e — F. Sologub: Sticii — N. Minskij: Malyj soblazn

Kn. 13. 1910. 296 s. L. Andreev: Gaudeamus — Bor. Zajcev: Smert' — Saša Černyj: Stichi — Gr. Al. N. Tolstoj: Svatobstvo — Al. Remizov: Krestovyja sestry

Kn. 14. 1911. 259 s. Gr. Al. N. Tolstoj: Dve žizni (č. I) — Bor. Zajcev: Aktrisa — G. Čulkov: Svireľ — L. Andreev: Razskaz zmei o tom, kak u neja pojavolis' jadovitye zuby — S. Sergeev-Censkij: Pristav Derjabin

Kn. 15. 1911. 271 s. Gr. Al. N. Tolstoj: Dve žizni (č. II) — M. Prišvin: Krutojarskij zver' — F. Sologub: Lesnoj pestun — Bor. Zajcev: Usaďba Laninych

Kn. 16. 1911. 305 s. L. Andreev: Saška Žegulev — A. Remizov: Petušok — Ju. Žulavskij: Konec Messii (perevod Al. Voznesenskago)

Kn. 17. 1912. 231 s. O. Dymov: Tomlenie ducha — Tèffi: Stichotvo-renija — A. Remizov: Dokuka i balagur'e: skazki

Kn. 18. 1912. 231 s. F. Sologub: Založniki žizni — A. Remizov: Pjataja jazva — M. Prišvin: Starokolennyj

Kn. 19. 1913. 277 s. Al. Tolstoj: Zavolož'e — F. Sologub: Stichi — N. Minskij: Malyj soblazn — A. Šnicler: Frau Beata i eja syn (perevod Zin. Vengerovoj) — L. Andreev: Ekaterina Ivanovna

Kn. 20. 1913. 231 s. Bor. Zajcev: Daľnij kraj — Pierre Mille: Ljubovnoe priključenie Amandy Manžen (per. N. Minskago) — Ch. N. Bjalik: Noj i Marinka (per. s evrejskago pod red. avtora)

Kn. 21. 1913. 218 s. Bor. Zajcev: Daľnij kraj (č. II) — Ju. Verchovskij: Zolotoj Cvetok — L. Rejsner: Atlantida

Literaturnoe nasledstvo. T. 16-18: Puškin. Moskva: Žurnaľno-gazetnoe ob''edinenie, 1934. 1 s.: ill. (10.000)

Litvinova, Elizaveta Fedorovna

N. I. Lobačevskij, ego žizn' i naučnaja dejatel'nost': biografičeskij očerk E. F. Litvinovoj. S portretom Lobačevskago, gravirovannym v Lejpcige Gedanom. S.-Peterburg: Tipogr. P. P. Sojkina, 1895. 79 s. (Žizn' zamečatel'nych ljudej)

S. V. Kovalevskaja (ženščina-matematik), eja žizn' i naučnaja dejatel'nost': biografičeskij očerk E. F. Litvinovoj. S portretom Kovalevskoj, gravirovannym v Lejpcige Gedanom. S.-Peterburg: Tipogr. P. P. Sojkina, 1894. 92 s. (Žizn' zamečatel'nych ljudej)

Ljackij, E. A. —> Byliny... —> Ruš' straždajuščaja... —> Skazki, utechi, dosužija...

Lobačevskij, N.I.—> Litvinova, E.F.: N.I. Lobačevskij...

Loboda, Andryj Mytrofanovyč

Russkij bogatyrskij èpos: opyt kritiko-bibliografičeskago obzora trudov po russkomu bogatyrskomu èposu. Kiev: Tipogr. Imperatorskago Universiteta Sv. Vladimira, 1896. 236 s.

Lomonosov, Michail Vasil'evič

Drevnjaja rossijskaja istorija ot načala rossijskago naroda do končiny velikago knjazja Jaroslava Pervago ili do 1054 goda sočinennaja Michailom Lomonosovym, statskim sovetnikom, professorom chimii i členom Sanktpeterburgskoj Imperatorskoj i Korolevskoj Švedskoj Akademii Nauk. V Sanktpeter-

burge: Pri Imperatorskoj Akademii Nauk, 1766. 140 s.

Sočinenija M. V. Lomonosova v stichach. Pod red. Ars. I. Vvedenskago. S biografičeskim očerkom i portretom Lomonosova, gravirovannym na stali I. F. Dejningerom v Mjunchene. 2-oe izd. S.-Peterburg: Izd. A. F. Marksa, 1897. 352 s.

—> L'vovič-Kostrica, A.I.: M. V. Lomonosov, ego žizn'...

Longinov, A. V.

Istoričeskoe izsledovanie skazanija o pochode severskago knjazja Igora Svjatoslaviča na polovcev v 1185 g. A. V. Longinova. Odessa: Ėkonomičeskaja tipogr., 1892. 261 s.

Lozovskij, A.

Moskva ili Amsterdam. Reč' proiznesennaja na Kongrese nezavisimych s. d. v Galle 14-go nojabrja 1920 goda. Moskva: Gos. izd. 1921. 29 s. (Biblioteka Professional'nogo Dviženija. Serija meždunarodnaja, 3; 30.000)

Lugovoj, A. —> Majak...

Lugovskoj, Vladimir Aleksandrovič

Muskul: vtoraja kniga stichov. Moskva: Federacija, 1929. 119 s. (2.000)

Lunačarskij, Anatolij Vasil'evič

Ètjudy: sbornik statej. Moskva-Peterburg: Gos. izd., 1922. 342 s. (7.000)

Ivan v raju: mif v pjati kartinach. Moskva: Gos. izd., 1920. 40 s.: ill.

Korolevskij bradobrej: p'esa. Izd. 2-oe. Petrograd: Gos. izd., 1918. 110 s.

Magi: dramatičeskaja fantazija. Moskva-Petrograd: Gos. izd. 1919. 66 s. (Teatral'nyj otdel Narodnogo Komissariata po Prosveščeniju)

O Tolstom: sbornik statej. Moskva-Leningrad: Gos. izd. 1928. 140 s.

Lundel', I. A. —> K novym daljam...

L'vov-Rogačevskij, V.
(Vasilij L'vovič Rogačevskij)

Novejšaja russkaja literatura. 7-e izd., pererabotannoe avtorom. Moskva: Kooperativnoe izd. Mir, 1927. 423 s. (5.200)

L'vovič-Kostrica, Aleksandr Iulianovič

M. V. Lomonosov, ego žizn', naučnaja, literaturnaja i obščestvennaja dejatel'nost': biografičeskij očerk A. I. L'vovič-Kostrica. S portretom Lomonosova, gravirovannym v Peterburge K. Adtom. S.-Peterburg: Tipogr. Ju. N. Èrlich, 1892. 86 s. (Žizn' zamečatel'nych ljudej)

Lyzlov, V.

Istorija zemli varjažskoj Rusi i bor'by russkago naroda s latinskoj propagandaju v predelach eja. Sostavitel' V. Lyzlov. Vil'na: Tipogr. M. B. Žirmunskago, 1886. 326 s.

M. Gor'kij: materialy i issledovanija. Pod red. V. A. Desnickogo. T. 1. Leningrad: Izd. Akademii Nauk SSSR, 1934. 552 s. (Institut Russkoj Literatury. Literaturnyj Archiv)

M. Gor'kij v portretach i fotografičeskich snimkach. K 35-letiju literaturnoj dejatel'nosti 1892–1927. Moskva: Akc. Izd. T-vo Ogonek, 1927. 46 s.: ill.

M. Gor'kij 1868–1928: katalog knig. Moskva: Gos. izd., 1928. 52 s. (25.000)

Majak: literaturno-publicističeskij sbornik. S.-Peterburg: Izd. A. Lugovogo, 1906. 275 s.: ill.

Majakovskij, Vladimir Vladimirovič

Rasskaz o dezertire. Tekst i risunki V. V. Majakovskogo. Moskva: Gos. izd., 1921. 15 s.: ill. (Otdel voennoj literatury pri Revoljucionnom Voennom Sovete Respubliki; 200.000)

Majkov, Apollon Nikolaevič

Polnoe sobranie sočinenij A. N. Majkova. 6 izd., ispr. i dopoln. avtorom. V trech tomach. S.-Peterburg: Tipogr. A. F. Marksa, 1893.
   T. 1: Lirika. 600 s.
   T. 2: Kartiny. 560 s.
   T. 3: Poèmy. 506 s.

Majkov, Leonid Nikolaevič

Batjuškov, ego žizn' i sočinenija. Izd. vtoroe, vnov' peresmotr. S portretom K. N. Batjuškova, gravirovannym na stali F. A. Brokgauzom i pečatannym na japonskoj bumage. S.-Peterburg: Izd. A. F. Marksa, 1896. vi, 287 s.

Istoriko-literaturnye očerki: Krylov, Žukovskij, Batjuškov, Puškin, Pletnev, Pogodin, Fet. S.-Peterburg: Izd. L. F. Panteleeva, 1895. 309 s.

Maksim Gor'kij. Moskva: Nikitinskie Subbotniki, 1927. 223 s. (Biblioteka Sovremennych Pisatelej dlja Školy i Junošestva pod red. E. F. Nikitinoj. Kritičeskaja serija; 4.000)

Malis, Ju. G.

N. I. Pirogov, ego žizn' i naučno-obščestvennaja dejatel'nost': biografičeskij očerk Ju. G. Malisa. S portretom Pirogova, gravirovannym v Peterburge K. Adtom. S.-Peterburg: Tipogr. P. P. Sojkina, 1893. 96 s. (Žizn' zamečatel'nych ljudej)

Mandel'štam, Iosip Emil'janovič

O charaktere Gogolevskago stilja: glava iz istorii russkago literaturnago jazyka. S.-Peterburg-Gel'singfors: Novaja tipogr. Guvudstadsbladet, 1902. 405, ix s.

Opyt ob"jasnenija obyčaev (indo-evropejskich narodov) sozdannych pod vlijaniem mifa. Č. 1-ja. S.-Peterburg: Tipolitogr. A. E. Landau, 1882. 336 s.

Markov, A. —> Belomorskija byliny...

Maslov, V.

Načal'nyj period bajronizma v Rossii: kritiko-bibliografičeskij očerk. Kiev-Petrograd: Tipogr. Imperatorskago Universiteta Sv. Vladimira, 1915. 132 s. (250)

Materialy dlja istorii gonenija studentov pri Aleksandre II. 2-oe izd. (Materialien zur Geschichte der Verfolgung von Studenten unter Alexander II. Zweite Auflage). Leipzig: É. L. Kasprovič; Berlin: J. Ladyschnikow. 183 s. (Meždunarodnaja biblioteka, 31)

Materialy i čerty k biografii Imperatora Nikolaja I i k istorii ego carstvovanija. Izd. pod red. I. F. Dubrovina. S.-Peterburg: Tipogr. I. N. Skorochodova, 1896. 702 s.

Mazepa, getman —> Umanec, F. M.: Getman Mazepa...

Mej, Lev Aleksandrovič

Polnoe sobranie sočinenij L. A. Meja. V pjati tomach s portretom avtora. Izd. N. G. Martynova. S.-Peterburg, 1887.
T. 1: Liričeskija stichotvorenija. S primečanijami. lxxxvi, 320 s.
T. 2: Liričeskija stichotvorenija. Perevody s grečeskago, anglijskago, nemeckago i francuzskago jazykov. vi, 349 s.
T. 3: Proza. Perevody s českago, pol'skago, anglijskago i francuzskago. 341 s.
T. 4: Dramatičeskija proizvedenija. S istoričeskimi primečanijami: Carskaja nevesta — Pskovitjanka — Servilija

— Dmitrij Samozvanec, tragedija Šillera — Lager Valenštejna, dramatičeskoe stichotvorenie F. Šillera — Burja, drama Šekspira. 444 s.

T. 5: Povesti i razskazy — Stat'i različnago soderžanija. S portretom avtora. 408 s.

Mejerchol'd, V. È. —> Volkov, N. D.: Mejerchol'd...

Mel'nikov, Pavel Ivanovič

Polnoe sobranie sočinenij P. I. Mel'nikova (Andreja Pečerskago). 2 izd. S kritiko-biografičeskom očerkom A. A. Izmajlova i s priloženiem portreta P. I. Mel'nikova-Pečerskago. T. 1-7. S.-Peterburg: Izd. T-va A. F. Marks, 1909. (Priloženie k žurnalu Niva na 1909 god)
T. 1: Razskazy. 288 s.
T. 2-3: V lesach. 554, 519 s.
T. 4-5: Na Gorach. 568, 483 s.
T. 6: Stat'i i razskazy. 422 s.
T. 7: Očerki i popovščiny. 589 s.

Menšikov, A.D.—>Porozovskaja, B.D.: A.D. Menšikov...

Merežkovskij, Dmitrij Sergeevič

Bylo i budet: dnevnik 1910—1914. Petrograd, 1915. 360 s.

Christos i Antichrist: trilogija. 1-3. S.-Peterburg: Tip. N. N. Klobukova, 1902-1905.
T. 1: Smert' bogov (Julian otstupnik). 2 izd. l902. 328 s.   ·
T. 2: Voskresšie bogi (Leonardo da Vinči). 1902. 685 s.
T. 3: Antichrist (Petr i Aleksej). S.-

Peterburg: Izd. M. V. Pirožkova, 1905. 608 s.

Gogol': tvorčestvo, žizn' i religija. SPB: Panteon, 1909. 231 s.

Gogol' i čert: izsledovanie. Obložka raboty N. Feofilaktova. Moskva: Skorpion, 1906. 218 s.

Grjaduščij cham. Čechov i Gor'kij D. S. Merežkovskago. SPB: Izd. M.V. Pirožkova, 1906. 185 s.
Grjaduščij cham — Čechov i Gor'kij — Teper' ili nikogda — Strašnyj sud nad russkoj intelligenciej — Sv. Sofija — O novom religioznom dejstvii

L. Tolstoj i Dostoevskij D. S. Merežkovskago. T. 1-2. S.-Peterburg, 1901-1903.
T. 1. S.-Peterburg. Izd. žurnala Mir iskusstva, 1901. 366 s.
T. 2: Religija L. Tolstogo i Dostoevskago. 2 izd. S.-Peterburg: Izd. M. V. Pirožkova, 1903. xl, 530 s.

Lica svjatych: ot Iisusa k nam. T. 1: Pavel — Avgustin. Berlin: Petropolis, 1936. 262 s.

Ljubov' silnee smerti — Nauka ljubvi — Mikel' Anželo — Svjatoj Satir. Moskva: Knigoizd. Skorpion, 1902. 178 s.

Messija. 1-2. Paris: Knigoizd. Vozroždenie, [n.d., ca. 1929]. 183, 135 s.

Novyja stichotvorenija 1891–1895. S.-Peterburg, 1896. 104 s.

O pričinach upadka i o novych tečenijach sovremennej russkoj literatury. S.-Peterburg: Tipo-litografija B. M. Vol'fa, 1893. 192 s.

Pavel I [trilogija: Pavel I. Aleksandr I.

Nikolaj I — Dekabristy]. Peterburg: Gos. izd., 1920. 223 s.

Polnoe sobranie sočinenij D. S. Merežkovskago. 1-17. S.-Peterburg-Moskva: Izd. T-va M. O. Vol'f, 1911–1913.

T. 1-5: Christos i Antichrist: trilogija. 1911–12. xi, 336, 348, 376, 264, 275 s. T. 1, s. ixi: Dmitrij Sergeevič Merežkovskij: kritiko-biografičeskij očerk M. A. Ljackago; 3 portr.

T. 6: Povesti i legendy: Ljubov' silnee smerti — Nauka ljubvi — Mikel' Anželo — Svjatoj Satir — Dafnis i Chloja. 1911. 248 s.

T. 7-9: Tolstoj i Dostoevskij: žizn', tvorčestvo i religija. 1912. 310, 222, 251 s.

T. 10: Ne mir no meč: k buduščim kritikam christianstva — Gogol': tvorčestvo, žizn' i religija — M. Ju. Lermontov: poèt sverch čelovečestva. 1911. 334 s.

T. 11: Grjaduščij cham — Čechov i Gor'kij — Teper' ili nikogda — Strašnyj sud nad russkoj intelligenciej — Sv. Sofija — O novom religioznom dejstvii (otkrytoe pis'mo N. A. Berdjaevu) — Prorok russkoj revoljucii (K jubileju Dostoevskago). 1911. 224 s.

T. 12: Vol'naja Rossija — V tichom omute. 1912. 358 s.

T. 13: Večnye sputniki. 1911. 362 s.

T. 14: Tragedii: Èschil: skovannyj prometej — Sofokl: Èdip-car — Sofokl: Èdip v kolone — Sofokl-Antigona — Èvripid-Medej — Èvripid-Ippolit. 1912. 389 s.

T. 15: Stichotvorenija – O pričinach upadka i o novych tečenijach sovremennoj russkoj literatury. 1912. 305 s.

T. 16-17: Aleksandr l. 1913. 335, 342 s.

Roždenie bogov: Tutankamon na Krite. Praga: Plamja, 1925. 189 s.

Mater' bogov – Labirint – Pazifaja — Vakchanki — Minotavr — Krest

Simvoly (pesni i poèmy): Bog — Smert' — Francisk Assizkij — Vera — Legendy — Semejnaja Idillija — Konec Veka — Voron — Vozvraščenie k Prirode — Prometej. S.-Peterburg: Izd. A. S. Suvorina, 1892. 424 s.

Tajna trech: Egipet i Vavilon. Praga: Plamja, 1925. 364 s.

Tajna Zapada: Atlantida-Evropa. Belgrad: Russkaja tipografija, 1920. 532, xx s. (Russkaja biblioteka, 17; 1.500). Portr.

Večnye sputniki: portrety iz vsemirnoj literatury. 2 izd. S.-Peterburg: Tipogr. M. Merkuševa, 1899. 552 s.

Akropol' — Dafnis i Chloja — Mark Avrelij — Plinij Mladšij — Kal'deron — Servantes — Monten' — Flober — Ibsen — Dostoevskij — Gončarov — Majkov — Puškin

14 dekabrja. Pariž: Knigoizd. Russkaja zemlja, 1921. 496 s.

Der Zar und die Revolution [von] Dmitri Mereschkowski, Zinaida Hippius, Dmitri Philosophoff. München und Leipzig: R. Piper, 1908. 203 s.

Meščerskij, Vladimir Petrovič

Moi vospominanija. Č. 1-2. S.-Peterburg: Tipogr. knjaza V. P. Meščerskago, 1897–98.

Č. 1: 1850–1865. 1897. 453 s.
Č. 2: 1865–1881. 1898. 514 s.

Merime, P. —> Mérimée, Prosper

Mérimée, Prosper

Žakerija. Perevod Z.A. Vengerovoj pod red. E. G. Lundberga. Moskva: Gos. izd., 1919. 169 s.

Mezier, Avgusta Vladimirovna

Russkaja slovesnost' s XI po XIX stoletija vključiteľno. Bibliografičeskij ukazateľ proizvedenij russkoj slovesnosti v svjazi s istoriej literatury i kritikoj. Knigi i žurnalnyja stať'i. Sost. A.V. Mezier. S.-Peterbourg: Tipogr. A. Porochovščikova, 1899–1902.
T. 1: Russkaja slovesnost' s XI po XVIII v. 1899. 161 s.
T. 2: Russkaja slovesnost' XVIII i XIX st. S predisloviem N. A. Rubakina. 1902. 650 s.

Mežov, Vladimir Izmajlovič

Sistematičeskij katalog russkim knigam prodajuščimsja v knižnom magazine Aleksandra Fedoroviča Bazunova, kommissionera Imperatorskoj Akademii Nauk, Morskago Učenago Komiteta, Ministerstv Justicii i Finansov v S.-Peterburge..., s ukazaniem 20.000 kritičeskich stať'ej, recenzij i bibliografičeskich zametok, kasajuščichsja knig, pomeščennych v kataloge, izvlečennych iz vsech periodičeskich izdanij i sbornikov, vyšedšich v svet s 1825 vplot' do 1869 goda; a takže bolee 400 ukazanij perevodov russkich sočinenij na inostrannye jazyki, vyšedšich otdeľnymi izdanijami. Sost. V. I. Mežov. S.-Peterburg: Izd. knigoprodavca A. F. Bazunova, 1869. xiii, 995 s.

Michajlovskij, N. G. —> Garin, N.

Michajlovskij, Nikolaj Konstantinovič

Kritičeskie opyty N. K. Michajlovskago.
T. 3: Ivan Groznyj v russkoj literature — Geroj bez vremen'ja. Izd. O.N. Popovoj. S.-Peterburg: Tipo-litogr. B.M. Voľfa, 1895. 163 s.

Michnevič, Vladimir Osipovič

Istoričeskie ètjudy russkoj žizni. T. 1-2. S.-Peterburg 1879–1882.
T. 1: Očerk istorii muzyki v Rossii v kuľturno-obščestvennom otnošenii. 1879. 359 s.
T. 2: Narodnaja kopilka Christa radi — Istorija russkoj borody —Istorija odnogo "prokljatago" voprosa — Ob"ediniteli — Pljaski na Rusi v chorovode, na balu i v balete — Izvraščenie narodnago pesnotvorčestva — Lodka.1882. 429 s.

Russkaja ženščina XVIII stoletija: istoričeskie ètjudy. Kiev-Char'kov: Južno-russkoe knigoizd. F.A. Iogansona, 1895. 402 s.

Mickevič, A. —> Mjakotin, V. A.: A. Mickevič...

Miljukov, Aleksandr Petrovič

Literaturnyja vstreči i znakomstva. S.-Peterburg: Izd. A. S. Suvorina, 1890. 279 s.
Vospominanija o F. F. Kokoškine — D. I. Jazykov — Vstreča s N. V. Gogolem — Irinarch Ivanovič Vvedenskij — Znakomstvo s O. I. Senkovskim — Ja. P. Bytkov — Znakomstvo s A.I. Gercenom — Fedor Michajlovič Dostoevskij — Ap. Grigor'ev i L. A. Mej

Miljukov, Pavel Nikolaevič

Glavnyja tečenija russkoj istoričeskoj mysli. T. 1-2. Izd. red. žurnala Russkaja mysl'. Moskva 1898. 396 s.

Očerki po istorii russkoj kul'tury. Č. 1-2. S.-Peterburg: Izd. red. žurnala Mir Božij, 1900–1899.
    Č.1: Naselenie, ėkonomičeskij, gosudarstvennyj i soslovnyj stroj. 4-e izd., ispr. i dopoln. 1900. 239 s.
    Č. 2: Cerkov' i škola (vera, tvorčestvo, obrazovanie). 2-e izd., ispr. i dopoln. 1899. 373 s.

Miller, Orest Fedorovič

Slavjanstvo i Evropa: stat'i i reči Oresta Millera 1865–1877. S.-Peterburg: Tipogr. G. E. Blagosvetova, 1877. xvi, 417 s.

Miller, Vsevolod Fedorovič

Očerki russkoj narodnoj slovesnosti: byliny. Moskva: Tipogr. T-va I. D. Sytina, 1897. xiv, 464 s.

Minskij, N. M.
(Nikolaj Maksimovič Vilenkin)

Stichotvorenija. 3 izd. S.-Peterburg: Tipogr. M. M. Stasjuleviča, 1896. 34 s.

Mirskij, Dmitrij Svjatopolk

Contemporary Russian literature 1881-1925 by prince D. S. Mirsky. London: George Routledge, 1926. xi, 372 s.

A history of Russian Literature: from the earliest times to the death of Dostoevsky (1881) by prince D. S. Mirsky. London: George Routledge, 1927. xi, 388 s.

Mišeev, Nikolaj Isidorovič

Na rassvete: p'esa v 4-ch dejstvijach. Peterburg: Gos. izd., 1920. 79 s. (Ser. Repertuar: Russkij teatr)

Mjakotin, Venedikt Aleksandrovič

A. Mickevič, ego žizn' i literaturnaja dejatel'nost': biografičeskij očerk V. A. Mjakotina. S portretom A. Mickeviča, gravirovannym v Lejpcige Gedanom. S.-Peterburg: Tipogr. T-va Obščestvennaja pol'za, 1891. 93 s. (Žizn' zamečatel'nych ljudej)

A. S. Puškin i Dekabristy. Berlin: Izd. Plamja, 1923. 89 s.

Protopop Avvakum, ego žizn' i dejatel'nost': biografičeskij očerk V. A. Mjakotina. Bez portreta Avvakuma, kotorogo nigde nel'zja dostat'. S.-Peterburg: Tipogr. T-va Obščestvennaja pol'za, 1893. 160 s. (Žizn' zamečatel'nych ljudej)

Modzalevskij, Boris L'vovič

Anna Petrovna Kern. Po materialam Puškinskogo doma. Leningrad: Izd. M. i S. Sabašnikovych, 1924. 141 s.: ill. (Druz'ja Puškina pod red. M. O. Geršenzona)

Moor, D.
(Dimitrij Stachievič Orlov)

Azbuka krasnoarmejca. Napisal i nari-
soval D. Moor. Moskva: Otdel voennoj
literatury pri Revoljuconnom voennom
Sovete Respubliki. Gos. izd., 1921. [28]
s.: ill.

Mordvinkin, V.

Egoruškina žizn'. Moskva: Gos. izd.,
1920. 30 s.: ill. (Krasnaja knižka, 18)

Morozov, Petr Osipovič

Minuvšij vek: literaturnye očerki. S.-
Peterburg: Izd. red. žurnala Obrazo-
vanie, 1902. 524 s.
    Iz istorii karikatury — Russkaja li-
teratura XIX veka — Iz istorii russkoj
literaturnoj kritiki — Puškin — Pote-
chin — Ostrovskij — Gercen

Očerki iz istorii russkoj dramy XVII-
XVIII stoletij. S.-Peterburg: Tipogr. V. S.
Balaševa, 1888. vi, 389 s.

Morozov, N. —> Alfavitnyj ukazatel' uzakonenij...

Morozov, V. S.

Za odno slovo: razskaz. S predisloviem
L. N. Tolstogo. Berlin: J. Ladyschnikow, [n.d.]. 23 s.

Moskovskij sbornik. Izd. K. P. Pobedo-
nosceva. 4-e dopoln. izd. Moskva: Sinodal'naja tipogr. 1897. 331 s.

Mujžel, Viktor Vasil'evič

Rasskazy. T. 1. Peterburg: Gos. izd.,
1920. 295 s.

Muratov, Pavel Pavlovič

Ėgerija: roman. Berlin-Peterburg-Moskva: Izd. Z. I. Gržebina, 1922. 304 s.

Načalo: stichi. Leningrad-Moskva: Gos.
izd. chudožestvennoj literatury, 1931.
93 s. (Sovremennaja proletarskaja literatura: Prizyv udarnika; 3.000)
    Stichi rabočich Leningrada A. Alfe-
eva, R. Zernova, Ja. Zlatopol'skogo, S.
Kaufmana, N. Levitova, F. Ružanskogo,
I. Celikova, M. Čertkova i B. Šmidta.

Nadson, Semen Jakovlevič

Stichotvorenija S. Ja. Nadsona. S portretom, faksimile i biografičeskim očerkom. 18-oe izd. S.-Peterburg: Tipogr.
I. N. Skorochodova, 1900. lxxxviii, 320
s. (Sobstvennost' Obščestva dlja posobija nuždajuščimsja literatoram i učenym)

Narodnyja russkija legendy —> Afanas'ev,
A. N.

Narodnyja russkija skazki—> Afanas'ev,
A. N.

Naumov, Nikolaj Ivanovič

Sobranie sočinenij N. I. Naumova. V
dvuch tomach. S.-Peterburg: Tipogr.
I. N. Skorochodova, 1897.

T. 1: Umališennyj — Poskotnik — Pautina — Poslednee prosti — Kajuščijsja — Jašnik — U perevoza — Kuda ni kin' - vse klin — Zažora — Jurovaja – Gornaja idillija — Krest'janskie vybory. 514 s.

T. 2: Derevenskij aukcion — Mirskoj učet — Noč' na ozere — Pogorel'cy — Odin iz sposobov sbliženija s narodom — Svjatoe ozero — Furgonščik — Ež — Kak auknetsja, tak i otkliknetsja — Derevenskij torgaš — Nefedovskij počinok — Sarbyska — Èskizy bez tenej — Kartinka s natury. 377 s.

Navrockij, Aleksandr Aleksandrovič
(N. A. Vrockij)

Dramatičeskija proizvedenija. T. 1. S.-Peterburg: Tipogr. V. Bezobrazova, 1900. 185 s.
Gosudar'-car' Ioann III Vasil'evič: tragedija v 5-ti dejstvijach, v stichach — Bojarskoe pravlenie: otryvok iz dramatičeskoj chroniki

Skazanija minuvšago: russkija byliny i predanija v stichach. Kn. 1-2. S.-Peterburg: Tipogr. V. S. Balaševa, 1896-1899. 257, 280 s.

Naživin, Ivan Fedorovič

Intimnoe: kniga tichago razdum'ja. 2 izd. Berlin: K-vo Ikar, 1922. 126 s.

Nelidov, Vladimir Aleksandrovič

Teatral'naja Moskva (sorok let moskovskich teatrov). Berlin-Riga: Pečatano v tipogr. Globus, 1931. 443 s.

Nekrasov, Ivan Stepanovič

Opyt istoriko-literaturnago izsledovanija o proischoždenii drevne-russkago domostroja. Sočinenie I. S. Nekrasova. Moskva: Izd. Imperatorsago Obščestva Istorii i Drevnostej Rossijskich pri Moskovskom Universitete, 1873. 183 s.

Nekrasov, Nikolaj Alekseevič

Izbrannye stichotvorenija N. A. Nekrasova: sbornik dlja detej staršego vozrasta. Moskva: Gos. izd., 1920. 111 s. (Biblioteka detskogo čtenija. 50.000)

Komu na Rusi žit' chorošo: poèma. Berlin: Izd. T-va I. P. Ladyžnikova, 1917. 260 s.

Neizdannye stichotvorenija, varianty i pis'ma: iz rukopisnych sobranij Puškinskogo doma pri Rossijskoj Akademii Nauk. Petrograd: Izd. M. i S. Sabašnikovych, 1922. 303 s. 3 portreta avtora, portret Z. N. Nekrasovoj, snimok s rukopisi sticha ”Poèzija”

Polnoe sobranie stichotvorenij N. A. Nekrasova v dvuch tomach. 1-2. 7 izd. s portretom, faksimile i biografičeskim očerkom. S.-Peterburg: Tipogr. A. S. Suvorina, 1899
T. 1: 1842–1872. xxix, 608 s.
T. 2: 1873–1877. 566 s.

Stichotvorenija. Sbornik II. Peterburg: Literaturno-izdatel'skij Otdel Narodnogo Komissariata po Prosveščeniju, 1919. 102 s.

Stichotvorenija N. Nekrasova. 2-oe izd., popoln. neizdannymi ešče stichotvorenijami 1874 goda. Berlin: B. Behr's Buchhandlung, 1874. 285 s.

—> Russkaja biblioteka, 7: N.A. Nekrasov...

Nemirov, Grigorij Aleksandrovič

"Rus'" i "Varjag": proischoždenie slov. Zametki dlja vyjasnenija drevnejšej istorii Peterburgskago kraja. S.-Peterburg: Tipogr. Imperatorskoj Akademii Nauk, 1898. 44 s. (Otdel'nyj ottisk XIII vypuska "Opyta istorii S.-Peterburgskoj birži v svjazi s istoriej S.-Peterburga")

Nemirovič-Dančenko, Vasilij Ivanovič

Bankirskij dom: nravy našej buržuazii. Izd. 5-oe. Petrograd: Izd. Petrogradskogo Soveta Rabočich i Krasnoarmejskich Deputatov, 1919. 215 s.

Skobelev: ličnyja vospominanija i vpečatlenija V. I. Nemiroviča-Dančenko. S 4-mja gravjurami i faksimile pis'ma M.D. Skobeleva. S.-Peterburg: Izd. A.F. Devriena, 1882. 358 s.

Večnaja pamjat'. Petrograd: Gos. izd., 1919. 228 s.

Neverov, Aleksandr
(Aleksandr Sergeevič Skobelev)

Baby: p'esa v 4-ch dejstvijach. Moskva: Gos. izd., 1920. 88 s. (Krasnaja knižka, 23)

Nezelenov, Aleksandr Il'ič

Literaturnyja napravlenija v Ekaterinskuju êpochu. Sočinenie A. Nezelenova. S portretami Imperatricy Ekateriny II, Cheraskova, Fonvizina, Kapnista, Novikova. S.-Peterburg: Izd. Knigoprodavca N.G. Martynova, 1889. vi, 395 s.

Nikitin, Afanasij

Choždenie za tri morja Afanasija Nikitina. V 1466–1471 gg. Čtenija I.I. S-go. S.-Peterburg 1857.

Nikitin, Ivan Savvič

Sočinenija I. S. Nikitina. S ego portretom, faksimile i biografiej sost. i vnov' ispr. M. F. De-Pule. T. 1-2. Moskva: Tipogr. Ė. Lissner i Ju. Roman, 1883. 496, 347 s.

—> F. E. Sivickij: I. S. Nikitin, ego žizn'...

Nikitina, Evdokija Fedorovna

Russkaja literatura ot simvolizma do našich dnej: literaturno-sociologičeskij seminarij. S predisloviem N.K. Piksanova. Moskva: Nikitinskie Subbotniki, 1926. 544 s. (4.100)

Nikitina, E.F. & Šuvalov, S.V.

Belletristy sovremennniki: stat'i i issledovanija. 1-4. Moskva: Nikitinskie Subbotniki, 1928–1931.
    1. A. P. Bibik — F. V. Gladkov — A.S. Neverov — A. S. Novikov-Priboj — P.S. Romanov. 2 dopoln. izd. 1928. 207 s. (3.000)
    2. I. E. Vol'nov — N. N. Ljaško — L.N. Sejfulina — A. S. Serafimovič — A.S. Jakovlev. 1929. 290 s. (4.000)
    3. Leonid Leonov — A. Malyškin — Ju. Libedinskij — A. A. Fadeev. 1930. 307 s. (3.000)

4. Artem Veselyj — Michail Šolochov — Georgij Nikiforov — N. Panferov — A. P. Čapygin. 1931. 209 s. (5.000)

Nikodim Pavlovič Kondakov. K vos'midesjatiletiju so dnja roždenija. So stat'jami E. Minnsa, A. Myn'osa, M. I. Rostovceva, S. A. Žebeleva i I. I. Tolstogo. Praga: Plamja, 1924. 85.

Nikolaj I —> Dubrovin, N. F.: Materialy i čerty k biografii...

Nikol'skij, Jurij Aleksandrovič

Turgenev i Dostoevskij: istorija odnoj vraždy. Sofija: Rossijsko-bolgarskoe knigoizd., 1921. 108 s.

Nikon, patriarch —> Bykov, A. A.: Patriarch Nikon... —> Delo o patriarche Nikone...

Nižegorodskij sbornik. S.-Peterburg: Izd. T-va Znanie, 1905. 345 s.

Nobel', brat'ja

Dvadcatipjatiletie Tovariščestva neftjanogo proizvodstva Br. Nobel' 1879-1904. S.-Peterburg: T-vo R. Golike i A. Vil'borg, 1904. 171 s.: ill.

Mechaničeskij zavod Ljudvig Nobel' 1862–1912. S.-Peterburg: T-vo R. Golike i A. Vil'borg, 1912. 112 s.: ill., tabl.

Na pamjat' o dne pjatidesjatiletija Ėmanuila Ljudvigoviča Nobel'. Izd. Komissiej služaščich Tovariščestva neftjanogo proizvodstva brat'ev Nobel', 1909.

47, 115 s., 22 tabl. ill.

Na pamjat' o dne pjatidesjatiletija Ėmanuila Ljudvigoviča Nobel' 10 ijunja 1909 goda. S.-Peterburg: Izd. Komissiej služaščich Tovariščestva neftjanogo proizvodstva Brat'ev Nobel', 1909. 44 tabl. ill.

Naftaproduktionsbolaget Bröderna Nobel St. Petersburg: några bilder af naftans vinning och bearbetning, bolagets nederlag samt sjö- och flodtransportmedel. 1914. 74 s. ill.

Prazdnovanie dvadcatipjatiletija Tovariščestva neftjanogo proizvodstva Brat'ev Nobel' 1879–1904. S.-Peterburg 1905. 141 s.: ill.

Novikov, Nikolaj Ivanovič

Truten' 1769–1770. 3 izd. P. A. Efremova. S portretom N. I. Novikova i dvumja snimkami s zaglavnych listkov Trutnja 1769 i 1770 gg. S.-Peterburg: Tipogr. I. I. Glazunova, 1865. 370 s.

Živopisec. 1772–1773. Izbrannyja stat'i iz Živopisca — Izvlečenie iz Trutnja — Materialy dlja izučenija pisatelja. S.-Peterburg: Tipogr. Glazunova, 1896. 106 s. (Russkaja klassnaja biblioteka izd. pod red. A. N. Čudinova)

—> Usova, S. E.: N. I. Novikov, ego žizn'...

Novikov-Priboj, Aleksej Silyč

Cusima. Ill. P. Pavlinova. Kn. [1]-2. Moskva: Sovetskij pisatel', 1934–1935. 373, 333 s.

Ženščina v more: roman. Riga: M.

Didkovska izdevnieciba, [1935]. 160 s.

Novyj ènciklopedičeskij slovar'. Izd. pod obščej red. početnogo akademika K. K. Arsen'eva. Izdateli: F. A. Brokgauz (Lejpcig) i I. A. Efron (S.-Peterburg). T. 1-25, 27-28. S.-Peterburg: Tipogr. Akcionnoe Obščestvo Brokgauz-Efron, 1915–1916.

O Dostoevskom: sbornik stat'ej pod red. A. L. Bema. 1-3. Praga 1929–1936.
    1. 1929. 162 s. S. i-viii,1-89: Slovar' ličnych imen u Dostoevskogo (400)
    2. 1933. 124, viii, 89 s. Slovar' ličnych imen u Dostoevskogo
    3.: U istokov tvorčestva Dostoevskogo: Griboedov, Puškin, Gogol', Tolstoj i Dostoevskij. 1936. 214 s.

Ob Aleksandre Bloke: stat'i N. Anciferova, Ju. Verchovskogo, V. Žirmunskogo, Vl. Pjasta, A. Slonimskogo, Ju. Tynjanova, B. Èjchenbauma, B. Èngel'gardta. Peterburg: Knigoizd. Kartonnyj Domik, 1921. 336 s. (1.000)

Obradovič, Sergej Aleksandrovič

Sdvig: stichi. Moskva: Vserossijskaja Associacija Proletarskich Pisatelej, 1921. 13 s.

Odoevskij, Aleksandr Ivanovič

Polnoe sobranie stichotvorenij knjazja Aleksandra Ivanoviča Odoevskago (dekabrista). S biografičeskim očerkom i portretom avtora. Moskva: Tipogr. F. K. Iogansona, 1890. 140 s.

Sočinenija knjazja A. I. Odoevskago. S biografičeskim očerkom i primečanijami sost. M. N. Mazaevym. S.-Peterburg: Izd. Evg. Evdokimova, 1893. 83 s. (Ežemesjačnoe priloženie k žurnalu Sever za ijul' 1893)

Ogarev, Nikolaj Platonovič

Stichotvorenija N. Ogareva. 3 izd. K. Soldatenkova. Moskva: V tipogr. V. Gračeva, 1863. 167 s.

Ogarkov, V. V.

A. V. Kol'cov, ego žizn' i literaturnaja dejatel'nost': biografičeskij očerk V. V. Ogarkova. S portretom Kol'cova i alfavitnym ukazatelem ego stichotvorenij položennych na muzyku. S.-Peterburg: Tipogr. T-va Obščestvennaja pol'za, 1891. 95 s. (Žizn' zamečatel'nych ljudej)

Demidovy — osnovateli gornago dela v Rossii: biografičeskij očerk V. V. Ogarkova. S portretom Akinfija Demidova, gravirovannym v Lejpcige Gedanom. S.-Peterburg: Tipogr. T-va Obščestvennaja pol'za, 1891. 95 s. (Žizn' zamečatel'nych ljudej)

E. P. Daškova, eja žizn' i obščestvennaja dejatel'nost': biografičeskij očerk V. V. Ogarkova. S portretom Daškovoj, gravirovannym v Lejpcige Gedanom. S.-Peterburg: Tipogr. T-va Obščestvennaja pol'za, 1893. 78 s. (Žizn' zamečatel'nych ljudej)

G. A. Potemkin, ego žizn' i obščestvennaja dejatel'nost': biografičeskij očerk V. V. Ogarkova. S portretom Potemkina, gravirovannym v Lejpcige Geda-

nom. S.-Peterburg: Tipogr. Ju. N. Ėrlich, 1892. 80 s. (Žizn' zamečatel'nych
ljudej)

V. A. Žukovskij, ego žizn' i literaturnaja
dejatel'nost': biografičeskij očerk V. V.
Ogarkova. S portretom V. A. Žukovskago, gravirovannym v Lejpcige Gedanom. S.-Peterburg: Tipogr. T-va Obščestvennaja pol'za, 1894. 80 s. (Žizn'
zamečatel'nych ljudej)

Voroncovy, ich žizn' i obščestvennaja
dejatel'nost': biografičeskie očerki V. V.
Ogarkova. S portretom knjazja M. S.
Voroncova, travirovannym v Lejpcige
Gedanom. S.-Peterburg: Tipogr. T-va
Obščestvennaja pol'za, 1892. 96 s.
(Žizn' zamečatel'nych ljudej)

Ognev, N.
(Michail Grigor'evič Rozanov)

Kostja Rubcov v Vuze: prodolženie na-
šumevšej knigi "Dnevnik Kosti Rubco-
va". Riga: Knigoizd. Gramatu Draugse,
1929. 205 s.

Okulov, Aleksej Ivanovič

Tam, gde smert': ėpizod graždanskoj
vojny v odnom dejstvii. Moskva: Gos.
izd., 1919. 32 s. (Teatral'nyj otdel Narodnogo Komissariata po Prosveščeniju)

Oleša, Jurij Karlovič

Zavist'. Gravjury na dereve V. Kozlin-
skogo. Moskva: Sovetskaja literatura,
1933. 163 s.: ill.

Oliger, Nikolaj Fridrichovič

Prazdnik vesny: roman. S.Pb.: Knigoizd. Osvoboždenie, 1911. 220 s. (Sobranie sočinenij, 4)

> *Ded.:* D-ru A. Iensenu v znak glu-
> bokago uvaženija i priznatel'nosti
> — ot avtora. Odessa 1911

Razskazy. T. 3: Volki — Belye lepestki
— Pustynja — Predatel' — Osennjaja
pesnja. S. Pb.: Kn-vo Prometej, 1910.
236 s.

Orlov, D. S. —> Moor, D. (pseud.)

Ostromirovo Evangelie 1056-1057 g.

Vtoroe fotolitografičeskoe izd. Iždiveni-
em Potomstvennago Početnago Gražda-
nina Il'i Kirilloviča Savinkova. S.-Peter-
burg: Foto-Litogr. A. F. Markova, 1889.
[ca. 600 s., folio]

Ostrovskij, Aleksandr Nikolaevič

Bednost' ne porok: komedija v trech
dejstvijach. Petrograd: Literaturno-
izdatel'skij Otdel Komissariata Narodnogo Prosveščenija, 1919. 69 s. (Narodnaja biblioteka)

Dochodnoe mesto: komedija v pjati
dejstvijach. Petrograd: Literaturno-
izdatel'skij Otdel Komissariata Narodnogo Prosveščenija, 1919. 97 s. (Narodnaja biblioteka)

Dramatičeskija sočinenija A. Ostrovskago i N. Solov'eva. Moskva: Izd. knižn.
mag. V. V. Dumnova, 1897. 379 s.

Sčastlivyj den' — Ženiťba Belugina — Na poroge k delu — Dikar'ka

Ne tak živi, kak chočetsja: narodnaja drama v trech dejstvijach. Petrograd: Literaturno-izdateľskij Otdel Komissariata Narodnogo Prosveščenija, 1919. 50 s.

Sočinenija A. N. Ostrovskago. S dvumja portretami i biografičeskim očerkom. 1-10. 10 izd. Moskva: Izd. knižn. mag. V. Dumnova, 1896.
T. 1: A. Nos: A. N. Ostrovskij: biografičeskij očerk — Semejnaja kartina — Svoi ljudi - sočtemsja — Utro molodogo čeloveka — Bednaja nevesta — Ne v svoi sani ne sadis'. lv, 319 s.
T. 2: Bednosť ne porok — Ne tak živi, kak chočetsja — V čužom piru pochmeľe — Dochodnoe mesto — Prazdničnyj son – do obeda — Ne sošlis' charakterami. 331 s.
T. 3: Svoi sobaki gryzutsja, čužaja ne pristavaj — Za čem pojdeš' to i najdeš' — Staryj drug lučše novych dvuch — Vospitannica — Groza — Tjažolye dni. 344 s.
T. 4: Grech da beda na kogo ne živet — Koz'ma Zachar'ič Minin, Suchoruk — Šutniki — Voevoda (Son na Volge). Novaja redakcija. 407 s.
T. 5: Pučina — Na bojkom meste — Dmitrij Samozvanec i Vasilij Šujskij. 267 s.
T. 6: Tušino — Vasilisa Melent'eva — Na vsjakago mudreca dovoľno prostoty. 288 s.
T. 7: Ne vse kotu maslenica — Les — Bešeny den'gi — Gorjačee serdce. 432 s.
T. 8: Ne bylo ni groša, da vdrug altyn — Komik XVII stoletija — Sneguročka — Pozdnjaja ljubov'. 367 s.
T. 9: Trudovoj chleb — Bogatyja nevesty — Volki i ovcy — Pravda – cho-

rošo, a sčasť e lučše — Poslednjaja žertva. 504 s.
T. 10: Bezpridannica —Serdce ne kamen' — Nevol'nicy — Talanty i poklonniki — Krasavec-mužčina —Bez viny vinovatye — Ne ot mira sego. 652 s.

Sočinenija A. N Ostrovskogo. T. 1. Peterburg: Gos. izd., 1919. lxxiii, 396 s. Portret A. N. Ostrovskogo
N. Dolgov: A. N. Ostrovskij: očerk žizni i tvorčestva — Semejnaja kartina — Svoi ljudi – sočtemsja — Utro molodogo čeloveka — Neožidannyj slučaj — Bednaja nevesta — Ne v svoi sani ne sadis' — Priloženie: Zapiski zamoskvoreckogo žitelja — Literaturno-sceničeskie primečanija.

Ozerov, Vladislav Aleksandrovič

Ėdip v Afinach: tragedija v pjati dejstvijach, v stichach s chorami — Dmitrij Donskoj: tragedija v pjati dejstvijach v stichach. 2 izd. S.-Peterburg: Izd. A. S. Suvorina, 1890. 155 s. (Deševaja biblioteka, 49)

Sočinenija V. A. Ozerova. Č. 1-2. Sanktpeterburg: V tipogr. Ivana Glazunova, 1816–1823.
Č. 1: V. Kapnist: O žizni i sočinenijach V. A. Ozerova 1816. 38 s.— Ėdip v Afinach: tragedija. 3 izd. 1823. 72 s. — Fingal: tragedija. 1823. 50 s.
Č. 2: Dmitrij Donskoj: tragedija. 3 izd. 1819. 82 s. — Poliksena: tragedija. 2 izd. 1819. 94 s.

Sočinenija Ozerova. 3 izd. Mavrikija Osipoviča Voľfa. Sanktpeterburg: V knižnom magazine M. O. Voľfa, 1856. 430 s. (Polnoe sobranie sočinenij russkich avtorov)

Panaev, Ivan Ivanovič

Literaturnyja vospominanija s priloženiem pisem. 3 izd. S.-Peterburg: Izd. N. G. Martynova, 1888. 419 s.

Pervoe polnoe sobranie sočinenij I. I. Panaeva v šesti tomach. S portretom avtora. S.-Peterburg: Izd. knigoprodavca N. G. Martynova, 1888–1889.
   T. 1: Povesti i razskazy 1834– 1840. 1888. xv, 400 s.
      S. vii-xv: Ot izdatelja. Nekrolog I. I. Panaeva
   T. 2: Povesti, razskazy i očerki 1840–1844. 1888. 484 s.
   T. 3: Romany i povesti 1847–1852. 1888. 470 s.
   T. 4: Povesti, razskazy i očerki 1845–1858. 1888. 570 s.
   T. 5: Očerki iz peterburgskoj žizni v dvuch častjach — Stichotvorenija i parodii. 1889. 658, 110 s.
   T. 6: Literaturnyja vospominanija s priloženiem pisem raznych lic. 1888. 419 s.

Pasternak, Boris Leonidovič

Devjat'sot pjatyj god. Moskva-Leningrad: Gos. izd., 1927. 100 s.

Poverch bar'erov: stichi raznych let. Moskva-Leningrad: Gos. izd., 1929. 159 s.

Sestra moja žizn': leto 1917 goda. Berlin-Peterburg-Moskva: Izd. Z. I. Gržebina, 1923. 115 s.
   Portret avtora raboty Ju. Annenkova 1921

Pavel I: sobranie anekdotov, otzyvov, charakteristik, ukazov i pr. Sost. Aleksandr Geno i Tomič. S priloženiem portreta. S.-Peterburg: Sinodal'naja tipogr., 1901. 300 s.

Pavlenko, Petr Andreevič

Barrikady. Risunki G. Fillipskogo. Moskva: Federacija, 1932. 216 s.: ill.
   Nabljudenie dejstviem — Dombrovskij — Tret'e maja — Ulica Turnon, 15 — Gljadi na puli

Pavlov, N. M.

Russkaja istorija ot drevnejših vremen: pervye pjat' vekov rodnoj strany (862–1362). T. 1-2. Moskva: Tipo-litografija T-va I. N. Kušnerev, 1896–1899. 405, 356 s.

Pečerskij, A. —> Mel'nikov, P. I.

Pekarskij, Petr Petrovič

Novyja izvestija o V. N. Tatiščeve. S portretom Tatiščeva i snimkom ego počerka. S.-Peterburg, 1864. 66 s. (Priloženie k IV-mu tomu Zapisok Imp. Akademii Nauk)

Pereverzev, Valer'jan Fedorovič

Tvorčestvo Dostoevskogo. Moskva: Gos. izd., Moskovskoe otdelenie, 1922. 252 s. (4.000)

Perov, V. G. —> Diterichs, L. K.: V. G. Perov, ego žizn'...

Pervol'f, Iosif Iosifovič

Germanizacija baltijskich slavjan. Iz-sledovanie Iosifa Pervol'fa, ėkstraordi-narnago professora Imperatorskago varšavskago universiteta. S.-Peterburg: Tipogr. V. S. Balaševa, 1876. 260 s.

Peskovskij, Matvej Leont'evič

A. V. Suvorov, ego žizn' i voennaja deja-tel'nost': biografičeskij očerk M. L. Pes-kovskago. S portretom Suvorova, gra-virovannym v Lejpcige Gedanom. S.-Peterburg: Tipogr. Ju. N. Ėrlich, 1899. 102 s. (Žizn' zamečatel'nych ljudej)

Baron N. A. Korf, ego žizn' i obščest-vennaja dejatel'nost': biografičeskij očerk M. L. Peskovskago. S portretom N. Korfa, gravirovannym v Peterburge K. Adtom. S.-Peterburg: Tipogr. T-va Obščestvennaja pol'za, 1893. 95 s. (Žizn' zamečatel'nych ljudej)

K. D. Ušinskij, ego žizn' i pedagogiče-skaja dejatel'nost': biografičeskij očerk M. L. Peskovskago. S portretom Ušin-skago, gravirovannym v Lejpcige Geda-nom. S.-Peterburg: Tipogr. Ju. N. Ėr-lich, 1893. 80 s. (Žizn' zamečatel'nych ljudej)

Pesni sobrannyja P. V. Kireevskim. Izd. Obščestvom Ljubitelej Rossijskoj Slovesnosti. 1-10. Moskva: V tipogr. Bachmeteva, 1861–1874.

Pesni sobrannyja P.V. Kireevskim. Novaja serija. Izd. Obščestvom Ljubi-telej Rossijskoj Slovesnosti pri Impera-torskom Moskovskom Universitete. Pod red. dejstviteľnych členov Obščestva akademika V. F. Millera i prof. M. N. Speranskago. Vyp. I (pesni obradovy-ja). S portretom P. V. Kireevskago. Moskva, 1911. lxxiii, 353 s.

Pesni sobrannyja P. N. Rybnikovym. Narodnyja byliny, stariny i pobyvaľ-ščiny. Č. 1-2. Moskva: V tipogr. A. Se-mena, 1861–1862. 488, xxvi, 354, ccclxxi s. (Sobstvennosť sobiratelja)

Petr I

Pis'ma i bumagi Imperatora Petra Veli-kago. T. 1-3. S.-Peterburg: Gosudarst-vennaja tipogr., 1887–1893.
    T. 1: 1688–1701. 1877. xxxii, 888, lii s.
    T. 2: 1702–1703. 1899. xxiii, 721, lxii s.
    T. 3: 1704–1705. 1893. xxxi, 1065, lxiv s.

—> Ivanov, I. M.: Petr Velikij, ego žizn'...—> Kovalevskij, P. I.: Petr Velikij...

Petropavlovskij, Nikolaj Eľpidiforo-vič (Karonin, pseud.)

Snizu vverch. Pod red. E. G. Lundber-ga. Peterburg-Moskva: Gos. izd., 1920. 118 s. (Narodnaja biblioteka)

Petrov, Grigorij Spiridonovič

Brat'ja pisateli. 7-e izd. S.-Peterburg: Tipogr. P. Voščinskoj, 1904. 151 s.

Christos voskres!: sbornik razskazov dlja detej svjaščennika G. Petrova. 2 izd. Moskva: Tipogr. T-va I. D. Sytina, 1903. 48 s.

Zatejnik. svjaščen. G. S. Petrova. Č. 1-3. 2 izd. s risunkami. S.-Peterburg: Tipogr. P. F. Voščinskoj, 1904–1905. 192, 159, 190 s.: ill.

Petrov, Stepan Gavrilovič
(Skitalec, pseud.)

Razskazy i pesni. T. 1. Izd. 5-oe. S.-Peterburg: Izd. T-va Znanie, 1903. 273 s.

Pil'njak, Boris Andreevič

Byl'e. Revel': Izd. Bibliofil, 1922. 132 s.
    Nad ovragom —U Nikoly, čto na Belych Kolodezjach — Polyn' — Arina — Proselki — Imenie Belokonskoe — Kolumen'–gorod — Smertel'noe manit — Pozemka — God ich žizni — Tysjača let

Golyj god: roman. Peterburg-Berlin: Izd. Gržebina, 1922. 142 s.

Krasnoe derevo. Berlin: Petropolis, 1929. 76 s.

O'kėj: amerikanskij roman. Moskva: Federacija, 1933. 373 s. (10.200)

Prostye rasskazy. Obložka, titul'nyj list, zastavki, koncovki i zaglavnye bukvy raboty D. I. Mitrochina. Peterburg: Izd. Vremja, 1923. 79 s.: ill. (4.000).
    Celaja žizn' — Smertel'noe manit — Smerti — Prostye rasskazy: Vsegda komandirovka; Volčyj ovrag; Pervyj den' vesny; Morja i gory — Vešči

Volga vpadaet v Kaspijskoe more: roman. Moskva: Izd. Nedra, 1930. 263 s. (10.000)

Pirogov, Nikolaj Ivanovič

Sočinenija N. I. Pirogova. S priloženiem stat'i: Proščanie Kievskago učebnago okruga s N. I. Pirogovym, s portretom i faksimile avtora i s dvumja risunkami... T. 1-2, 2 izd. S.-Peterburg: Tipogr. M. M. Stasjuleviča, 1900. 552, 525 s.

—> Malis, Ju. G.: N. I. Pirogov, ego žizn'...

Pisarev, Dmitrij Ivanovič

Sočinenija D. I. Pisareva. Polnoe sobranie v šesti tomach. S portretom avtora i stat'ej Evgenija Solov'eva (avtora biografii Pisareva). Portret avtora i stat'ja o ego literaturnoj dejatel'nosti poмеščeny pri šestom tome. 3-e izd. F. Pavlenkova. 1-6. S.-Peterburg: Tipogr. Ju. N. Ėrlicha, 1900–1901.

—> Kazanovič, E.: D. I. Pisarev... —> Solov'ev, E. A.: D. I. Pisarev, ego žizn'...

Pisemskij, Aleksej Feofilaktovič

Polnoe sobranie sočinenij A. F. Pisemskago. 2-oe posmertnoe polnoe izd., dopoln., sverennoe i vnov' prosmotr. po rukopisjam. T. 1-24. Izd. T-va M.O. Vol'f, 1895–1896.
    T. 1: Bibliografija A. F. Pisemskago — V. Zelinskij: A. F. Pisemskij, ego žizn' i literaturnaja dejatel'nost' — P. Annenkov: A. F. Pisemskij kak chudožnik i prostoj čelovek — Avtobiografija i pis'ma — Bojarščina: roman v dvuch častjach. xiii, cclxxiv, 211 s.
    T. 2: Tjufjak: povest' — Komik: razskaz. 1895. 324 s.
    T. 3: Lešij — Piterščik — Batmanov — Fanfaron — Vinovata-li ona? 1895. 393 s.

T. 4: Bogatyj ženich — Nina — Plotnič'ja artel' — Staraja barynja. 1895. 405 s.

T. 5: Sergej Petrovič Chozarov i Mari Stupicyna — Starčeskij grech — Bat'ka. 1895. 334 s.

T. 6: Uže otcvetšie cvetki — Russkie lguny — Putevye očerki — Zapiski Salatuški — Obličitel'noe pis'mo iz ada — Fel'etony Nikity Bezrylova — Zaveščanie moim detjam Vasiliju i Nikolaju — Po povodu sočinenija N. V. Gogolja, najdennago posle ego smerti: "Pochoždenija Čičikova ili Mertvyja duši" — čast' vtoraja. 1895. 374 s.

T. 7: Tysjača duš: roman. Č. 1-2. 185. 276 s.

T. 8: Tysjača duš. Č. 3-4. 1895. 334 s.

T. 9: Vzbalamučennoe more. Č. 1-3. 1895. 321 s.

T. 10: Vzbalamučennoe more. Č.4-6. 1895. 288 s.

T. 11: Ljudi sorokovych godov. Č. 1-2. 1895. 393 s.

T. 12: Ljudi sorokovych godov. Č. 3. 1895. 221 s.

T. 13: Ljudi sorokovych godov. Č. 4-5. 1896. 417 s.

T. 14: V vodovorote. Č. 1-2. 1896. 374 s.

T. 15: V vodovorote. Č. 3. 1896. 221 s.

T. 16: Masony. Č. 1-2. 1896. 343 s.

T. 17: Masony. Č. 3. 1896. 211 s.

T. 18: Masony. Č. 4. 1896. 234 s.

T. 19: Masony, Č. 5. 1896. 229 s.

T. 20: Meščane. Č. 1-2. 1896. 278 s.

T. 21: Meščáne. Č. 3. 1896. 163 s.

T. 22: Dramatičeskija proizvedenija 1: Ipochondrik — Razdel — Chiščniki — Finansovyj genij. 1896. 356 s.

T. 23: Dramatičeskija proizvedenija 2: Veteran i novobranec — Gor'kaja sud'bina — Samoupravcy — Poručik Gladkov — Byvye sokoly — Prosve-

ščennoe vremja. 1896. 488 s.

T. 24: Dramatičeskija proizvedenija 3: Ptency poslednjago sveta — Miloslavskie i Naryškiny — Bojcy i vyžidateli — Materi-sopernicy — Semejnyj omut. 1896. 243 s.

—> Skabičevskij, A. M.: A. F. Pisemskij, ego žizn'...

Platonov, Sergej Fedorovič

K istorii Poltavskoj bitvy 27 ijunja 1709 g. S.-Peterburg: Tipogr. Nadežda, 1909. 9 s.

Pleščeev, Aleksej Nikolaevič

Povesti i razskazy A. N. Pleščeeva. S portretom gravirovannym Brokgauzom i biografičeskim očerkom. Pod red. P.V. Bykova. T. 1-2. Izd. A. A. Pleščeeva. S.-Peterburg: Tipogr. M.M. Stasjuleviča, 1896–1897.

T. 1: 1647–1859. 1896. xxvi, 742 s.

T. 2: 1859–1868. 1897. 724 s.

Stichotvorenija A. N. Pleščeeva (1844-1891). 3 dopoln. izd. S portretom avtora, snimkom s pamjatnika na ego mogile, biografičeskim očerkom i bibliografiej stichotvorenij. Pod red. P. V. Bykova. Izd. A. A. Pleščeeva. S.-Peterburg: Tipogr. A. S. Suvorina, 1898. xxxv, 824 s.

Pobedonoscev, K. P. —> Moskovskij sbornik...

Poètika: sborniki po teorii poètičeskogo jazyka. I-II. Petrograd: 18-ja Gos. tipogr., 1919. 168 s.

1. Viktor Šklovskij, L. P. Jakubinskij, E. P. Polivanov, O. Brik
2. Viktor Šklovskij, B. M. Ėjchenbaum

Pod"jačev, Semen Pavlovič

Doma: Ivanovy zapiski. Moskva: Gos. izd., 1920. 46 s.: ill. (Krasnaja knižka, 10)

Prošenie. Moskva: Gos. izd. 1920. 32 s. (Krasnaja knižka, 7)

Pogodin, Michail Petrovič

G. Gedeonov i ego sistema o proischoždenii varjagov i Rusi. S.-Peterburg 1864. 102 s. (Priloženie k VI-mu tomu Zapisok Imp. Akademii Nauk, 2)

Pogodin, Nikolaj Fedorovič

Aristokraty: komedija v 4 dejstvijach. Izd. vtoroe. Moskva-Leningrad: Gos. Ob"edinennoe Izdat. Iskusstvo, 1936. 87 s. (5.000)

Pokrovskij, Michail Nikolaevič

Russkaja istorija v samom sžatom očerke (ot drevnejšich vremen do vtoroj poloviny 19-go stoletija). Moskva: Gos. izd., 1920. 224 s.

Pokrovskij, V.

Sokraščennaja istoričeskaja chrestomatija. Posobie pri izučenii russkoj slovesnosti dlja učenikov staršich klassov sredneučebnych zavedenij. Sost. V.

Pokrovskij. 1-7. Moskva: Tipogr. G. Lissnera, 1899–1904. 675, 656, 818, 798, 856, 1115, 505 s.

Pokrovskij, V. —> Anton Pavlovič Čechov... Sost. V. Pokrovskij

Polevoj, Nikolaj Alekseevič

Abbaddonna. Č. 1-4. S.-Peterburg: Izd. A. S. Suvorina, [n.d.]. 297, 275 s. (Deševaja biblioteka)

Polevoj, Petr Nikolaevič

Istoričeskie razskazy i povesti P. N. Polevogo. S 65 original'nymi risunkami i vin'etkami K. V. Lebedeva. S.-Peterburg: Izd. A. F. Marksa, 1892. 472 s.: ill.

Istorija russkoj literatury v očerkach i biografijach. Sočinenie P. Polevogo. Č. 1-2. 5 izd. Sankt-Peterburg, 1883-1890.
Č. 1: Drevnij period. 1883. 288 s.: ill.
Č. 2: Novyj i novejšij periody — Ot Kantemira i do našego vremeni. 5 dopoln. izd. 1890. 356 s.: ill.

Poležaev, Aleksandr Ivanovič

Stichotvorenija A. I. Poležaeva. Pod red. Ars. I. Vvedenskago. S biografičeskim očerkom i portretom A. I. Poležaeva, gravirovannym na stali F. A. Brokgauzom v Lejpcige. S.-Peterburg: Izd. A. F. Marksa, 1892. 327 s.

Poljakov, Aleksandr Sergeevič

O smerti Puškina (po novym dannym). Peterburg: Gos. izd., 1922. 113 s. (Trudy Puškinskogo Doma pri Rossijskoj Akademii Nauk)

Polnyj pesennik: dragocennyj podarok ljubiteljam penija. Sobranie pesen':
novejšich, narodnych, čerkeskich, cyganskich, gruzinskich i soldatskich
različnych romansov, komičeskich kupletov, operetok, šansonetok, jumoristič eskich i satiričeskich stichotvorenij ljubimych sovremennych avtorov: Puškina, Nekrasova, Beranže, Kol'cova, Lermontova i proč. Sostavlen kružkom ljubitelej penija. V četyrech častjach. S.-Peterburg-Moskva, 1882. 636, xx s.

Polonskij, Jakov Petrovič

Polnoe sobranie sočinenij Ja. P. Polonskago. T. 1-10. Izd. Ž. A. Polonskoj. S.Peterburg: Tipogr. R. Golike, 18851886.

T. 1: Stichotvorenija 1841–1885. 1885. viii, 488 s.

T. 2: Stichotvorenija raznych godov — Kuznečik-muzykant — Bol'noj pisatel' — Svežee predanie — Noč' v Letnem sadu — V konce sorokovych godov — U Satany — Mišen'ka — Kukly. 1886. 360 s.

T. 3: Poėmy, povesti i stichotvorenija. 1886. 490 s.

T. 4: Povesti i razskazy. 1886. 577 s.

T. 5: Priznanija Sergeja Čalygina: roman. 1886. 375 s.

T. 6: Nečajanno: povest' v dvuch čast jach. 1886. 530 s.

T. 7: Deševyj gorod: chronikaroman. 1886. 562 s.

T. 8-9: Krutyja gor'ki: roman. Č. 12. 1885–86. 371, 312 s.

T. 10: Pod goru: roman (okončanie "Krutych gorok"). 1886. 392 s.

Stichotvorenija Ja. P. Polonskago. Sanktpeterburg: V tipogr. I. Fišona, 1855. 226, viii s.

Polonskij, Vjačeslav
(Vjačeslav Pavlovič Gusin)

Maksim Gor'kij: očerk s četyr'mja portretami. Moskva: Izd. Vserossijskogo Central'nogo Ispolnitel'nogo Komiteta Soveta Rab., Kr., Krasn. i Kaz. Dep., 1919. 23 s.

O sovremennoj literature. S portretami raboty Natana Al'tmana. Moskva-Leningrad: Gos. izd. 1928. 240 s.: ill. (4.000)

Babel', Pil'njak, V. V. Veresaev, A. Tolstoj, S. Malaškin, Artem Veselyj, S. Esenin, Furmanov

Očerki literaturnogo dviženija revoljucionnoj ėpochi (1917–1927). MoskvaLeningrad: Gos. izd., 1928. 334 s. (3.000)

Polovcov, A. A. —> Russkij biografičeskij slovar'...

Pomjalovskij, Nikolaj Gerasimovič

Polnoe sobranie sočinenij N. G. Pomjalovskago. S portretom avtora i biografičeskim očerkom sost. N. A. Blagoveščenskim. T. 1-2. S.-Peterburg: Izd. T-va A. F. Marks, 1912. (Priloženie k žurnalu Niva na 1912 g.)

T. 1: N. G. Pomjalovskij — biografičeskij očerk — Vukol — Meščanskoe sčastie — Molotov. 406 s.

T. 2: Očerki bursy — Neokončennyja sočinenija — Priloženie: Pis'ma k Ja. P. Polonskomu. 343 s.

Popov, A. S. —> Serafimovič, A. (pseud.)

Porickij, I. E.

Maksim Gor'kij i ego proizvedenija. S priloženiem otzyvov o Gor'kom Michajlovskago, Men'šikova, Skabičevskago, Minskago i dr., i izbrannych iz ego proizvedenij aforizmov. Sost. i perevel s nemeckago N. I. Gasfel'd. S priloženiem portreta M. Gor'kago. Varšava: Izd. M. A. Kovnera, 1903. 80 s.

Porochovščikov, Aleksandr Aleksandrovič

Rossija: nakanun XX stoletija. Vyp. 1-3. Moskva: Tipogr. br. Verner, 1889. xvii, 89, 213, 236 s.

Porošin, Semen Andreevič

Semena Porošina zapiski, služaščija k istorii ego imperatorskago vysočestva blagovernago gosudarja cesareviča i velikago knjazja Pavla Petroviča. Izd. 2-e, ispr. i značiteľno dopoln. S.-Peterburg: Tipogr. V. S. Balaševa, 1881. 635 s.

Porozovskaja, B. D.

A. D. Menšikov, ego žizn' i gosudarstvennaja dejateľnost': biografičeskij očerk B. D. Porozovskoj. S portretom Menšikova, gravirovannym v Lejpcige Gedanom. S.-Peterburg: Parovaja skoropečatnaja A. Porochovščikova, 1895. 92 s. (Žizn' zamečateľnych ljudej)

Poržezinskij, V.

Kratkoe posobie k lekcijam po istoričeskoj grammatike russkogo jazyka čitannym na b. Vysšich Ženskich Kur-

sach prof. V. Poržezinskim. Vvedenie i fonetika. Novoe izd. (tret'e) peresm. i dopoln. Moskva: Gos. izd., 1920. 151 s. (15.000)

Posoškov, Ivan Tichonovič

Zaveščanie otečeskoe. Sočinenie I. T. Posoškova. Novoe izd., dopoln. vnov' otkrytoju vtoroju polovinoju "Zaveščanija". Izd. Vysočajše učreždennoju Komissieju dlja opisanija archiva Svjatejšago Praviteľsvujuščago Sinoda, pod red. člena eja E. M. Priležaeva. Sanktpeterburg: Sinodaľnaja tipogr. 1893. ciii, 388 s.

Potapenko, Ignatij Nikolaevič

Povesti i razskazy I. N. Potapenko. T. 1-12. 2-oe izd. F. Pavlenkova. S.-Peterburg: Tipogr. P. P. Sojkina, 1895-1899.

T. 1: Svjatoe iskusstvo — Potešnaja istorija — Zdravyja ponjatija — Nikogda! 1896. 315 s.

T. 2: Na dejstviteľnoj službe — Sekretar' ego prevoschoditeľstva — Redkij prazdnik — Prokljataja slava. 1895. 320 s.

T. 3: General'skaja doč' — Krylatoe slovo — Otečestvo v opasnosti — Obščij vzgljad — Achmetka saratovskij — Icek Šmuľ, brilliantščik. 1898. 347 s.

T. 4: Šestero — Derevenskij roman — Semejka — Domašnij sud — Radi chozjajstva — Illjuzija i pravda. 1899. 335 s.

T. 5: Samorodok — Tože žizn' — Pis'mo — Zadača — Tajna — Smysl žizni — Kusok chleba — Otstuplenie — Na vdovice — Grech deda Martyna. 1901. 306 s.

T. 6: Do i posle — Ostroumno — Žestokoe sčast'e — Vragi — Nezamenimaja utrata. 1901. 333 s.

T. 7: Na pensiju — Nebyvaloe delo — Povozka — Pozdno — Prjamoj razčet — Stydno — Pravo na sčast'e. 1893. 324 s.

T. 8: Ispolnitel'nyj organ — Zemlja — Semejnaja istorija — Ampir — Nachodka — Tret'ja. 1894. 343 s.

T. 9: Rečnye ljudi — Prostaja slučajnost' — Klavdija Michajlovna — Gorjačaja stat'ja — Sčastlivyj — Razvjazannyj uzel — Beglyj. 1896. 317 s.

T. 10: Grechi — Gore-devica — Peterburgskaja istorija — Sorvalos' — Baba zamešalas' — Azorka. 1896. 340 s.

T. 11: Podval'nyj ėtaž — Mišuris — Rešilsja — Gastroler — Oktava — Tysjača talantov — Kreščenskie dni — Postnaja kolbasa — Dvenadcatyj — Pis'mo — Poėzija. 1897. 329 s.

T. 12: Ustav — Dve polosy — Mužickaja kanitel' — Sfinks. 1899. 338 s.

Potemkin, G. A. —> Brikner, A. G.: Potemkin... —> Ogarkov, V. V.: G. A. Potemkin, ego žizn'...

Pridvornyj, E. A. —> Bednyj, Dem'jan (pseud.)

Protopopov, Michail Alekseevič

Literaturno-kritičeskija charakteristiki. S.-Peterburg: Izd. red. žurnala Russkoe bogatstvo, 1896. 522 s.

V. G. Belinskij — Lev Tolstoj — N. V. Šelgunov — Vsevolod Garšin — S. T. Aksakov — A. M. Žemčužnikov — Gleb Uspenskij — F. M. Rešetnikov — N. N. Zlatovratskij — N. E. Petropavlovskij (Karonin)

V. G. Belinskij, ego žizn' i literaturnaja dejatel'nost': biografičeskij očerk M. A.

Protopopova. S portretom Belinskago, gravirovannym v Lejpcige Gedanom. 2-e izd. S.-Peterburg: Tipogr. T-va Obščestvennaja pol'za, 1894. 77 s. (Žizn' zamečatel'nych ljudej)

Prokof'ev, Aleksandr Andreevič

Pobeda: tret'ja kniga stichov. Leningrad-Moskva: LAPP. Gos. izd. chudožestvennoj literatury, 1931. 95 s. (Sovremennaja proletarskaja literatura)

Prutkov, Koz'ma (pseud.)

Polnoe sobranie sočinenij Koz'my Prutkova. S portretom, faksimile i biografičeskimi svedenijami. 8 izd. S.-Peterburg: Tipogr. M. M. Stasjuleviča, 1900. 253 s.

Prževal'skij, N. —> Ėngel'gardt, M. A.: N. Prževal'skij, ego žizn'...

Ptička-sinička: sbornik rasskazov i stichotvorenij. Risunki A. N. Komarova. Izd. T-va I. D. Sytina, [1921?]. 16 s.: ill. (Izd. zaregistrirovano v Otdele Pečati M.S.R. i Kr. D.)

Puškin, Aleksandr Sergeevič

Boris Godunov: tragedija. Peterburg: Literaturno-izdatel'skij Otdel Narodnogo Komissariata po Prosveščeniju, 1919. 119 s. (Narodnaja biblioteka)

Evgenij Onegin: roman v stichach. Peterburg: Gos. izd., 1919. 318 s. (Narodnaja biblioteka)

S. 3-44: Vstupitel'nyj očerk M. L. Gofmana

Kapitanskaja dočka. Peterburg: Gos. izd., 1920. 144 s.: ill. (Narodnaja biblioteka)

Neizdannyj Puškin. Sobranie A.F. Onegina. Peterburg: Izd. Atenej, 1922. 235 s. (Trudy Puškinskogo Doma pri Rossijskoj Akademii Nauk)

Polnoe sobranie sočinenij Puškina. T. 1-5. S.-Peterburg: Izd. Brokgauz-Efrona, 1907-1911. vii, 648; 640; 619; 560, lxxix; 552, lxxx s.: ill. (Biblioteka velikich pisatelej pod red. S. A. Vengerova)

Sočinenija A. S. Puškina. Izd. 3-e, ispravl. i dopoln., pod red. P. A. Efremova. T. 1-6. S.-Peterburg: Izd. Ja. A. Isakova, 1880–1881. viii, 584; 448; 492; 456; 544; 526 s.

Sočinenija A. S. Puškina. Polnoe sobranie v odnom tome. So stať'ej A. Skabičevskago: Aleksandr Sergeevič Puškin (biografičeskij očerk), s portretom avtora, gravirovannym V. Matz, i 160 illjustracijami. 7-e izd. S.-Peterburg: Knigopečatnaja Šmidt, 1907. 1738 stb.: ill.

Sočinenija Puškina. S priloženiem materialov dlja ego biografii, portreta, snimkov s ego počerka i s ego risunkami, i proč. Izd. P. V. Annenkova. T. 1-6. Sanktpeterburg: V voennoj tipogr. 1855.
    T. 1: Materialy dlja biografii A. S. Puškina. 487 s.: ill.
    T. 2-4: Stichotvorenija. viii, 551, 558, 466 s.
    T. 5-6: Proizvedenija v proze. 638, 561 s.

Sočinenija Puškina. Izd. Imperatorskoj Akademii Nauk. Prigotovil i primečanijami snabdil Leonid Majkov. T. 1-4, 11. 1905–1914. xx, 459; xxii, 527; xii, 533; xii, 447, x, 479+364 s.: ill.

Vystrel — Metel'. Obložka i illjustracii chudož. I. Simakova. Peterburg: Gos. izd., 1919. 36 s.: ill. (Narodnaja biblioteka)

—> Al'bom Puškinskoj vystavki... —> Avenarius, V. P.: Puščin v sele Michajlovskom... —> Brjusov, V. Ju.: Moj Puškin... —> Dostoevskij i Puškin... —> Gofman, M.L.: Puškin: pervaja glava nauki... —> Gofman, M. L.: Puškin — Don Žuan... —> Grossman, L. P.: Ėtjudy o Puškine... —> Mjakotin, V. A.: A. S. Puškin i Dekabristy... —> Modzalevskij, B. L.: Anna Petrovna Kern... —> Poljakov, A. S.: O smerti Puškina... —> Puškin. Dostoevskij. (Pervyj sbornik Doma Literatury)... —> Russkaja biblioeka. 1: A. S. Puškin... —> Sakulin, P. N.: Puškin i Radiščev...—> Skabičevskij, A. M.: A. S. Puškin... —> Slovar' literaturnych tipov: Puškin... —> Solov'ev, V. S.: Suď'ba Puškina... —> Tynjanov, Ju. N.: Puškin...

Puškin. Dostoevskij. (Pervyj sbornik Doma Literatorov). Peterburg: Izd. Doma Literatorov, 1921. 147 s. (3.000)
    Predislovie — Deklaracija o ežegodnom čestvovanii pamjati Puškina — M. A. Kuzmin: Puškin — A. Blok: O naznačenii poėta — V. F. Chodasevič: Koleblemyj trenožnik — A. F. Koni: Obščestvennye vzgjady Puškina — B.M. Ėjchenbaum: Problemy poėtiki Puškina — A. G. Gornfeľd: Dva sorokaletija — A. M. Remizov: Ognennaja Rossija

Pypin, Aleksandr Nikolaevič

Charakteristiki literaturnych mnenij ot dvadcatych do pjatidesjatych godov. Izd. vtoroe, ispr. i dopoln. Sanktpeterburg 1890. 519 s.
    Romantizm. Žukovskij — Puškin — Narodnosť official'naja — Projavlenija

skepticizma. Čaadaev — Razvitie naučnych izsledovanij narodnosti — Slavjanofil'stvo — Gogol' — Belinskij — Zaključenie

Istorija russkoj ètnografii. T. 1-4. S.-Peterburg: Tipogr. M. M. Stasjuleviča, 1890–1892.
    T. 1-2. Obščij obzor izučenij narodnosti i ètnografija velikorusskaja. 1890. viii, 424, viii, 428 s.
    T. 3: Ètnografija malorusskaja. 1891. viii, 425 s.
    T. 4: Belorussija i Sibir'. 1892. 488 s.

Istorija russkoj literatury. T. 1-3. S.-Peterburg: Tipogr. M. M. Stasjuleviča, 1898–1899.
    T. 1: Drevnjaja pis'mennost'. 1898. 484 s.
    T. 2: Drevnjaja pis'mennost'. Vremena Moskovskago carstva. Kanun preobrazovanij. 1898. 566 s.
    T. 3: Sud'by narodnoj poèzii. Èpocha preobrazovanij Petra Velikago. Ustanovlenie novoj literatury. Lomonosov. 1899. 535 s.
    T. 4: Vremena Imp. Ekateriny II. Devjatnadcatyj vek. Puškin i Gogol'. Utverždenie nacional'nago značenija literatury. 1899. 647 s.

Obščestvennoe dviženie v Rossii pri Aleksandre I. Izd. tret'e, s dopoln. S.-Peterburg: Tipogr. M. M. Stasjuleviča, 1900. xi, 587 s.

Obzor istorii slavjanskich literatur A.N. Pypina i V. D. Spasoviča. S.-Peterburg: Izd. O. I. Baksta, 1865. 536 s.

Radek, Karl Berngardovič

Na službe germanskoj revoljucii (perevod s nemeckogo). Moskva: Gos. izd.,
1921. 269 s. (20.000)

Radiščev, Aleksandr Nikolaevič

Putešestvie iz Peterburga v Moskvu. Sanktpeterburg, 1905.

—> Sakulin, P. N.: Puškin i Radiščev... —> Suchomlinov, M. I.: A. N. Radiščev...

Radlov, Èrnest Leopol'dovič

Očerk istorii russkoj filosofii. 2-e dopoln. izd. Peterburg: Knigoizd. Nauka i Škola, 1920. 98 s.

Raduga: al'manach Puškinskogo doma. Peterburg: Kooperativnoe izd. literatorov i učenych, 1922. 308 s. (3.000)

Razskazy očevidcev o dvenadcatom gode. [Sobral] T. N. Moskva: V universitetskoj tipogr., 1872. 54 s.

Remizov, Aleksej Michajlovič

Car' Maksimilian: teatr Alekseja Remizova po svodu V. V. Bakrylova. Peterburg: Gos. izd., 1920. 126 s.

Časy: roman. S.-Petersburg: Knigoizd. EOS, 1908. 174 s.

Prud: roman. S.-Petersburg: Izd. Sirius, 1908. 284 s.

Sočinenija. T. 1-8. S.-Peterburg: Izd. Šipovnik. [1911–1912]
    T. 1: Razskazy: Neuemnyj buben' — Carevna Mymra — Čortik — Sud Božij — Žertva — Zanofa — Slonenok. 224 s.

T. 2: Razskazy: Časy — V plenu — Požar. 212 s.

T. 3: Razskazy: Krepost' — Svjatoj večer — Bez pjati minut barin — Pridvornyj juvelir — Serebrjanyja ložka — Muzykant — Opera — Kazennaja dača — Émaliol' — Novyj god — Bebka — Bedovaja dolja. 213 s.

T. 4: Prud: roman. Izd. vtoroe. 369 s.

Ded.: Alfred Jensen — A. Rémisoff.
1911, 9/22.X

T. 5: Razskazy: Krestovyja sestry — Čertychanec —Galstuk — Maka. 233 s.

T. 6: Skazki: Posolon' — Vesna krasna — Leto krasnoe — Osen' temnaja — Zima ljutaja — K morju-okeanu — Myšinymi norami. Zmeinymi tropami — Primečanija. 270 s.

T. 7: Otrečennyja povest: Limonar' — Paralipomenon. 203 s.

T. 8: Rusal'nyja dejstvija: Besovskoe dejstvo — Tragedija o Iude — Dejstvo o Georgii Chrabrom — Primečanija. 284 s.

Šumy goroda. Revel'. Izd. Bibliofil, 1921. 174 s.

Vesennee poroš'e. S.-Peterburg: Izd. Sirin, 1915. 328 s.

Ded.: Alfredu Jensenu
s uvaženiem Aleksej Remizov.
915 g. 1 janvarja

Za svjatuju Rus': dumy o rodnoj zemle. Petrograd: Izd. žurnala Otečestvo, 1915. 53 s.

Za svjatuju Rus' — Nikolin zavet — Nikola milostivyj-ugodnik Božij — Polonnoe terpenie — Kubiki — Svet neoborimyj — O dnjach poslednich — Červlenyj ščit.

Rešetnikov, Fedor Michajlovič

Jaška. Moskva: Gos. izd., 1919. 64 s.

Podlipovcy. Moskva: Gos. izd., 1920. 135 s. (Narodnaja biblioteka)

Sočinenija F. M. Rešetnikova v dvuch tomach. S portretom avtora i vstupitel'noj stat'ej M. Protopopova. Deševoe izd. F. Pavlenkova. T. 1-2. S.-Peterburg: Tipogr. T-va Obščestvennaja pol'za, 1890-1896.

T. 1: F. Rešetnikov, kak pisatel' i kak čelovek – vstupitel'naja stat'ja M. A. Protopopova — Podlipovcy — Glumovy — Gde lučše? — Stavlennik. 1896. 694 s.

T. 2: Svoj chleb — Meždu ljud'mi — Melkie razskazy — Gornorabočie (načalo neokončennago romana). 1890. 747 s.

Rogačevskij, V. L. —> L'vov-Rogačevskij, V.

Romanov, Pantelejmon Sergeevič

Novaja skrižal': roman. Berlin: Petropolis, 1928. 206 s.

Razskazy. Riga: Knigoizd. Literatura, 1927. 220 s. (Naša biblioteka, 6)

Ruš. Moskva: Izd. M. i S. Sabašnikovych, 1923. 134 s. (2.000)

Tovarišč Kisljakov (tri pary šelkovych čulok). Berlin: Kniga i scena, 1931. 295 s.

Romias, S. —> Karpova-Mongird, V. A.

Roni Staršij —> Rosny Ainé, J.-H.

Rosny Ainé, J.-H.
(Roni Staršij, pseud.)

Bor'ba za ogon': doistoričeskij roman. Moskva: Gos. izd.,1920. 107 s. (10.000)

Rossija: polnoe geografičeskoe opisanie našego otečestva. Nastol'naja i dorožnaja kniga dlja russkich ljudej pod red. V.P. Semenova i pod obščim rukovodstvom P.P. Semenova i V.I. Lamanskago. T. 1-3, 5-7, 9, 14, 16, 18-19. S.-Peterburg: Izd. A.F. Devriena, 1899-1914.
T. 1: Moskovskaja promyšlennaja oblast' i Verchnee Povolž'e. 1899. xi, 484 s.: ill.
T. 2: Srednerusskaja černozemnaja oblast'. 1902. viii, 717 s.: ill.
T. 3: Ozernaja oblast'. 1900. ix, 456 s.: ill.
T. 5: Ural i Priural'e. 1914. viii, 669 s.: ill.
T. 6: Srednee i Nižnee Povolž'e i Zavolž'e. 1901. vii, 599 s.: ill.
T. 7: Malorossija. 1903. ix, 517 s.: ill.
T. 9: Verchnee Podneprov'e i Belorussija. 1905. iv, 619 s.: ill.
T. 14: Novorossija i Krym. 1910. viii, 983 s.: ill.
T. 16: Zapadnaja Sibir'. 1907. viii, 588 s.: ill.
T. 18: Kirgizskij Kraj. 1903. v, 478 s.: ill.
T. 19: Turkestanskij Kraj. 1913. x, 861 s.

Rostopčina, Evdokija Petrovna

Sočinenija grafini E. P. Rostopčinoj s eja portretom. T. 1-2. S.-Peterburg: Tipogr. I. N. Skorochodova, 1890.
T. 1: Stichi. 346 s.
T. 2: Proza: Činy i den'gi — Poedinok — Palacco Forli — Sčastlivaja žen-

ščina. 461 s.

Rozanov, M. G. —> Ognev, N. (pseud.)

Rozanov, Vasilij Vasil'evič

Uedinennoe. Počti na pravach rukopisi. S priloženiem stat'i Viktora Chovina "Predsmertnyj Rozanov". Pariž: Izd. Očarovannyj strannik, 1928. 136 s. (500)

L'Apocalypse de notre temps. Précédé de Esseulement. Traduit du russe par Vladimir Pozner et Boris de Schlœzer. Paris: Librairie Plon, 1930. 281 s.

Rozenbljum, Vitol'd Konstantin Nikolaevič (K. L'dov, pseud.)

Otzvuki duši: stichotvorenija. S.-Peterburg: Tipogr. V.V. Komarova, 1899. 87, vii s.

Rus' straždajuščaja: stichi narodnye o ljubvi i skorbi: venec mnogocvetnyj. Vstupitel'naja stat'ja E. A. Ljackago. Izd. vtoroe. Stokchol'm: Severnye ogni, 1920. 175 s.

Rusakov, Viktor

Maksim Gor'kij v karrikaturach i anekdotach. S 48 illjustracijami. S.-Peterburg, 1903. 77 s.: ill.

Rusanov, N. S. (N. E. Kudrin)

Socialisty Zapada i Rossii: Fur'e. Marks. Éngel's. Lassal'. Žjul'. Vallès. Uilliam Morris. Černyševskij. Lavrov.

Michajlovskij. S.-Peterburg: Tipogr. M. M. Stasjuleviča, 1908. 393 s.

Russkaja biblioteka. 1-9. Sankt Peter-burg 1874–1879.

1: A. S. Puškin. 1874. 340 s. Por-tret, biografija, Belinskij i Gogol' o Puš-kine

2: M. Ju. Lermonov. 2 izd. 1876. 243 s. Portret, biografija, Belinskij o poèzii Lermontova

3. N. V. Gogol'. 1874. Portret, bio-grafija, Belinskij o Gogole

4: V. A. Žukovskij. 1875. 365 s. Por-tret, biografija, Belinskij o poèzii Žu-kovskago

5: A. S. Griboedov. 1875. 260 s. Por-tret, biografija, iz kritiki Belinskogo

6: I. S. Turgenev. 1876. 434 s. Por-tret, biografija

7: N. A. Nekrasov. 1877. 260 s.

8: M. E. Saltykov. 1878. 438 s. Por-tret, biografija

9. Graf Lev Nikolaevič Tolstoj. 1879. 384 s. Portret, biografija

Russkaja poèzija: sobranie proizvede-nij russkich poètov, čast'ju v polnom sostave, čast'ju v izvlečenijach, s važ-nejšimi kritiko-biografičeskimi stat'ja-mi, biografičeskimi primečanijami i portretami, izdaetsja pod red. S. A. Vengerova. T. 1

Vyp. 1-6. XVII vek: èpocha klassi-cizma. S 23 portretami S.-Peterburg: Tipo-Litografija A. È. Vineke, 1897. 886, 413 s.

Vyp. 7. 1. Polnoe sobranie stichotvo-renij Ju. A. Neledinskago-Meleckago. 2 Polnoe sobranie stichotvorenij N. M. Ka-ramzina. S. Peterburg 1901. 143 s.: ill.

La Russie à la fin du 19-e siècle. Ouvrage publié sous la direction de M.

W. de Kovalevsky, adjoint du Ministre des Finances de Russie. Paris: Paul Dupont/Guillaumin, 1900. xx, 989 s.: ill., tabl.

Russkij bibliofil: illjustrirovannyj vest-nik dlja sobiratelej knig i gravjur. Vy-chodit 8 raz v god = Le bibliophile rus-se: revue illustrée des amateurs de liv-res et de gravures. Parait 8 fois par an. S.-Peterburg

1912: 1-8; Priloženie: P. N. Siman-skij: Suvorovskij otdel v biblioteke P. N. Simanskago.

1913: 1-8.

1914: 1-8.

Russkij biografičeskij slovar'. Izd. pod nabljudeniem predsedatelja Imperator-skago russkago istoričeskago obščestva A. A. Polovcova. T. 1-18. S.-Peterburg: Tipogr. I. N. Skorochodova, 1896-1913.

Russkij Parnas. Sost. Aleksandr i Da-vid Éliasberg. Leipzig: Insel-Verlag, 1920. 330 s. (Bibliotheca Mundi)

Russkija byliny: staroj i novoj zapisi. Pod red. N. S. Tichonravova i V. F. Mil-lera. Moskva: Ètnografičeskij otdel Im-peratorskago Obščestva Ljubitelej Es-testvoznanija, Antropologii i Ètnografii, 1894. viii, 88, 304 s.

Russkija drevnosti v pamjatnikach iskusstva, izd. grafom I. Tolstym i N. Kondakovym. Vyp. pjatyj. Kurgannyja drevnosti i klady domongol'skago pe-rioda. S 225-ju risunkami v tekste. S.-Peterburg, 1897. 163 s.: ill.

Rybnikov, P. N. —> Pesni sobrannyja P. N. Rybnikovym...

Ryleev, Kondratij Fedorovič

Sočinenija i perepiska Kondratija Fedoroviča Ryleeva. Izd. 2-e ego dočeri pod red. P. A. Efremova. Sanktpeterburg: Tipogr. I. I. Glazunova, 1874. x, 346 s.

Sočinenija K. F. Ryleeva izd. pod red. M. N. Mazaeva. S biografičeskim očerkom i primečanijami. S.-Peterburg: Izd. Evg. Evdokimova, 1893. 183 s.

Šackij, Stanislav Teofilovič

Gody iskanij. Izd. 2-e. Moskva: Izd. T-va Mir, 1925. 270 s. (Pedagogičeskaja studija; 3.000)

Sadof'ev, Il'ja Ivanovič

Dinamo-stichi. Izd. 4-e. Petrograd: Proletkul't, 1919. 61 s.

Šaginjan, Mariètta Sergeevna

Gidrocentral': roman. Moskva: Gos. izd. chudožestvennoj literatury, 1934. 522 s: ill. Portr. (7.500)

Sakulin, Pavel Nikitič

Puškin i Radiščev: novoe rešenie starogo voprosa. Moskva: Al'ciona, 1920. 75 s. (Istoriko-literaturnye èskizy; 15.000)

Salias, Evgenij Andreevič

Sobranie sočinenij grafa E. A. Saliasa. 1-27. Izd. A. A. Karceva. Moskva 1894-1901.
   1: Iskra bož'ja – T'ma — Manžaža — Evrejka — Volga. 1894. 480 s.
   2: Pugačevcy. Č. 1-4. 1901. 483 s.
   3: Pugačevcy. Č. 5-8. 1901. 551 s.
   4: Najdenyš — Samokrutka. 1894. 470 s.
   5: Na Moskve. 1894. 631 s.
   6: Peterburgskoe dejstvo. 1894. 651 s.
   7: Ataman Ustja — Svadebnyj bunt. 1894. 495 s.
   8: Putešestvenniki — Madonna — Četvertoe izmerenie. 1895. 467 s.
   9: Graf Tjatin Baltijskij — Šir' i mach — Poèt namestnik. 1895. 542 s.
   10: Služitel' Boga — Vedun'ja. 1895. 512 s.
   11: Kudesnik — Jaunkundze. 1895. 476 s.
   12: Samozvanka. 1895. 583 s.
   13: Brigadirskaja vnučka — Krutojarskaja carevna — Donskie gišpancy. 1895. 501 s.
   14: Baryni-krest'janki — Frejlina Marii Leščinskoj. 1895. 495 s.
   15: Džettatura — Pan krul — Zaira. 1896. 525 s.
   16: Andaluzskija legendy — Los Novios — Kamer-jungfera — Filosof. 1896. 406 s.
   17: Pjatoe koleso — Bylye gusary — Izbuška na kur'ich nožkach — Senatskij sekretar'. 1896. 385 s.
   18: Nevesta fin de siècle — Melkie razskazy. 1896. 512 s.
   19: Melkie razskazy. 1896. 441 s.
   20: Novaja Sandril'ona. 1896. 463 s.
   21: Izlomannye ljudi — Francuz — Rubikon. 1899. 552 s.
   22: Èkzotika — Vanja — Prestiž. 1899. 486 s.

23: Geroj svoego vremeni. 1900. 643 s.

24: Las Espanas: putevye očerki Ispanii (1864 g). 1900. 512 s.

25: Vladimirskie monomachi. 1901. 462 s.

26: Nazvanec — Podložnyj samoubijca — Ina Nina — Panduročka — Sa-e-ij Pa-ic — Maškerad — V Muromskich lesach. 1901. 492 s.

27: Zmej-gorynyč. 1901. 191 s.

Saltykov-Ščedrin, Michail Evgrafovič

Polnoe sobranie sočinenij M. E. Saltykova (N. Ščedrina). 1-12. 4 izd. S.-Peterburg: Izd. A. F. Marksa, 1900.

T. 1: Gubernskie očerki (1856-1857) — Materialy dlja biografii M. E. Saltykova. S portretom avtora, ego faksimile i mogil'nym pamjatnikom. 684 s.

T. 2: Gospoda Golovlevy (1872-1876) — Satiry v proze (1860-1862). 688 s.

T. 3: Pompadury i Pompadurši (1863-1873) — Nevinnye razskazy (1857-1863). 687 s.

T. 4: Blagonamerennyja reči (1872-1876) — Kul'turnye ljudi (1876). 720 s.

T. 5: Meloči žizni (1886–1887) – Sbornik (1869–1879). 720 s.

T. 6: Skazki (1880–1885) — Pestryja pis'ma (1884–1886) — Nedokončennyja besedy (1873–1884). 686 s.

T. 7: Istorija odnogo goroda (1869-1870) — Ubežišče Monrepo (1878-1879) — Priznaki vremeni (1866-1869). 674 s.

T. 8: Dnevnik provinciala v Peterburge (1872–1873) — Za rubežom (1880-1881). 719 s.

T. 9: Gospoda taškentcy (1869-1872) — Pošechonskie razskazy (1883-1884) — Kruglyj god (1879). 768 s.

T. 10: V srede umerennosti i akkuratnosti (1874–1877) — Pis'ma o provincii (1868–1870)—Itogi (1876). 688s.

T. 11: Sovremennaja idillija (1877-1883) — Pis'ma k teten'ke (1881-1882). 712 s.

T. 12: Pošechonskaja starina (1887-1889) — Brusin (1849). 709 s.

—> Krivenko, S. N.: M. E. Saltykov...

Samarin, Jurij Fedorovič

Sočinenija Ju. F. Samarina. T. 2, 5 Izd. D. Samarina. Moskva: Tipogr. A. I. Mamontova, 1878. 1880.

T. 2: Krest'janskoe delo do Vysočajšago reskripta 20 nojabrja 1857 goda. 1878. xi, 444 s.

T. 5: Stefan Javorskij i Feofan Prokopovič. 1880. xcii, 463 s.

Sannikov, Grigorij Aleksandrovič

Dni. Vjatka: Kuznica, 1921. 30 s.

Lirika. Moskva: Vserossijskaja Associacija Proletarskich Pisatelej, 1921. 14 s.

Savina, M. G. —> Turgenev, I. S.: Turgenev i Savina...

Sbornik armjanskoj literatury. Pod red. M. Gor'kago. Petrograd: Knigoizd. Parus A. N. Tichonova, 1916. 316 s.

Sbornik postanovlenij i rasporjaženij Glavpolitprosveta. 1921 g. Moskva: Gos. izd., 1921. 32 s. (5.000)

Sbornik revoljucionnych stichov dlja deklamacii. Moskva: Gos. izd., 1921. 32 s. (Krasnaja knižka, 46; 30.000)

Sbornik Tovariščestva Znanie. Kn. I-XX, XXIII-XXXX. S.-Peterburg 1904-1913.

1903: Kn. I. 1904. 325 s.
L. Andreev: Žizn' Vasilija Fivejskago — I. Bunin: Stichotvorenija — V. Veresaev: Pered zavesoj — N. Garin: Derevenskaja drama — M. Gor'kij: Čelovek — S. Gusev: V prichode — A. Serafimovič: V puti — N. Telešov: Meždu dvuch beregov

1903: Kn. II. 1904. 318 s.
A. Kuprin: Mirnoe žitie — Skitalec: Stichotvorenija — A. Čechov: Višnevyj sad — E. Čirikov: Na porukach — S. Juškevič: Evrei.

1904: Kn. III. 1905. 348 s.
Skitalec: Pamjati Čechova — A. Kuprin: Pamjati Čechova — M. Gor'kij: Dačniki — I. Bunin: Pamjati Čechova — L. Andreev: Krasnyj smech

1904: Kn. IV. 1905. 378 s.
S. Najdenov: Avdoťina žizn' — S. Gusev-Orenburgskij: Strana otcov — A. Luk'janov: Kuznec—M. Gor'kij: Tjur'ma

1904: Kn. V. 1905. 307 s.
E. Čirikov: Ivan Mironyč — N. Telešov: Černoju nočju — A. Serafimovič: Zajac — Skitalec: Kandaly — D. Ajzman: Ledochod — L. Andreev: Vor — M. Gor'kij: Razskaz Filippa Vasil'eviča

1905: Kn. VI. 1905. 320 s.
A. Kuprin: Poedinok — Iv. Bunin: Stichotvorenija — M. Gor'kij: Bukoemov — Skitalec: Stichotvorenija

Ded.: G-nu Iensenu ot A. Kuprina

1905: Kn. VII. 1905. 340 s.
M. Gor'kij: Deti solnca — Al. Kipen: Birjučij ostrov — Iv. Bunin: Vostok —

Skitalec: Polevoj sud — Gustav Danilovskij: Na ostrove — Iv. Rukavišnikov: Stichotvorenie

1906: Kn. VIII. 1906. 372 s.
Semen Juškevič: Golod — A. Luk'janov: Meč vragov — Mario Rapisardi: Rudokopy — E. Čirikov: Mužiki — Skitalec: Les razgoralsja — Iv. Rukavišnikov: Tri znameni

1906: Kn. IX. 1906. 322 s.
M. Gor'kij: Varvary — Iv. Bunin: Stichotvorenija — N. Telešov: Nadziratel' — A. Serafimovič: Sredi noči; Pochoronnyj marš — L. Suleržickij: Puť — Skitalec: Stichotvorenija

1906: Kn. X. 1906. 301 s.
L. Andreev: K zvezdam — Ėmil Vercharn: Vozstanie — A. Serafimovič: Na Presne — A. Luk'janov: Slepcy i bezumcy — Luidži Merkantini: Gimn garibaľdijcev — Skitalec: Ogarki

1906: Kn. XI. 1906. 352 s.
Ėmil Vercharn: Zori — A. Kipen: V oktjabre — L. Andreev: Savva — M. Gor'kij: Gorod Želtago D'javola

1906: Kn. XII. 1906. 320 s.
M. Gor'kij: Carstvo skuki; "Mov"; Čarli Mėn — S. Juškevič: V gorode — Zinovij Pė: Dom — Ėmil Vercharn: V derevne — A. Serafimovič: V sem'e — Uolt Uitman: Stichotvorenie — M. Novorusskij: V Šlisselburge — Evg. Tarasov: Stichotvorenija — Evg. Čirikov: V tjur'me — Skitalec: Stichotvorenie

1906: Kn. XIII. 1906. 363 s.
M. Gor'kij: Korol', kotoryj vysoko deržit svoe znamja.; Prekrasnaja Francija; Car'; Odin iz korolej respubliki; Tovarišč — Uolt Uitman: Stichotvorenija — G. Ėrastov: Otstuplenie

1906: Kn. XIV. 1906. 320 s.
M. Gor'kij: Vragi — Iv. Bunin: Stichotvorenija — A. Tennison: Godiva — Vera Figner: Mojanjanja — Evg. Tarasov: Černyj sud — S. Juškevič: Korol'

1907: Kn. XV. 1907. 303 s.

S. Najdenov: Steny — A. Serafimovič: On prišel — Skitalec: Na Volge — N. Telešov: Kramola — Iv. Bunin: Stichotvorenija — M. Gor'kij: Žrec morali — E. Čirikov: Legenda starogo zamka
1907: Kn. XVI. 1907. 339 s.

G. Flober: Iskušenie sv. Antonija — Iv. Bunin: Stichotvorenija — M. Gor'kij: Mat' (čast' 1) – Skitalec: Četvero — D. Ajzman: Serdce bytija — L. Andreev: Iuda Iskariot i drugie
1907: Kn. XVII. 1907. 310 s.

M. Gor'kij: Mat' (prodolženie) — A. Čeremnov: Stichotvorenija — V. Veresaev: Na vojne — N. Garin: Inženery
1907: Kn. XVIII. 1907. 327 s.

M. Gor'kij: Mat' (prodolženie) — V. Veresaev: Na vojne: zapiski (prodolženie) — N. Garin: Inženery (prodolženie) — Šolom Aš: Bog mesti
1907: Kniga XIX. 1907. 348 s.

M. Gor'kij: Mat' (prodolženie) – N. Garin: Inženiery (prodolženie) – V. Veresaev: Na vojne (prodolženie) — Šolom Aš: Bog mesti (prodolzenie)
1908: Kn. XX. 1907. 348 s.

D. Ajzman: Krovavyj razliv — Iv. Bunin: Razskazy v stichach — V. Veresaev: Na vojne (prodolženie) — Evg. Čirikov: Na poroge žizni — A. Fedorov: Stichotvorenija — G. Gauptmann: Založnica Karla Velikago — N. Šrejter: Stichotvorenija — M. Gor'kij: Mat' (prodolženie)
1908: Kn. XXIII. 1908. 369 s.

M. Gor'kij: Ispoved' — S. Gusev-Orenburgskij: Skazki zemli — A. Zolotarev: V Staroj Lavre
1908: Kn. XXIV. 1908. 292 s.

M. Gor'kij: Žizn' nenužnogo čeloveka — Iv. Bunin: Sonety — A. Amfiteatrov: Knjaginja Nastja — Rikard Demel': Demon želanij; Osvoboždennyj Prometej
1908: Kn. XXV. 1908. 77; 5; 174; 112 s.

S. Konduruškin: Moisej — Iv. Bunin: Iudeja — Skitalec: Ėtapy — Oktav Mirbo: Očag
1908: Kn. XXVI. 1908. 128; 221 s.

L. Andreev: Dni našej žizni — Knut Gamsun: Roza
1909: Kn. XXVII. 1909. 151; 4; 18; 14; 114 s.

M. Gor'kij: Leto — Iv. Bunin: Senokos; Beden bes — I. Kasatkin: V uezde — F. Krjukov: Zyb
1909: Kn. XXVIII. 1909. 69; 16; 33; 195 s.

M. Gor'kij: Gorodok Okurov — Šolom Aš: Zimoju — S. Konduruškin: V solnečnuju noč' — Knut Gamsun: Strannik igraet pod surdinku
1909: Kn. XXIX. 1909. 87; 10; 109; 2; 46, 8, 12; 6 s.

M. Gor'kij: Gorodok Okurov (prodolženie) – Iv. Kasatkin: Veselyj batja — S. Razumovskij: Svetloe zatočenie — Iv. Bunin: Stichi — Gol'debaev: Galčenok — K. Jasjukajtis: Na bulvare — Iv. Voronov: Stichi — N. Karžanskij: Cvety
1910: Kn. XXX. 1910. 107; 27; 34; 6; 118; 10 s.

M. Gor'kij: Matvej Kožemjakin — Iv. Kasatkin: S dokukoj — N. Garin: Zajac — Iv. Bunin: Stichi — L. Nikiforova: Dve lestnicy — Iv. Voronov: Stichi
1910: Kn. XXXI. 1910. 91; 12; 18; 61; 110 s.

M. Gor'kij: Matvej Kožemjakin (prodolženie) — A. Čeremnov: Stichotvorenija — V. Jazvickij: V Tajbole — S. Karcevskij: Jamkarka — Iv. Šmelev: Pod gorami
1910: Kn. XXXII. 1910. 152; 8; 42; 65; 11 s.

M. Gor'kij: Čudaki — A. Čeremnov: Stichi — Jak. Okunev: "Dar'ja Avilova s synov'jami" — E. Milicyna: V ožidanii prigovora — Iv. Voronov: Stichi
1910: Kn. XXXIII. 1910. 144; 63; 114; 9 s.

M. Gor'kij: Vassa Železnova – S. Gusev-Orenburgskij: Rycar' Lančelot — L. Nikiforova: Artel' — A. Čeremnov: Krym

1911: Kn. XXXIV. 1911. 156; 6; 169 s.

Knut Gamsun: U žizni v lapach — A. Čeremnov: Belorussija — N. Karžanskij: Pariž

1911: Kn. XXXV. 1911. 142; 10; 131; 10 s.

M. Gor'kij: Matvej Kožemjakin (II čast') — German Lazaris: Stichi — A. Zolotarev: Na čužoj storone — A. Čeremnov: Sonety

1911: Kn. XXXVI. 1911. 141; 174 s.

M. Gor'kij: Matvej Kožemjakin (III čast') — Iv. Šmelev: Čelovek iz restorana

1911: Kn. XXXVII. 1911. 203; 4; 48; 24; 6 s.

M. Gor'kij: Matvej Kožemjakin (okonč.) — A. Čeremnov: Stichi — Iv. Kasatkin: Selo Mikul'skoe — V. Vinničenko: Kuz' i Grycun' — Iv. Voronov: Stichi

1912: Kn. XXXVIII. 1912. 22; 4; 22; 218; 10 s.

M. Gor'kij: Skazka — A. Blok: Stichi — Iv. Bunin: Zachar Vorob'ev – S. Gusev-Orenburgskij: V gluchom uezde — A. Čeremnov: Stichi

1912: Kn. XXXIX. 1912. 38; 10; 260 s.

M. Gor'kij: Slučaj iz žizni Makara — A. Čeremnov: Stichi — Il'ja Surgučev: Gubernator

1913: Kn. XXXX. 1913. 70; 6; 24 s.

S. Najdenov: Roman teti Ani — S. Astrov: Stichi — A. Zolotarev: Vo edinu ot subbot

Sčepkin, M. S.—> Jarcev, A. A.: M.S. Sčepkin, ego žizn'...

Sčerbačev, Grigorij Dmitrievič

Idealy moej žizni. Vospominanija iz vremen carstvovanij imperatorov Nikolaja I-go i Aleksandra II-go, s priloženiem stat'i togo že avtora: Kak sdelat' našu žizn' najbolee sčastlivoj?. S zametkoj o darvinizme i ob učenii grafa L. N. Tolstogo. Moskva: Tipo-litogr. V. Richter, 1895. 368 s.

Sčit: literaturnyj sbornik pod red. Leonida Andreeva, Maksima Gor'kago i Fedora Sologuba. Izd. tret'e, dopoln., Russkago Obščestva dlja izučenija evrejskoj žizni. Moskva: 1916. 256 s.

L. Andreev: Pervaja stupen'; Ranenyj — K. Arsen'ev: Respice inem! — M. Arcybašev: Evrej — K. Bal'mont: Golos ottuda — M. Bernackij: Evrei i russkoe narodnoe chozjajstvo — Akad. V. Bechterev: "Mne otmščenie i Az vozdam"; Iz mraka k svetu — V. Brjusov: Paschal'naja vstreča — S. Bulgakov: Sion — I. Bunin: Den' gneva; Tora; Grobnica Rachili; ***; Stolp ognennyj — V. V.: Nemeckie intelligenty o duchovnoj cennosti evreev — Z. Gippius: *** — M. Gor'kij: ***; Mal'čik — S. Gusev-Orenburgskij: Evrejčik — L. Dobronravov: Životvorjaščee — Kn. Pav. Dolgorukov: Vojna i položenie evreev — S. El'pat'evskij: Vyselency — Vjačeslav Ivanov: K ideologii evrejskago voprosa — A. Kartašev: Izbrannye i pomilovannye — M. Kovalevskij: Ravnopravie evreev i ego vragi – F. Kokoškin: Korni antisemitizma — Vl. Korolenko: Mnenie mistera Džaksona o evrejskom voprose — F. Krjukov: Sestra Ol'švanger (iz zakavkazskich vpečatlenij) — I. Boduen-de-Kurtenè: Svoeobraznaja "krugovaja poruka" — Ek. Kuskova: Kak i čem pomoč'? — P. N. Maljantovič: Russkij vopros o evrejach — D. Merežkovskij: Evrejskij vopros, kak russkij — P. Miljukov: Evrejskij vopros v Rossii — D. Ovsjaniko-Kulikovskij: Dva slova ob antisemitizme — A. Pešechonov: Bez viny vinovatye — Vl. Solov'ev: O nacionalizme (reč' na universitetskom obede 8 fevr. 1890) — Poliksena Solov'eva: Večernjaja molitva; Pesnja — F. Sologub: Otečestvo dlja vsech; Brat'jam; Vse vmeste; Svet večernij; Večnyj žid — Tėffi: Dva estestva — Tichoberežskij: Smert' ravvina (iz sobytij na zapadnom teatre vojny) — Gr. Aleksej N. Tolstoj: Anna Ziserman — Gr. Iv. Tolstoj: Po povodu pravovogo položenija evreev; Narodnoe prosveščenie v Rossii i evrei — T. Ščepkina-Kupernik: Evrejke — A. Fedorov: Iz proroka Isaii — V. Korolenko: Otryvok iz pis'ma k Vl. Solov'evu — Vjač. Ivanov: Istinno, ėto – kara Bož'ja... — V. Brjusov: Al Ha-schchitah — L. Tolstoj: Pis'ma k F. B. Gecu — Iv. Bunin: Da ispolnjatsja sroki

Šejn, P. V. —> Velikoruss...

Sel'vinskij, Il'ja L'vovič

Komandarm 2. Moskva-Leningrad: Gos. izd., 1930. 159 s. Portr. (3.000)

Tichookeanskie stichi. Moskva: Moskovskoe tovariščestvo pisatelej, 1934. 123 s. (5.100)

Uljalaevščina: ėpopeja. Ispravl. i dopoln. tekst. Izd. 2-e. Moskva-Leningrad:; Gos. izd., 1930. 159 s. (3.000)

Sel'vinskij, I. —> Biznes... —> Gosplan literatury...

Semenov, P. P. —> Rossija...

Semenov, V. P. —> Rossija...

Semenovskij, D. M.

Krasnyj uzor: rasskaz. Moskva: Gos. izd., 1921. 16 s. (Krasnaja knižka, 38; 50.000)

Sementkovskij, Rostislav Ivanovič

A. D. Kantemir, ego žizn' i literaturnaja dejatel'nost': biografičeskij očerk R. I. Sementkovskago. S portretom Kantemira, gravirovannym v Lejpcige Gedanom. S.-Peterburg: Tipogr. T-va Obščestvennaja pol'za, 1893. 96 s. (Žizn' zamečatel'nych ljudej)

E. F. Kankrin, ego žizn' i gosudarstvennaja dejatel'nost': biografičeskij očerk R.I. Sementkovskago. S portretom Kankrina, gravirovannym v Peterburge K. Adtom. S.-Peterburg: Tipogr. T-va Obščestvennaja pol'za, 1893. 94 s. (Žizn' zamečatel'nych ljudej)

Semevskij, Michail Ivanovič

Carica Katerina Alekseevna, Anna i Villiam Mons. 1692-1724. Izd. 2-e, peresm. i dopoln. Izd. redakcii žurnala Russkaja starina. S.-Peterburg: Tipogr. V. S. Balaševa, 1884. 344 s.: ill. (Očerki i razskazy iz russkoj istorii XVIII v.)

Semevskij, Vasilij Ivanovič

Krest'janskij vopros v Rossii v XVII i pervoj polovine XIX veka. T. 1-2. S.-

Peterburg: Tipogr. T-va Obščestvennaja poľza, 1888.
T. 1: Krest'janskij vopros v XVIII i
pervoj četverti XIX veka. liii, 517 s.
T. 2: Krest'janskij vopros v carstvo-
vanie imperatora Nikolaja. 625 s.

M. V. Butaševič-Petraševskij i Petraševev-
cy. Pod red. V. Vodovozova. Č. 1. Moskva: Zadruga, 1922. 217 s. (2.000)

Senigov, Iosif Petrovič

Istoriko-kritičeskija izsledovanija o nov-
gorodskich letopisjach i o rossijskoj istorii V. N. Tatiščeva. Moskva: V Universitetskoj tipog., 1887. viii, 434 s.

Kak voeval Petr Velikij so švedami. 2-e
izd. S.-Peterburg: Tipogr. Doma prizr.
maloletn. bedn. 1897. 55 s.: ill.

O drevnješem letopisnom svode Velikago Novgoroda. Izsledovanie I. P. Seni-
gova. Izd. Archeografičeskoj Komissii.
S.-Peterburg: Tipogr. brat. Panteleevych, 1885. 125 s.

Šenšin, A. —> Fet. A. A. (pseud.)

Šepelevič, Lev Julianovič

Naši sovremenniki: istoriko-literatur-
nye očerki. S.-Peterburg: Tipogr. M. M.
Stasjuleviča, 1899. 253 s.
Poľ Burže — Gi de Mopassan —
Éduard Rod — Gergard Gauptman —
Choze Éčegaraj — Senkevič – kak psi-
cholog-romanist — Istoričeskie romany
Senkeviča — Romany Chuana Valery
— Tri romana Zolja

Serafimovič, A.
(Aleksandr Serafimovič Popov)

Ljubov' i drugie rasskazy. Moskva: Gos.
izd., 1920. 257 s. (10.000)
Ljubov' — Cholodnaja ravnina —
Strannaja noč' — Brillianty — Naden'-
ka — Slučaj — Večerinka — V sem'e —
Sereža.

Serapionovy brat'ja. Aľmanach per-
vyj. Peterburg: Alkonost, 1922. 125 s.
M. Zoščenko: Viktorija Kazimirovna
— L. Lunc: V pustyne — V. Ivanov:
Sinij zverjuška — M. Slonimskij: Dikij
— N. Nikitin: Dezi — K. Fedin: Pes'i
duši — V. Kaverin: Chronika goroda
Lejpciga

Sergeev, M. S.

Dom'e [Daumier]: Osada. Tekst M. S.
Sergeeva. Moskva: Gos. izd., 1920. 14
s., 8 tabl. ill. (20.000)

Sergeev-Censkij, Sergej Nikolaevič

Razskazy. S.-Peterburg T. 1-2. 1907-
1908.
1. Knigoizd. Mir Božij, 1907. 353 s.
2. Izd. Šipovnik, 1908. 241 s.

Serov, A. N. —> Bazunov, S. A.: A. N. Serov

Šestov, Lev
(Lev Isaakovič Švarcman)

Na vesach Iova: stranstvovanija po du-
šam. Pariž: Izd. Sovremennyja zapiski,
1929. 368 s.

Načala i koncy: sbornik stať ej. S.-Peterburg: Tipogr. M. M. Stasjuleviča, 1908. xi, 197 s.

Tvorčestvo iz ničego (A. P. Čechov) — Proročeskij dar — Pochvala Gluposti — Predposlednija slova

Dostoevski und Nietzsche: Philosophie der Tragödie. Köln: F. J. Marcan, 1924. xxxi, 388 s.

Ševčenko, T. G. —> Jakovenko, V. I.: T.G. Ševčenko, ego žizn'...

Severnye cvety sobrannyja izdatel'stvom Skorpion. 1-4. Moskva: 1901-1904.

1. 1909. 202 s.: ill.

Dramy i razskazy: Z. Gippius: Svjataja krov' — A. P. Čechov: Noč'ju — Iv. Bunin: Pozdnej noč'ju — M. Krinickij: Umnyj i glupyj — Ju. Baltrušajtis: Kapli — Stichi: Fet, K. Pavlova, A. Dobroljubov, K. Fofanov, K. Slučevskij, K. Bal'mont, F. Sologub, M. Lochvickaja, Vladimir G..., B., P. Percov, Anastasija Mirovič, A. Kursinskij, L. G. Ždanov, A. Fedorov, A. L. Miropoľ skij, Ivan Konevskoj, D. Fridberg, Ju. Baltrušajtis, V. Brjusov — Pis'ma, memuary, stať i: A. S. Puškin, F. I. Tjutčev, A. Fet, Vladimir Solov'ev, Kn. A. I. Urusov, V. Rozanov, Ivan Konevskoj, V. Brjusov

2. 1902. 253 s.: ill.

Nebesnyja slova — V. Brjusov: Teper', kogda ja prosnulsja — M. Krinickij: Angel stracha — F. Sologub: Obruč — A. Mirovič: Jaščericy; Ěľ za — Ju. Baltrušajtis: Obrazy — Stichi: Ja. Polonskij, A. Fet, K. Slučevskij, D. Merežkovskij, Z. Gippius, N. Korin, A. Mirovič, V. Brjusov, Iv. Konevskoj, A. L. Miropoľ skij, L. Viľ kina, V. G. M., Ju. Baltrušajtis, P. Percov, K. Bal'mont,

Lionel' — Stať i, pis'ma: A. S. Puškin, N. Nekrasov, I. Turgenev, A. Fet, Iv. Konevskoj, N. Černogubov, A. Volynskij — Primečanija

3. 1903. 191 s.: ill.

F. I. Tjutčev: Samosoznanie: stichi — A. Belyj: Prišedšij: misterija; Prizyvy: stichi — K. Bal'mont: Čuvstvo ličnosti: stať ja; Toľ ko ljubov': stichi — Z. Gippius: Messa: perevodnaja kartinka — V. Brjusov: Mysli: stichi — V. V. Rozanov: Zverinoe čislo — A. Blok: Stichi o prekrasnoj dame – M. Krinickij: Ulica: razskaz — M. Vološin: V vagone: stichi — A. Dobroljubov: Iz sumasšedšago doma; Stichi — A. Remizov: Ěpitafija — A. L. Miropoľ skij: Mitja: razskaz – V. Gofman: Tri stichotvorenija — A. Krylov: Nenapisannyja basni — N. M. Minskij: O dvuch putjach dobra — Z. Gippius: Čisla: stichi — V. V. Rozanov: Mimoletnoe: zametka — Raznoglas'e: stichi K. K. Slučevskago, L. N. Viľ kinoj, S. L. Rafaloviča, D. N. Fridberga, Vjačeslava Ivanova, F. Sologuba i Avrelja — D. S. Merežkovskij: Petr i Aleksej — Jurgis Baltrušajtis: Napevy: stichi — F. I. Tjutčev: Četyre sticha; Faksimile stichov

4. 1905: Severnye cvety assirijskie. 250 s.: ill. Obložka, pjať risunkov vo vsju stranicu, zastavki i koncovki raboty N. Feofilaktova po obrazcam assirijskago iskusstva K. Bal'mont: tri rascveta: drama — Stichi: V. Brjusov, Vjačeslav Ivanov, S. Solov'ev, M. Vološin, F. Sologub, L. Viľ kina, N. Minskij, S. Rafalovič, L. Semenov, A. Remizov — Razskazy: Z. Gippius: Tvar' — M. Krinickij: Korabl' — F. Sologub: V plenu – Ju. Čereda: Ugoľ ki; Rascvet — M. Pantjuchov: Skazka o tumane — A. Medelung: Cvet poznanija — L. Zinov'eva-Annibal': Teni sna — V. Brjusov: Zemlja: tragedija iz buduščich vremen v 5 dejstvijach i 9 kartinach — Vjačeslav

Ivanov: Tantal': tragedija

Sidorov, Aleksej Alekseevič

Stejnlen: chudožnik parižskogo prole-
tariata. Očerk prof. A. A. Sidorova.
Moskva: Gos. izd. 1919. 25 s., 16 tabl.
ill.

Šilo, Ivan

Licemery: istoričeskaja komed' v pjati
raznovidnostjach i tridcati kartinach s
prologom i épilogom. Moskva: Gos. izd.,
1920. 30 s.

Šipovnik —> Literaturno-chudožestvennyj
al'manach izd. Šipovnik...

Sipovskij, Vasilij Vasil'evič

Iz istorii russkago romana i povesti.
(Materialy po bibliografii, istorii i teorii
russkago romana). Čast' I: XVIII vek.
Izd. 2-go Otd. Imperatorskoj Akademii
Nauk. Sanktpeterburg, 1903. xiii, 333
s.

Širjaev, V. F.

Kak organizovat' kommunu ili artel':
kratkoe rukovodstvo dlja organizatorov
i rukoviditelej sel'sko-chozjajstvennych
kommun i zemledel'českich artelej.
Moskva: Gos. izd., 1921. 15 s. (Raboče-
krest'janskie listovki, 57; 50.000)

Šiškov, Vjačeslav Jakovlevič

Čujskie byli. Peterburg: Gos. izd.,
1920. 30 s.

Staryj mir: melodrama v 4-ch dejstvijach. Peterburg: Gos. izd., 1920. 67 s.

Van'ka Chljust. Peterburg: Gos. izd.,
1920. 32 s.

Sistematičeskij katalog russkim knigam —>
Mežov, V. I.: Sistematičeskij katalog...

Sivačev, Michail Gordeevič

Proškino gore. Moskva: Gos. izd.,
1920. 31 s. (Krasnaja knižka, 4)

Sivickij, F. E.

I. S. Nikitin, ego žizn' i literaturnaja dejatel'nost'.: biografičeskij očerk F. E. Si-
vickago. S portretom Nikitina, gravirovannym v Lejpcige Gedanom. S.-Peter-
burg: Tipogr. T-va Obščestvennaja pol'-
za, 1893. 78 s. (Žizn' zamečatel'nych
ljudej)

Skabičevskij, Aleksandr Michajlovič

A. F. Pisemskij, ego žizn' i literaturnaja
dejatel'nost': biografičeskij očerk A. M.
Skabičevskago. S portretom Pisemskago, gravirovannym v Peterburge K. Adtom. S.-Peterburg: Tipogr. T-va Obščestvennaja pol'za, 1894. 95 s. (Žizn'
zamečatel'nych ljudej)

A. S. Griboedov, ego žizn' i literaturnaja dejatel'nost': biografičeskij očerk
A. M. Skabičevskago. S portretom Griboedova, gravirovannym v Lejpcige Gedanom. S.-Peterburg: Tipogr. T-va Obščestvennaja pol'za, 1893. 87 s. (Žizn'
zamečatel'nych ljudej)

A. S. Puškin, ego žizn' i literaturnaja dejatel'nost': biografičeskij očerk A. M. Skabičevskago. S 15 portretami Puškina i mnogimi risunkami. 3-e izd. S.-Peterburg: Tipogr. T-va Obščestvennaja pol'za, 1899. 80 s.: ill. (Žizn' zamečatel'nych ljudej)

Belletristy-narodniki: F. Rešetnikov, A. Levitov, Gl. Uspenskij, N. Zlatovratskij: kritičeskie očerki. S.-Peterburg: Tipogr. V. S. Balašova, 1888. 315 s.

Istorija novejšej russkoj literatury 1848-1898. Izd. 4-e, ispravl. i dopoln. S 52 portretami v tekste. S.-Peterburg: Tipogr. T-va Obščestvennaja pol'za, 1900. 490 s.

M. Ju. Lermontov, ego žizn' i literaturnaja dejatel'nost': biografičeskij očerk A. M. Skabičevskago. S portretom Lermontova, gravirovannym v Peterburge K. Adtom, i mnogimi risunkami. S.-Peterburg: Tipogr. T-va Obščestvennaja pol'za, 1891. 100 s. (Žizn' zamečatel'nych ljudej)   .

N. A. Dobroljubov, ego žizn' i literaturnaja dejatel'nost': biografičeskij očerk A. M. Skabičevskago. S portretom N. A. Dobroljubova, gravirovannym v Lejpcige Gedanom. S.-Peterburg: Tipogr. T-va Obščestvennaja pol'za, 1894. 95 s. (Žizn' zamečatel'nych ljudej)

Očerki istorii russkoj cenzury (1700-1863) A. M. Skabičevskago S.-Peterburg: Izd. F. Pavlenkova, 1892. 495 s.

Sočinenija A. Skabičevskago v dvuch tomach: kritičeskie ètjudy, publicističeskie očerki, literaturnyja charakteristiki. S portretom avtora gravirovannym v Lejpcige Gedanom, po fotografii Ju. Štejnberga. Izd. 2-e. S.-Peterburg:

Tipogr. T-va Obščestvennaja pol'za, 1895. 811 stb., 887 stb.

Skal'kovskij, Konstantin Apollonovič

Očerki i fantazii. S.-Peterburg: Tipogr. A. S. Suvorina, 1903. 384 s.

U skandinavov i flamandcev: putevye vpečatlenija K. Skal'kovskago. S.-Peterburg: Tipogr. A. S. Suvorina, 1880. 202 s.

Skazki: utechi dosužija. Vstupitel'naja stat'ja E. A. Ljackago. Izd. 2-e. Stokchol'm: Izd-vo Severnye ogni, 1920. 190 s.
  Orig. izd. Petrograd: Ogni, 1915

Skitalec —> Petrov, Stepan Gavrilovič

Šklovskij, Viktor Borisovič

Mater'jal i stil' v romane L'va Tolstogo "Vojna i mir". Moskva: Izd. Federacija, 1928. 249 s.: ill. (3.000)

Udači i poraženija Maksima Gor'kogo. Tiflis: Akc. O-vo Zakkniga, 1926. 65 s. Portr. (4.000)

Skobcova, E.
(Mat' Marija)

Mirovozrenie Vl. Solov'eva. Paris: YMCA Press, 1929. 48 s.

Skobelev, M. D. —> Filippov, M. M.: M. D. Skobelev...

Skvoruška: sbornik rasskazov i stichotvorenij. Risunki A. N. Komarova. Izd.
T-va I. D. Sytina, [1921]. 16 s.: ill. (Izd.
zaregistrirovano v Otdele Pečati M.S.R.
i Kr.D.)

**Slovar' členov Obščestva ljubitelej
rossijskoj slovesnosti** pri Moskovskom Universitete. 1811-1911. Moskva:
Pečatnaja A. Snegirevoj, 1911. 342 s.

Slovar' literaturnych tipov. Red. N. D.
Noskova. S.-Peterburg: Knigoizd. Vscho-
dy-Izd. Slovar' Lit. Tipov
    T. 2: Literaturnye tipy Lermontova.
Vyp. 3. [n.d.]. 114 s.
    T. 4: Tipy Aksakova. 1914.
    T. 5: Literaturnye tipy Griboedova.
Vyp. 6-j. [n.d.]. 114 s.
    T. 6: Tipy Puškina. 7-j i 8-j vyp.
Slovarja. 1912. 315 s.
    T. 7: Tipy Gončarova. Vyp. 9- i 10-j.
1914. 367 s.

Smidovič, V.V. —> Veresaev, V. V. (pseud.)

Šmidt, O.J. —> Bol'šaja sovetskaja ėnciklo-
pedija...

Smirnov, V. D.

A.I. Gercen, ego žizn' i literaturnaja
dejatel'nost': biografičeskij očerk V. D.
Smirnova. S.-Peterburg: Tipogr. T-va
Obščestvennaja pol'za, 1898. 160 s.:
ill. (Žizn' zamečatel'nych ljudej)

Aksakovy, ich žizn' i literaturnaja dejatel'nost': biografičeskij očerk V.D. Smirnova. S portretami Konstantina, Sergeja i Ivana Aksakovych. S.-Peterburg: Ti-

pogr. T-va Obščestvennaja pol'za, 1895.
87 s.: ill. (Žizn' zamečatel'nych ljudej)

Šmurlo, Evgenij Francevič

Vvedenie v russkuju istoriju. Praga:
Plamja, 1924. 178 s.

Sologub, Fedor
(Fedor Kuz'mič Teternikov)

Kniga skazok. Moskva: Knigoizd. Grif,
1905. [86] s.

Razskazy i stichi: Červjak — Teni — K
zvezdam — Stichi: kniga vtoraja. S.-Pe-
terburg: Tipogr. M. Merkuševa, 1896.
187 s.

Sobranie stichov: kniga III i IV: 1897-
1903 g. Moskva: Knigoizd. Skorpion,
1904. 188 s.

Stichi: kniga pervaja. S.-Peterburg: Tipogr. Morskago Ministerstva, 1896.
lxiv s.
    Ded.: A. Jensenu ot avtora na
    pamjat'. 1905 g.

Tjaželye sny: roman Fedora Sologuba.
S.-Peterburg: Tipo-litogr. A. E. Landau,
1896. 309 s.

Zaklinatel'nica zmej: roman. Danzig:
Knigoizd. Slovo, 1921. 313 s.

Žalo smerti: razskazy. Moskva: Knigoizd. Skorpion, 1904. 203 s.
    Žalo smerti — Zemle zemnoe — Ob-
ruč — Barančik — Krasota — Utešenie

—> Ščit: Literaturnyj sbornik...

Solov'ev, Evgenij Andreevič
(pseud. Andreevič)

D.I. Pisarev, ego žizn' i literaturnaja dejatel'nost': biografičeskij očerk Evgenija Solov'eva. S portretom Pisareva, gravirovannym v Lejpcige Gedanom. 3-e izd. S.-Peterburg: Tipogr. T-va Obščestvennaja pol'za, 1899. 160 s. (Žizn' zamečatel'nych ljudej)

F. Dostoevskij, ego žizn' i literaturnaja dejatel'nost': biografičeskij očerk Evgenija Solov'eva. S portretom Dostoevskago, gravirovannym v Lejpcige Gedanom. S.-Peterburg: Tipogr. T-va Obščestvennaja pol'za, 1898. 96 s. (Žizn' zamečatel'nych ljudej)

I. A. Gončarov, ego žizn' i literaturnaja dejatel'nost': biografičeskij očerk E. A. Solov'eva. S portretom Gončarova, gravirovannym v Peterburge K. Adtom. S.-Peterburg: Tipogr. T-va Obščestvennaja pol'za, 1895. 80 s. (Žizn' zamečatel'nych ljudej)

Ioann Groznyj, ego žizn' i gosudarstvennaja dejatel'nost': biografičeskij očerk E.A. Solov'eva. S portretom Ioanna Groznago, gravirovannym v Lejpcige Gedanom. S.-Peterburg: Tipogr. T-va Obščestvennaja pol'za, 1893. 87 s. (Žizn' zamečatel'nych ljudej)

I. S. Turgenev, ego žizn' i literaturnaja dejatel'nost': biografičeskij očerk Evgenija Solov'eva. S portretom Turgeneva, gravirovannym v Peterburge K. Adtom. S.-Peterburg: Tipogr. Kontragentsva žel. dorog., 1894. 96 s. (Žizn' zamečatel'nych ljudej)

Kniga o Maksime Gor'kom i A. P. Čechove. S priloženiem avtobiografii Gor'kago i portretov Gor'kago i Čechova.

[izd.] Andreevič. S.-Peterburg: Tipogr. A. E. Kolpinskago, 1900. 259 s.

L. N. Tolstoj, ego žizn' i literaturnaja dejatel'nost': biografičeskij očerk Evgenija Solov'eva. S portretom Tolstogo, gravirovannym v Lejpcige Gedanom. 2-e izd. S.-Peterburg: Tipogr. T-va Obščestvennaja pol'za, 1897. 160 s. (Žizn' zamečatel'nych ljudej)

N. M. Karamzin, ego žizn' i naučno-literaturnaja dejatel'nost': biografičeskij očerk Evgenija Solov'eva. S portretom N. M. Karamzina, gravirovannym v Peterburge K. Adtom. S.-Peterburg: Tipogr. T-va Obščestvennaja pol'za, 1894. 80 s. (Žizn' zamečatel'nych ljudej)

Očerki po istorii russkoj literatury XIX veka. Evg. Solov'ev (Andreevič). S.-Peterburg: Tipogr. A. E. Kolpinskago, 1902. xvi, 554 s.

Solov'ev, N. —> Ostrovskij, A. N.: Dramatičeskija sočinenija...

Solov'ev, Sergej Michajlovič

Istorija Rossii s drevnejšich vremen. Kn. 1-6 (29 tomov). Moskva: Izd. T-va Obščestvennaja pol'za, 1896.

—> Bezobrazov, P. V. —> S.M. Solov'ev, ego žizn'...

Solov'ev, Vladimir Sergeevič

Sobranie sočinenij Vladimira Sergeeviča Solov'eva. T. 1-9. S.- Peterburg: Izd. T-va Obščestvennaja pol'za, 1901-1907.
　　T. 1: 1873-1877. 1901. 375 s. Portr.
　　T. 2: 1878-1880. 1901. 386 s.

T. 3: 1877-1884. 1901. 387. Portr.
T. 4: 1883-1887. 1901. 587 s.
T. 5: 1883-1897. 1902. 552 s.
T. 6: 1886-1896. 1904. 670 s.
T. 7: 1894-1897. 1903. 677 s.
T. 8: 1897-1900. [n.d.]. 586 s.
T. 9, dopoln. 1907. lv, 261 s.
S. i-lv: É. Radlov: V. S. Solov'ev,
biografičeskij očerk

Stichotvorenija. Izd. 5-e. Moskva: Izd.
S. M. Solov'eva, [n.d.]. xvi, 187 s.

Sud'ba Puškina. S.-Peterburg: Tipogr.
M. M. Stasjuleviča, 1898. 40 s.

—> Skobcova, E.: Mirovozrenie Vl. Solov'e-
va...

Solov'ev, Vsevolod Sergeevič

Sočinenija Vsevoloda Sergeeviča Solo-
v'eva. T. 1-7. S.-Peterburg: T-vo Ob-
ščestvennaja pol'za, 1887.
T. 1: Knjažna Ostrožskaja — Ka-
simovskaja nevesta — Russkie kresto-
noscy. 205, 238, 84 s.
T. 2: Car'-devica — Junyj impera-
tor. 286, 260 s.
T. 3: Sergej Gorbatov — Kapitan
Grenaderskoj roty. 410, 218 s.
T. 4: Vol'ter'janec — Magnit —
Svjatočnye razskazy. 424, 30, 74 s.
T. 5: Staryj dom — Staryja byli.
412, 128 s.
T. 6: Izgnannik — Kavkazskija
legendy — Kartinka venskoj žizni –
Bol'šoj čelovek. 384, 80 s.
T. 7: Navoždenie — Starik — Stichi
— Poslednie Gorbatovy. 160, 34, 30,
348 s.

Spasovič, Vladimir Danilovič

Sočinenija V. D. Spasoviča. S portre-

tom avtora. 1-10. S.-Peterburg: Kniž-
nyj magazin Br. Rymovič, 1889-1902.
T. 1: Predislovie — Vladislav Syro-
komlja — Šekspirovskij Gamlet —
Martin Matuševič i ego memuary —
Neskol'ko slov o Kaveline — Reč' o
Puškine — Vincentij Pol' i ego poèzija.
1889. 286 s.
T. 2: Literaturnye očerki i portrety:
Bajron i nekotorye ego predšestvenniki
— Mickevič v rannem perioede ego žizni (do 1830 g.) — Puškin i Mickevič u
pamjatnika Petra Velikago — Bajronizm u Puškina — Bajronizm u Lermontova. 1889. 406 s.
T. 3: Stat'i, dissertacii, lekcii juridi-
českago soderžanija. 1890. 544 s.
T. 4: Perežitoe — Polemika — Pu-
tevyja zametki — Kritika. 1891. 432 s.
T. 5-7: Sudebnyja reči. 1893–1894.
355, 378, 318 s.
T. 8-9: Poslednija raboty v devjano-
stych godach. 1896-1900. 474, 453 s.
T. 10: Politika — Istorija — Kritika.
1902. 498 s.

Speranskij, M.M. —> Južakov, S.N.: M.M.
Speranskij, ego žizn'...

Speranskij, V.

Istoriko-kritičeskie materialy k zadani-
jam po literature: M. Gor'kij - "Na dne".
Moskva: Kooperativnoe izd. Mir, 1925.
79 s. (Praktika Dal'ton-Plana; 5.000)

Sreznevskij, Izmail Ivanovič

Drevnie pamjatniki russkago pis'ma i
jazyka (X—XIV vekov). Obščee povre-
mennoe obozrenie. Trud I. I. Sreznev-
skago. 2-e izd. Sanktpeterburg: Tipogr.
Imperatorskoj Akademii Nauk, 1882.
390 s.

Stanjukovič, Konstantin Michajlovič

Sobranie sočinenij K. M. Stanjukoviča.
T. 1-2. Izd. A. A. Karceva. Moskva: Tipo-
litogr. G.I. Prostakova, 1902. 556, 543 s.

Stasov, Vladimir Vasil'evič

Sobranie sočinenij V. V. Stasova 1847-
1886. S priloženiem ego portreta i
snimka s podnesennago emu adresa.
T. 1-3. S.-Peterburg: Tipogr. M. M. Stasjuleviča, 1894.

T. 1: Chudožestvennyja stat'i: Istorija chudožestv i chudožestvennych
proizvedenij — Kritika chudožestvennych proizvedenij. 882, 768 stb.: ill.

T. 2: Chudožestvennyja stat'i: Kritika chudozestvennych izdanij i statej —
Očerki žizni i dejatel'nosti chudožnikov. 1050, 483 stb.: ill.

T. 3: Muzyka i teatr — Literatura —
Imperatorskaja publičnaja biblioteka
— Avtobiografija. 1790 stb.: ill.

Steinlen, Theophile Alexandre —> Sidorov,
A. A.: Stejnlen...

Steklov, Jurij Michajlovič

Poèžija revoljucionnogo socializma: pevcy trudovogo carstva vo Francii. Izd. 2-
oe, ispravl. i dopoln. Moskva: Gos. izd.,
1919. 111 s.

**Stepnjak-Kravčinskij, Sergej Michaj-
lovič**

Andrej Kožuchov: roman. Moskva: Gos.
izd., 1921. 199 s. (20.000)

Sobranie sočinenij. Č. 1-4. S.-Peter-
burg, 1907.

Č. 1: Štundist Pavel Rudenko. Dopoln. po rukopisi. S napisannymi dlja
nastojaščego izd. vospominanijami P.A.
Kropotkina i fototipičeskim portretom
Stepnjaka. Edinstvennoe razrešennoe
vdovoju avtora izd. xxxi, 224 s. (Biblioteka Svetoča pod red. S. A. Vengerova,
35-39)

Č. 2: Podpol'naja Rossija. 3-e razrešennoe vdovoju avtora izd. Dopoln.
stat'ej o Bardinoj i 7-ju fototipičeskimi
portretami. 262 s.: ill. (Biblioteka Svetoča, 6-9)

Č. 3: Domik na Volge — Novoobra-
ščennyj — Skazka o korejke. Dopoln.
po rukopisi. S fototipičeskim portretom
Stepnjaka. Edinstvennoe razrešennoe
vdovoju avtora izd. iv, 241 s. (Biblioteka Svetoča, 51-55)

Č. 4: Andrej Kožuchov. Perevod s
anglijskogo F. M. Stepnjak pod. red. i s
predisloviem P. A. Kropotkina. So sta-
t'ej Georga Brandesa i fototipičeskim
portretom Stepnjaka. 3-e razrešennoe
vdovoju avtora izd. xvi, 306 s. (Biblioteka Svetoča, 66-70)

Strachov, Nikolaj Nikolaevič

Bor'ba s Zapadom v našej literature. 1-
3. Izd. 3-e. Kiev: Izd. I. P. Matčenko,
1897.

T. 1: Gercen — Mill — Parižskaja
kommuna — Renan — Istoriki bez
principov — Štraus — Pomniki po I. S.
Aksakove. xiii, 386 s.

T. 2: Chod našej literatury, načinaja
ot Lomonosova — Rokovoj vopros —
Naša kul'tura i vsemirnoe edinstvo —
Darvin — Polnoe oproverženie darvi-
nizma. vi, 463 s.

T. 3: Izd. vtoroe.: Itogi sovremennago znanija — Renan — Tèn — Chod
i charakter sovremennago estestvozna-

nija — Spor ob "Rossii v Evrope" N. Ja. Danilevskago — Razbory knig — Belinskij. 296 s.

Kritičeskija stat'i ob I. S. Turgeneve i L. N. Tolstom (1862-1885). T. 1. Izd. 4-e. Kiev: Izd. I. P. Matčenko, 1901. xv, 387 s.

Stroev, V. A.

M. Gor'kij (Aleksej Maksimovič Peškov): k 50-letiju so dnja roždenija 14 marta 1869 — 14 marta 1919. Peterburg: Izd. Z. I. Gržebina, 1919. 32 s.

Šubin, N.

Strannik: dramatičeskij èskiz v odnom dejstvii dlja P'estro Gori prisposobil dlja sceny N. Šubin. Moskva: Gos. Izd., 1920. 32 s. (Krasnaja knižka, 26)

Šubinskij, Sergej Nikolaevič

Očerki iz žizni i byta prošlogo vremeni. S 30 gravjurami. S.-Peterburg: Tipografija A. S. Suvorina, 1888. 162, 7 s.: ill.

Suchomlinov, Michail Ivanovič

A. N. Radiščev, avtor "Putešestvija iz Peterburga v Moskvu", M. I. Suchomlinova. Sanktpeterburg: Tipogr. Imperatorskoj Akademii Nauk, 1883. 143 s.

Izsledovanija i stat'i po russkoj literature i prosveščeniju. T. 1-2. S.-Peterburg: Izd. A. S. Suvorina, 1889. 671, 516 s.

Sudrabs, Ja. F. —> Lacis, M. I. (pseud.)

Sumarokov, Aleksandr Petrovič

Izbrannyja dramatičeskija proizvedenija: Chorev — Sinav i Truvor — Opekun — Materialy dlja izučenija ego proizvedenij. Izd. I. Glazunova. S.-Peterburg: Tipogr. Glazunova, 1893. vi, 171 s. (Russkaja klassnaja biblioteka izd. pod red. A. N. Čudinova)

Šuvalov, S.V. —> Nikitina, E.E. & Šuvalov, S. V.: Belletristy...

Suvorin, Aleksej Sergeevič

Ivan Nikolaevič Kramskoj, ego žizn', perepiska i chudožestvenno-kritičeskija stat'i 1837-1887. Izdal Aleksej Suvorin. S faksimile i 2 portretami. Sanktpeterburg: Tipogr. A. S. Suvorina, 1888. 750 s.

Suvorov, A.V. —> Peskovskij, M.L.: A.V. Suvorov...

Svirskij, Aleksej Ivanovič

Mužik i Kapital: (Vol'noe skazanie). Obložka i ill. chudožnika I. Simakova. Peterburg: Gos. izd., 1920. 32 s.: ill.

T. N. —> Razskazy očevidcev...

Tatiščev, V. N. —> Pekarskij, P. P.: Novyja izvestija o V. N. Tatiščeve...

Telešov, Nikolaj Dmitrievič

Elka Mitriča: iz žizni sibirskich perese-
lencev. S ill. V. Spasskogo. Moskva:
Gos. izd., 1919. 23 s.: ill. (Literaturnaja Komissija pri Pedagogičeskom učre-
denii "Naš Dom")

Razskazy. Izd. 2-e. T. 1. S.-Peterburg
1904. 270 s.

Temnyj, N. A. —> Lazarev, Nikolaj Artemo-
vič

Terpigorov, Sergej Nikolaevič

Sobranie sočinenij S.N. Terpigorova (S.
Atavy). Red. S. N. Šubinskago. S biografičeskim očerkom, sost. P. V. Bykovym,
i portretom S. N. Terpigoreva. T. 1-6.
S.-Peterburg: Izd. A. F. Marksa, 1900.
    T. 1-2: Oskudenie; Želtaja kniga.
493, 542 s.
    T. 3: Potrevožennyja teni. 721 s.
    T. 4-5: Povesti i razskazy. 572, 588
s.
    T. 6: Istoričeskie razskazy — Dorož-
nye očerki. 640 s.

Teternikov, F. K. —> Sologub, Fedor

Tichonravov, N. S. —> Russkija byliny...

Tjutčev, Fedor Ivanovič

Sočinenija F. I. Tjutčeva: stichotvorenija i političeskija stat'i. S portretom i
snimkom s rukopisi avtora. Izd. vtoroe
ispr. i dopoln. S.-Peterburg: Tipogr. A.
S. Suvorina, 1900. 622, x s.

Tolstoj A. K. —> Prutkov, K.

Tolstoj, I. —> Russkija drevnosti...

Tolstoj, Lev L'vovič

Protiv obščiny. Tri stat'i: Mir durak —
Neizbežnyj put' — tormoz russkoj kul'-
tury. L. L. Tolstogo. Moskva: Tipo-litogr. I. N. Kušnerev, 1900. 77 s.

V Jasnoj Poljane: pravda ob otce i ego
žizni. Praga: Plamja, 1923. 102 s.

Tolstoj, Lev Nikolaevič

Čem ljudi živy i drugie rasskazy. Petrograd: Literaturno-izdatel'skij Otdel Komissariata Narodnogo Prosveščenija,
1918. xv, 107 s. (Narodnaja biblioteka)
    Čem ljudi živy — Upustiš' ogon' –
ne potušiš' — Gde ljubov', tam i Bog —
Dva starika — Kajuščijsja grešnik —
Tri starca
    S. iii-xv: Lev Nikolaevič Tolstoj

Chadži-Murat i drugie proizvedenija.
Peterburg: Gos. izd., 1920. 290 s.
    Chadži-Murat — Dva sputnika —
Zapiski sumasšedšago — O sude —
Vstuplenie k "Istorii materi" — Zapiski
materi — Otec Vasilij — Kto ubijcy —
Ieromonach Isidor — Chodynka — Dve
različnyja versii istorii ul'ja s lubočnoj
kryškoj — Posmertnyja zapiski starca
Fedora Kuz'miča — Primečanie V.
Čertkova k "Posmertnym zapiskam
starca Fedora Kuz'miča"

Detstvo i otročestvo grafa L. N. Tolstogo. Moskva: Tipogr. A. Torleckago,
1876. 140 s.

Dnevnik molodosti L'va Nikolaeviča
Tolstogo. Izd. pervoe pod red. V. G.
Čertkova. T. 1: 1847-1852. S portre-

tom 1851 g. Moskva: Tipogr. I. D. Sytina, 1917. 286 s.

I svet vo t'me svetit: drama. Berlin: J. Ladyschnikow 1912. 95 s.

Krug čtenija. T. 1-2. Berlin: Izd. I. P. Ladyžnikova, 1923. 615, 714 s.

Mnogo-li čeloveku zemli nužno. Obložka i ill. chudož. V. Michajlova-Severnogo. Petrograd: Gos. izd., 1920. 19 s.: ill.

Neizdannye razskazy i p'esy. Pod red. S. P. Mel'gunova... S predisloviem T. I. Polnera. Pariž: Izd. T-va N. P. Karbasnikov, 1926. 317 s.

Pervyj vinokur ili Kak čertenok krajušku zaslužil: komedija. Obložka i ill. chudož. I. Simakova. Peterburg: Gos. izd., 1920. 29 s.: ill. (Narodnaja biblioteka)

Pis'ma L. N. Tolstogo. T. 1-2. Sobrannyja i red. P. A. Sergeenko. Moskva: K-vo Kniga, 1910-1911. 367, xxx, 311 s.

Pis'ma L. N. Tolstogo k duchoborcam. Berlin: Izd. Gugo Štejnica, 1902. 53 s.

Pis'ma grafa L. N. Tolstogo k žene 1862–1910. Pod red. A. E. Gruzinskago. Moskva 1913. vi, 558 s.

Polnoe sobranie sočinenij. Pod obščej red. V. G. Čertkova pri učastii redaktorskogo komiteta... Izd. osuščestvljaetsja pod nabljudeniem gosudarstvennoj redakcionnoj komissii v sostave... T. 1-90. Moskva-Leningrad: Gos. izd., 1928-1958.

Posmertnyja chudožestvennyja proizvedenija. Pod red. V. G. Čertkova. Avtorizovannoe izd. T. 1-3. Berlin: J. La-

dyschnikow, 1912. 273, 320, 295 s.

Sočinenija grafa L. N. Tolstogo. Izd. 7-e. Č. 1-12. Moskva Tipogr. M. G. Volčaninova, 1887.
    Č. 1: Detstvo, otročestvo i junost'. 450 s.
    Č. 2-3: Povesti i razskazy. 561, 573 s.
    Č. 4: Pedagogičeskija stat'i. 625 s.
    Č. 5-8: Vojna i mir. 479, 520, 551, 479 s.
    Č. 9-11: Anna Karenina. 364, 479, 400 s.
    Č. 12: Proizvedenija poslednich godov. 742 s.

Sočinenija grafa L. N. Tolstogo. Izd. 9-oe. T. 1-14. Moskva Tipo-litogr. T-va I. N. Kušnerev, 1893-1898. Portr.
    T. 1: Detstvo, otročestvo i junost'. 1893. 367 s.
    T. 2-3: Povesti i razskazy. 1893. 436, 502 s.
    T. 4: Pedagogičeskija stat'i — Sočinenija i perevody dlja detej. 1893. 503 s.
    T. 5-8: Vojna i mir. 1893. 458, 393, 400, 441 s.
    T. 9-11: Anna Karenina. 1893. 296, 376, 325 s.
    T. 12-13: Proizvedenija poslednich godov. 1893. 552 s. 573 s.: ill.
    T. 14. Izd. 1-e. 1898. 560 s.
    + izd. 12-e. 1911

Sočinenija grafa L. N. Tolstogo. 12-e izd. Č. 1-5. Moskva: Lito-tipogr. I. N. Kušnerev, 1911.

Svečka: razskaz. Praga: Slavjanskoe izd. Kreml' v Češskoj Prage, [n.d.]. 14 s. (Izbrannye proizvedenija russkich pisatelej, 2)

V golodnye goda: (zapiski i stat'i). S illjustracijami. Moskva: Tipogr. T-va I. N. Kušnerev, 1900. 180 s.: ill.

Velikij grech. Izd. Posrednika. Moskva 1905. 48 s.

Živoj trup: drama v 6 dejstvijach i 12 kartinach. Izd. Aleksandry L'vovny Tolstoj, pod red. V. G. Čertkova. Moskva: Tipogr. T-va I. D. Sytina, 1912. 68 s. Portr.

Živye reči L. N. Tolstogo: (1885-1908). Odessa: Tipogr. gazety Odesskija novosti, 1908. 395 s.

—> Čertkov, V. G.: Uchod Tolstogo...—> Ėjchenbaum, B. M.: Lev Tolstoj. Kn. vtoraja... —> Graf Lev Tolstoj... —> L. N. Tolstoj — žizn' i tvorčestvo 1828-1908... —> Leont'ev, K. N.: O romanach gr. L. N. Tolstogo... —> Lunačarskij, A. V.: O Tolstom: sbornik statej... —> Russkaja biblioteka, 9: Graf Lev Nikolaevič Tolstoj...—> Šklovskij, V. B.: Material i stil'... —> Solov'ev, E. A.: L. N. Tolstoj... —> Strachov, N. N.: Kritičeskija stat'i...—> Tolstoj, L. L.: V Jasnoj Poljane...—> Velikoj pamjati L. N. Tolstogo...

Tretij Vserossijskij s''ezd professional'nych sojuzov 6-13 aprelja 1920 goda. Stenografičeskij otčet. Č. 1-ja: plenumy. Moskva: Gos. izd., 1921. 146 s.

Turgenev, Ivan Sergeevič

Bežin lug. Moskva: Gos. izd., 1920. 28 s. (Narodnaja biblioteka, 35)

Polnoe sobranie sočinenij I. S. Turgeneva. 3 izd. T. 1-10. S.-Peterburg: Tipogr. Glazunova, 1891.

Sočinenija I. S. Turgeneva (1844-1868-1874-1880). T. 2, 7. Moskva: Izd. Knižnago magazina naslednikov Brat'ev Salaevych, 1880

T. 2: Zapiski ochotnika. 413 s.
T. 7: Zatiše — Perepiska, Jakov Pasynkov — Faust — Poezdka v Poles'e — Asja — Pervaja ljubov'. 370 s.

Turgenev i Savina. Pis'ma I. S. Turgeneva k M. G. Savinoj. Vospominanija M. G. Savinoj ob I. S. Turgeneve. S predisloviem i pod red. A. F. Koni, pri bližajsem sotrudničestve A. E. Molčanova. Petrograd: Izd. Gosudarstvennych teatrov. 1918. xxxviii, 113 s.

—> Russkaja biblioteka, 6: I. S. Turgenev... —> Solov'ev, E. A.: I. S. Turgenev... —> Strachov, N. N.: Kritičeskija stat'i...

Tverskoj, Nikita

Vlast': dramatičeskoe predstavlenie v četyrech dejstvijach (pjati kartinach) Nikity Tverskogo. Moskva: Gos. izd., 1920. 47 s.

Tynjanov, Jurij Nikolaevič

Kjuchla. Leningrad-Moskva: Gos. izd. Chudožestvennoj literatury, 1931. 328 s. (5.000)

Puškin. Č. 1-2. Leningrad: Gos. izd. Chudožestvennoj literatury, 1936. 590 s. (150.000)

Rasskazy: Podporučik Kiže — Maloletnyj Vitušišnikov — Voskovaja persona. Moskva: Sovetskij pisatel', 1935. 348 s. (10.200)

Smert' Vazir-Muchtara. Leningrad: Priboj, 1929. 550 s. (7.000)

Uajl'd, O. —> Wilde, O.

Udar za udarom: literaturnyj al'manach pod red. A. Bezymenskogo. Udar vtoroj. Moskva-Leningrad: Gos. izd., 1930. 346 s. (3.000)

S. Semenov: Natal'ja Tarpova: p'esa — L. Grabar': Krasnobožskij Letopisec — N. Aseev: Antigenial'naja poėma — A. Kudrejko: Čumak: stich — L. Iochved: Topolja: rasskaz; Kaštanovyj cvet — A. Bezymenskij: Den' našej žizni: poėma — E. Mozol'kov: Polesskie stichi — Nik. Ušakov: Admiral zemlečerpalok: stich — P. Tyčina: N. Podvojskomu: stich — Ės. Chabib Vafa: Pjataja žena — L. Baril': Šekspir: novella — B. Solov'ev: Otryvok: stich — V. Ėrlich: O svine: stich — I. Sel'vinskij: Puštorg — O. Ėdberg: Dragij kamen' — Dela i ljudi: R. Landau: Čechoslovackij Ford - Tomas Batja — Napostovec: O Sofrone Selivestrove — Stat'i: G. Gorbačev: O putjach proletarskoj literatury — S. Rodov: Samokritika i proletarskaja literatura — E. Mistangova: "Krugovaja" poruka — A. Bek: Na ėtapach pervonačal'nogo nakoplenija — A. Kurella: Chudožestvennaja reakcija nastupaet — G. Gorbačev: Kak ponimat' dramu S. Semenova "Natal'ja Tarpova" — Za polnuju jasnost' — Protiv pereverzevščiny: F. Šemjakin: Metafizika V. F. Pereverzeva — G. Gorbačev: Pereverzevcy na proizvodstvennoj praktike — Satira i jumor: Literaturnyj panoptikum

Uėlls, G. —> Wells, H. G.

Umanec, Fedor Michajlovič

Getman Mazepa. Istoričeskaja monografija F. M. Umanca. S.-Peterburg: Tipogr. M. Merkušova, 1897. 455 s.

Umanov-Kaplunovskij, Vladimir Vasil'evič

Farisei: iz gallerei tipov konca XIX stoletija: roman v dvuch častjach. S.-Peterburg: Tipo-litogr. V. V. Komarova, 1905. 270 s.

Ušinskij, K.D. —> Peskovskij, M.L.: K.D. Ušinskij, ego žizn'...

Usova, S. E.

N. I. Novikov, ego žizn' i obščestvennaja dejatel'nost': biografičeskij očerk S. E. Usovoj. S portretom Novikova, gravirovannym v Peterburge K. Adtom. S.-Peterburg: Tipogr. T-va Obščestvennaja pol'za, 1891. 94 s. (Žizn' zamečatel'nych ljudej)

Uspenskij, Gleb Ivanovič

Sočinenija Gleba Uspenskago. S portretom avtora i vstupitel'noj stat'ej N. Michajlovskago. 4-e izd. F. Pavlenkova. 1-3. S.-Peterburg: Tipogr. Ju. N. Ėrlich, 1896-1898.

T. 1: Nravy rasterjaevoj ulicy — Rasterjaevskie tipy i sceny —Stoličnaja bednota — Razorenie — Novye vremena, novye zaboty — Očerki i razskazy — Meloči — Pis'ma iz Serbii — Koj-pročto - Iz putevych zametok. li, 1192 stb.

T. 2: Iz derevenskago dnevnika — Neporvannyja svjazi — Ovca bez stada — Malye rebjata — Beglye nabroski — Bog grecham terpit — Volej-nevolej — Krest'janin i krest'janskij trud — Vlast' zemli - Iz razgovorov s prijateljami — Prišlo na pamjat' — Skučajuščaja publika — Črez pen' kolodu — Očerki — Pis'ma s dorogi — Živyja cifry — Mimochodom. 1256 stb.

T. 3: Izd. 2-e.: Očerki perechodnago vremeni —Stat'i raznago soderžanija — Nevidimki — Poezdki k pereselencam — Mel'kom — Razskazy. 740 stb.

Uspenskij, G. I. —> Aptekman, O. V.: Gleb Ivanovič Uspenskij...

V zaščitu slova: Sbornik 1. 2 izd. bez peremen. S.-Peterburg: Tipogr. N. N. Klobukova, 1905. 255 s.

Vasil'ki: literaturno-chudožestvennyj sbornik. 50 belletrističeskich, 19 chudožestvennych i 6 muzykal'nych proizvedenij. S.-Peterburg 1901. 498 s.: ill. (k 25-ti-letnemu jubileju Julija Osipoviča Grjunberga)

Velikij kommunar: agitacionno-revoljucionnoe predstavlenie. Trilogija. Moskva: Gos. Izd., 1920. 48 s. (Krasnaja knižka, 27)

Velikoj pamjati L. N. Tolstogo. Kazanskij Universitet. 1828-1928. Kazan', Izd. Kazanskogo Gosuniversiteta imeni V. I. Lenina, 1928. 151 s.: ill. (500)
S. 146-151: Sommaire

Velikoruss v svoich pesnjach, obrjadach, obyčajach, verovanijach, skazkach, legendach i t.p.: materialy sobrannye i privedennye v porjadok P.V. Šejnom. T. 1 (vyp. pervyj). Sanktpeterburg: Izd. Imperatorskoj Akademii Nauk, 1898. lviii, 833 s.

Wells, Herbert G.

Kogda prosnetsja spjaščij: roman. Perevod s anglijskogo M. Šišmarevoj i Ė. Pimenovoj. Moskva: Gos. izd., 1920. 336 s. (Obščaja biblioteka, 65; 25.000)

Vel'tman, Elena Ivanovna

Priključenija koroleviča Gustava Irikoviča, ženicha carevny Ksenii Godunovoj: istoričeskij roman v pjati častjach. Sanktpeterburg: V tipogr. A. A. Kraevskago, 1867. 76, 83, 81, 101, 86 s. (Iz Otečestvennych zapisok 1867 g., 1-5)

Venevitinov, Dmitrij Vladimirovič

Polnoe sobranie stichotvorenij Venevitinova. S biografiej i portretom ego. Izd. 2-e. S.-Peterburg: Izd. A. S. Suvorina, 1886. x, 90 s. (Deševaja biblioteka)

Vengerov, Semen Afanas'evič

Istočniki slovarja russkich pisatelej. Sobral S. A. Vengerov. T. 1-3. Sanktpeterburg: Tipogr. Imperatorskoj Akademii Nauk
T. 1: Aaron-Gogol'. 1900. 814 s.
T. 2: Gogockaja-Karamzin. 1910. 598 s.
T. 3: Karamyšev-Lomonosov. 1914. 524 s.

Kritiko-biografičeskij slovar' russkich pisatelej i učenych (ot načala russkoj obrazovannosti do našich dnej). T. 1-6. S. Peterburg: Semenovskaja tipo-litografija, 1889-1904.
T. 1. Vyp. 1-21: A. 1889. xxii, 992 s.
T. 2. Vyp. 22-30: Babadžanov- Benzengr. 1891. 422 s.

T. 3: Benni-Boborykina. 1892. 444 s.
T. 4. Otdel 1: Boborykin-Bogojavlen-skij; Otdel 2: Vavilov-Vvedenskij. 1895. 262, 212 s.
T. 5: S alfavitnym ukazatelem ko vsem pjati tomam. 1897. 466 s.
T. 6: Istoriko-literaturnyj sbornik. S alfavitnym ukazatelem ko vsem 6 to-mam. 1897-1904. x, 465 s.

Očerki po istorii russkoj literatury. 2-e izd., bez peremen. S.-Peterburg 1907. 492 s. (Biblioteka Svetoča pod red. S. A. Vengerova, 56-65. Serija Istorija i teorija literatury, 4)

Russkija knigi. S biografičeskimi dan-nymi ob avtorach i perevodčikach (1708-1893). Red. S. A. Vengerova. Izd. G. V. Judina. T. 1-3. S.-Peterburg: Ti-po-litografija A. É. Vineke, 1897-1899. 476, 472, 476 s.

Sobranie sočinenij S. A. Vengerova. T. 1, 3, 5. S.-Peterburg: Knigoizd. Prome-tej, 1911. 205 s.
T. 1: Geroičeskij charakter russkoj literatury. 1911. 205 s.
T. 3: Peredovoj boec slavjanofil'stva Konstantin Aksakov. 1912. 247 s.
T. 2: Družinin. Gončarov. Pisem-skij. 1911. 275 s.

Vengerov, S. A. —> Russkaja poèzija...

Verchovskij, N. P.

Norvegija i Švecija: iz zapisnoj knižki slučajnago turista N. P. Verchovskago. Varšava: V tipogr. Gubernskago Prav-lenija, 1899. 75 s.

Veresaev, V. V.
(Vikentij Vikent'evič Smidovič)

Konec Andreja Ivanoviča: povest'. S.-Peterburg: Tipogr. E. Evdokimovych, 1900. 170 s.

Očerki i razskazy: Na mertvoj doroge — Tovarišči — Poryv — Prekrasnaja Ele-na — Zagadka — Bez dorogi — Povet-rie. Izd. 3-e. S.-Peterburg: Tipogr. A. E. Kolpinskago, 1901. 267 s.

Polnoe sobranie sočinenij V. V. Vere-saeva. T. 1-4. S.-Peterburg: Izd. T-va A. F. Marks, 1913.
T. 1-2: Razskazy — Zapiski vrača. 385, 319 s.s.
T. 3: Razskazy — Iz drevne-grečes-kich poètov. 403 s.
T. 4: Razskazy o vojne — Na vojne: zapiski. 343 s.

Razskazy. T. 1-3. S.-Peterburg: Tipogr. Al'tšulera, 1903.
T. 1. Izd. 5-e. 267 s.
T. 2. Izd. 2-e. 319 s.
T. 3. Izd. 2-e. 276 s.

Zapiski vrača. S.-Peterburg: Tipogr. A. E. Kol'pinskago, 1901. 310 s.

—> Bocjanovskij, V. T.: V. V. Veresaev...

Vereščagin, Aleksandr Vasil'evič

Doma i na vojne 1853-1881: vospomi-nanija i razskazy Aleksandra Vereščagi-na. Izd. 2-e. S.-Peterburg 1886. 572 s.

U bolgar i zagranicej 1881-1893: vos-pominanija i razskazy (prodolženie očerkov "Doma i na vojne"). S portre-tom. Izd. 2-e. S.-Peterburg 1896. 328 s.: ill.

Vereščagin, Vasilij Andreevič

Russkija illjustrirovannyja izdanija XVIII i XIX stoletija (1720-1870). Bibliografičeskij opyt. S.-Peterburg: Tipogr. V. Kiršbauma, 1898. 309 s.

Vereščagin, Vasilij Vasil'evič

Detstvo i otročestvo chudožnika V. V. Vereščagina. T. 1: Derevnja — Korpus — Risoval'naja škola. Moskva: Tipogr. T-va I. N. Kušnerevych, 1895. 315 s.

Literator: povest'. Moskva: Tipo-litogr. T-va I. N. Kušnerev, 1894. 239 s.

Na vojne v Azii i Evrope. S risunkami chudožnika V. V. Vereščagina. Moskva Tipogr. T-va I. N. Kušnerev, 1898. 391 s.: ill.

Očerki, nabroski, vospominanija V. V. Vereščagina. S risunkami. Sanktpeterburg: Tipogr. Ministerstva Putej Soobščenija, 1883. 155 s.: ill.

Veselovskij, Aleksej Nikolaevič

Zapadnoe vlijanie v novoj russkoj literature: istoriko-sravnitel'nye očerki. 2-oe pererab. izd. Moskva: Vysočajše utverždennoe Russkoe T-vo pečatnago i izdatel'skago dela, 1896. 256, 7 s.

Veselovskij, Jurij Alekseevič

Ėtjudy po russkoj literature. T. 1. Moskva: Zvezda, [1913?]. 163 s.
Poėzija gr. E. P. Rostopčinoj — K charakteristike literaturnych otgoloskov krepostnogo prava — Belinskij i Puškin — Belinskij i francuzskaja tra-

gedija — Nadson i ego poėzija

Literaturnye očerki. T. 1-2. Moskva: Tipo-litografija A. V. Vasil'eva, 1900-1910. 592, 428 s.

Russkaja literatura v Švecii. Moskva: Tipo-litografija T-va I. N. Kušnerev, 1912. 16 s.

Vetrinskij, Č.
(Vasilij Evgrafovič Češichin)

Gercen. S 4-mja fototipjami i 16-ju avtotipijami na melovoj bumage. Priloženie: A. G. Fomič: Bibliografija proizvedenij Gercena i literatura o nem. S.-Peterburg, 1908. 532 s.: ill. (Biblioteka Svetoča pod red. S. A. Vengerova, 101-112)

T. N. Granovskij i ego vremja: istoričeskij očerk. Moskva: Tipo-litogr. T-va I. N. Kušnerev, 1897. ix, 319 s.

V sorokovych godach: istoriko-literaturnye očerki i charaktereristiki (Dorevoljucionnoe vremja — Belinskij — Granovskij — Iskander — Botkin — Kol'cov — Gogol' — Nikitenko i I. Aksakov — Kn. V. Odoevskij — Cepkin). Moskva: Tipo-litogr. T-va I. N. Kušnerev, 1899. 387 s.

Wilde, Oscar

Ballada Rėdingskoj tjur'my. Perevod s anglijskogo, razmerom podlinnika, Valerija Brjusova. Moskva: Literaturno-izdatel'skij Otdel Narodnogo Komissariata po Prosveščeniju, 1919. 31 s. (Social'no-istoričeskie romany i dramy)
Vvedenie V. Brjusova

Vilenkin, N. M. —> Minskij, N. M. (pseud.)

Williams, Robert

Sovetskaja sistema za rabotoj. Otčet o poezdke v Sovetskuju Rossiju. S predisloviem V. Jarockogo. Moskva: Gos. izd., 1921. 24 s. (Biblioteka Professional'nogo dviženija. Serija meždunarodnaja, 2; 30.000)

Vinogradov, Pavel Gavrilovič

Učebnik vseobščej istorii. Č. 1: Drevnij mir. 9-e izd. Stokchol'm: Severnye ogni, 1921. 189 s.

Vjazemskij, Petr Andreevič

Pis'ma Petra Andreeviča Vjazemskago k A. A. Voejkovoj. S.-Peterburg: Tipogr. M. M. Stasjuleviča, 1913. 81 s.

Polnoe sobranie sočinenij knjazja P. A. Vjazemskago. Izd. grafa S. D. Šeremeteva. 1-10. S.-Peterburg: Tipogr. M. M. Stasjuleviča, 18781886.
T. 1: Literaturnye kritičeskie i biografičeskie očerki 1810-1827. 1878. lx, 355 s.
T. 2: Literaturnye kritičeskie i biografičeskie očerki 1827-1851. 1879. xvii, 426 s.
T. 3-4: Stichotvorenija. 453, 378 s.
T. 5: Fon-Vizin. 1880. 351 s.
T. 6: Lettres d'un vétéran russe de l'année 1812 sur la question d'orient publiées par P. d'Ostafievo. Francuzskij podlinnik s russkim perevodom. 1881. 515 s.
T. 7: Literaturnye kritičeskie i biografičeskie očerki 1855-1877 g. 1882. 514 s.
T. 8-9-10: Staraja zapisnaja knižka

— Adol'f: roman Benžamen-Konstana. 1883. 524, 320, 316+82 s.

Vladimirov, Petr Vladimirovič

Drevnjaja russkaja literatura kievskago perioda XI—XIII vekov. Kiev: Tipogr. Imperatorskago Universiteta sv. Vladimira, 1900. 375, vii, 46, 17, 4, 4, 10 s.
Priloženie: Ironičeskaja pesn' o pochode na Polovcev udel'nago knjazja Novagoroda-Severskago Igorja Svjatoslaviča. Moskva 1800 g.

Iz učeničeskich let Gogolja. Pis'mo N.V. Gogolja 1827 g. k G. I. Vysockomu i predpolagaemyj portret Gogolja-studenta. S četyr'mja snimkami i portretom. Kiev: Tipogr. Imperatorskago Universiteta sv. Vladimira, 1890. 46 s.

Načalo slavjanskago i russkago knigopečatanija v XV—XVI vekach. Kiev: tipogr. N. Piljuščenko, 1894. 34 s.

Vladislavlev, I. V.
(Ignatij Vladislavovič Gul'binskij)

Russkie pisateli. Opyt bibliografičeskogo posobija po russkoj literature XIX i XX st. 4-e pererab. i znač. dopoln. izd. S priloženiem obzorov: 1. Literatura revoljucionnogo perioda (1918-1923 gg.). 2. O proletarskom tvorčestve. 3. Voprosy poètiki. Moskva-Leningrad: Gos. izd. 1924. 445 s.

Russkie pisateli XIX—XX st. Opyt bibliografičeskago posobija po novejšej russkoj literature. 2-oe pererab. i dopoln. izd. Moskva: Knigoizd. Nauka, 1913. 244 s.
Chudožestvennaja literatura — Kritika i publicistika — Istorija literatury

— Ukazatel' po épocham, v svjazi s istoričeskimi i istoriko-literaturnymi materialami

Vodovozov, Vasilij Ivanovič

Očerki iz russkoj istorii XVIII veka. S priloženiem očerkov iz drevne-russkoj žizni i iz istorii do-petrovskago perechodnago vremeni. Sost. V. Vodovozov. S.-Peterburg: Tipogr. V. S. Balaševa, 1897. 535 s.

Volkonskij, Sergej Grigor'evič

Očerki russkoj istorii i russkoj literatury: publičnyja lekcii čitannyja v Amerike. 2-e izd. S. Pb.: Tipogr. R. R. Golike, 1897. vii, 345 s.

Zapiski Sergija Grigor'eviča Volkonskago (dekabrista). Izd. knjazja M. S. Volkonskago. S.-Peterburg: Sinodal'naja tipogr. 1901. vii, 545 s. (Portr.)

Volkov, F. G. —> A. A. Jarcev: F. G. Volkov, ego žizn'...

Volkov, Nikolaj Dmitrievič

Mejerchol'd. T. 1-2. Moskva-Leningrad: Izd. Academia, 1929.
  T. 1: 1874-1908. 403 s., [12] tabl.
  T. 2: 1908-1917. 490 s., [14] tabl.

Volynskij, A. L.

Bor'ba za idealizm: kritičeskija stat'i. S.-Peterburg: Izd. N. G. Molostvova, 1900. 542 s.
  Dostoevskij, Senkevič, Nicše, Strachov, Zolja, Kol'cov, Pypin, Ge, Tolstoj,

Meterlink, Oskar Uajl'd, Gercen, Ogarev, Turgenev, Gogol', Korolenko, Jasinskij, Mamin-Sibirjak, Mikulič, Sollogub, Krestovskaja, Luchmanova, Apuchtin, Čechov, Gor'kij, Sigma, Minskij, Merežkovskij, Bal'mont, Gippius, Lochvickaja, A. Dobroljubov, Brjusov, gr. Aleksis Žasminov, Korinfskij, Veličko, gr. Goleniščev-Kutuzov, Djagilev, Vlad. Solov'ev, Kareev, Men'šikov, Boborykin

Russkie kritiki: literaturnye očerki. S.-Peterburg: Tipogr. M. Merkuševa, 1896. 827 s.

Voroncovy —> Ogarkov, V. V.: Voroncovy, ich žizn'...

Vorovskij, Vaclav Vaclavovič

Literaturnye očerki. Moskva: Novaja Moskva, 1923. 230 s. (8.000)
  Priloženie: V. Friče: V. V. Vorovskij kak literaturnyj kritik

Vrockij, N. A. —> Navrockij, A. A. (pseud.)

Zabelin, Ivan Egorovič

Domašnij byt russkich carej v XVI i XVII st. Sočinenie Ivana Zabelina. 3-e izd. s dopoln. Č. 1. Moskva: T-vo tipogr. A. I. Mamontova, 1895. xxi, 759 s.

Zacharin, Ivan Nikolaevič

Teni prošlago: razskazy o bylych delach I. N. Zacharina (Jakutina). S.-Peterburg: Izd. A.S. Suvorina, 1885. 367 s.

Žadovskaja, Julija Valerianovna

Polnoe sobranie sočinenij V.Ju. Žadov-skoj v četyrech tomach. S portretom, faksimile i biografičeskim očerkom pod red. P. V. Bykova. T. 1-4. 2-e posmert-noe izd., ispravl. i dopoln. S.-Peter-burg: Izd. I. P. Perevoznikova, 1894.
    T. 1: Biografija — Stichotvorenija 1844-1859 — Povesti 1849-1859. xxvi, 372 s.
    T. 2: V storone ot bol'šogo sveta. 320 s.
    T. 3: Ženskaja istorija — Otstalaja. 352 s.
    T. 4: Stichotvorenija i perepiska. 280 s.

Zagoskin, Michail Nikolaevič

Polnoe sobranie sočinenij M. N. Zagos-kina. T. 1-10. S.-Peterburg: Izd. T-va M. O. Vol'f, 1898.
    T. 1: Biografičeskij očerk — Chro-nologičeskij perečen' sočinenij M. N. Zagoskina — Jurij Miloslavskij ili rus-skie v 1612 godu — Kuz'ma Roščin. cxvi, 341 s.
    T. 2: Brynskij les — Russkie v na-čale os'mnadcatago stoletija. 502 s.
    T. 3: Kuz'ma Petrovič Mirošev. 348s.
    T. 4: Roslavlev ili russkie v 1812 godu. 354 s.
    T. 5: Askol'dova mogila: povest' — Toska po rodine. 471 s.
    T. 6: Iskusitel' — Oficial'nyj obed — Večer na Chopre — Tri ženicha. 494 s.
    T. 7: Moskva i moskviči: zapiski Bogdana Il'iča Bel'skago izdavaemyja M. N. Zagoskinym. 526 s.
    T. 8-9-10: Komedii — Žurnal'nyja stat'i. 427, 374, 418 s.

Zaiončkovskaja, N. D. —> Krestovskij, V. (pseud.)

Zajcev, Boris Konstantinovič

Putniki. Pariž: Knigoizd. Russkaja zem-lja, 1921.
    Putniki — Ljudi Bož'i — Osennij svet — Golubaja zvezda — Prizraki

Razskazy. S.-Peterburg: Izd-vo Šipov-nik, 1906. 91 s.

Zakrževskij, Aleksandr Karlovič

Religija: psichologičeskija paralleli. Do-stoevskij — Z. Gippius — D. S. Merež-kovskij — N. M. Minskij — S. Bulgakov — N. A. Berdjaev — V. V. Rozanov — A. Belyj — Vjač. Ivanov — A. Blok — A. Dobroljubov. Kiev: Izd. žurnala Iskus-stvo, 1913. vii, 473 s.

Zapiski nabljudatelja: literaturnye sbor-niki. Kn. pervaja. Češsko-russkoe izd. v Prage, 1924. 256 s.: ill.

Zarevoj, Sergej
(Sergej Nikolaevič Koškarov)

Velikaja nov': stichi. Moskva: Gos. izd., 1920. 30 s. (Krasnaja knižka, 15)

—> Koškarov, S. N.

Ždanov, Ivan Nikolaevič

Russkij bylevoj épos: izsledovanija i materialy. 1-5. S.-Peterburg: Izd. L. F. Panteleeva, 1895. 631 s.

Zelinskij, K. —> Biznes... —> Gosplan lite-ratury...

Žemčužnikov, Aleksej Michajlovič

Stichotvorenija A. M. Žemčužnikova v dvuch tomach. S portretom avtora i avtobiografičeskim očerkom. 2-e izd. 1-2. S.-Peterburg: Tipogr. M. M. Stasjuleviča, 1898.

Žemčužnikov, A.M. —> Prutkov, K. (pseud.)

Zemlja. Sbornik 1, 12. Moskva 1908, 1913.

Sb. 1: L. Andreev: Prokljatie zverja — Šolom Aš: Grech — M. Švob: Krestovyj pochod detej — A. Fedorov: Petlja — A. Kuprin: Sulamif' — Iv. Bunin: Ten' pticy — Stichi: A. Blok, S. Gorodeckij, N. Morozov, E. Tarasov. Georg. Čulkov. 1908. 288 s.

Sb. 12: M. Arcybašev: Mstitel' — N. Krašeninnikov: Devstvennost'. 1913. 378 s.

Žizn' zamečatel'nych ljudej: biografičeskaja biblioteka F. Pavlenkova

Aksakovy —> V. D. Smirnov
Avvakum, protopop —> V. A. Mjakotin
V. G. Belinskij —> M. A. Protopopov
S. P. Botkin —> A. N. Belogolovyj
Bogdan Chmel'nickij —> V. I. Jakovenko
A. S. Dargomyžskij —> S. A. Bazunov
E. P. Daškova —> V. V. Ogarkov
Demidovy —> V. V. Ogarkov
G. R. Deržavin —> S. M. Briliant
N. A. Dobroljubov —> A. M. Skabičevskij
F. Dostoevskij —> E. Solov'ev
Fon-Vizin —> S. M. Briliant
A. I. Gercen —> V. D. Smirnov
M. I. Glinka —> S. A. Bazunov
N. V. Gogol' —> A. N. Annenskaja
I. A. Gončarov —> E. A. Solov'ev
A. S. Griboedov —> A. M. Skabičevskij

Ivan IV Groznyj —> E. A. Solov'ev
A. A. Ivanov —> A. I. Comakion
E. F. Kankrin —> R. I. Sementkovskij
A. D. Kantemir —> R. I. Sementkovskij
N. M. Karamzin —> E. Solov'ev
V. N. Karazin —> Ja. V. Abramov
A. V. Kol'cov —> V. V. Ogarkov
N. A. Korf, baron —> M. L. Peskovskij
S. V. Kovalevskaja —> E. F. Litvinova
I. A. Krylov —> S. M. Briliant
M. Ju. Lermontov —> A. M. Skabičevskij
N. I. Lobačevskij —> E. F. Litvinova
M. V. Lomonosov —> A. I. L'vovič-Kostrica
A. D. Menšikov —> B. D. Porozovskaja
A. Mickevič —> V. Mjakotin
I. S. Nikitin —> F. E. Sivickij
Nikon, patriarch —> A. A. Bykov
N. I. Novikov —> S. E. Usova
V. G. Petrov —> L. K. Diterichs
Petr I —> I. M. Ivanov
N. I. Pirogov —> Ju. G. Malis
D. I. Pisarev —> E. Solov'ev
A. F. Pisemskij —> A. M. Skabičevskij
G. A. Potemkin —> V. V. Ogarkov
N. Prževal'skij —> M. A. Engel'gardt
A. S. Puškin —> A. M. Skabičevskij
M. E. Saltykov —> S. N. Krivenko
M. S. Ščepkin —> A. A. Jarcev
A. N. Serov —> S. A. Bazunov
T. G. Ševčenko —> V. I. Jakovenko
M. D. Skobelev —> M. M. Filippov
S. M. Solov'ev —> P. V. Bezobrazov
M. M. Speranskij —> S. N. Južakov
A. V. Suvorov —> M. L. Peskovskij
L. N. Tolstoj —> E. Solov'ev
I. S. Turgenev —> E. Solov'ev
K. D. Ušinskij —> M. L. Peskovskij
F. G. Volkov —> A. A. Jarcev
Voroncovy —> V. V. Ogarkov
V. A. Žukovskij —> V. V. Ogarkov

Zlatovratskij, Nikolaj Nikolaevič

Sočinenija N. N. Zlatovratskago v trech tomach s portretom avtora. Izd. 3-e, dopoln. 1-3. Moskva: Tipogr. T-va I. N. Kušnerev, 1897.

T.1: Povesti, očerki i razskazy iz narodnoj žizni. 353 s.

T. 2: Ustoi: roman — Očerki krest'janskoj obščiny. 406 s.

T. 3: Povesti i razskazy (1878-95 gg.). 350 s.

Znanie —> Sbornik Tovariščestva Znanie...

Znosko-Borovskij, Evgenij Aleksandrovič

Russkij teatr načala XX veka: kratkij očerk russkogo teatra do XX veka; Moskovskij Chudožestvennyj Teatr; Bor'ba s naturalizmom i realizmom; Teatr i revoljucija; Zaključenie. Praga: Plamja, 1925. 441 s.

Zola, Émile

Osada mel'nicy: rasskaz. Moskva: Gos. izd., 1919. 56 s. (Biblioteka detskogo čtenija)

Zolja, É. —> Zola, Émile

Zoščenko, Michail Michajlovič

Blednolicye brat'ja: jumorističeskie rasskazy. Moskva: Akc. Izd. Ogonek, 1927. 47 s. (Biblioteka Ogonek, 267; 75.000)

Blednolicye brat'ja — Meloči žizni — Svad'ba — Limonad — Paschal'nyj slučaj — Volokita — Kačestvo produkcii — Carskie sapogi — Sila krasnorečija — Avantjurnyj rasskaz — Gosti — Mokroe delo — Literator

Meloči žizni. Na obložke risunok N. Radlova. Leningrad: Izd-vo Krasnaja gazeta, 1927. 39 s. (Biblioteka žurnala Begemot, 74)

Melkoe proisšestvie — Igra prirody — Puškin — Duševnaja prostota — Katorga — Ljubitel' — Operacija — Grimasa NÉPa — Administrativnyj vostorg — Kolpak — Rubaška-fantazi

Razskazy. 2-oe izd.. Riga: Knigoizd. Gramatu draugs, 1930. 224 s. (Biblioteka Novejšej Literatury, 3)

Uvažaemye graždane. 8-oe izd. Moskva-Leningrad: Zemlja i fabrika, 1928. 270 s. (Biblioteka satiry i jumora; 10.000)

Žukovskij, Vasilij Andreevič

Ballady V. A. Žukovskago. Polnoe sobranie ballad, s primečanijami, ob"jasnitel'nyja stat'i. S.-Peterburg: Izd. I. Glazunova, 1892. 295 s. (Russkaja klassnaja biblioteka izd. pod red A. N. Čudinova. Posobie pri izučenii russkoj literatury, V)

Sočinenija v stichach i proze. Izd. desjatoe, ispr. i dopoln. pod red. P. A. Efremova. S priloženiem četyrech portretov Žukovskago, ispolnennych chudožestvennoj fototipiej K. A. Fišera. S.-Peterburg: Izd. knigoprodavca I. Glazunova, 1901. xvi, 1007 s.

S. vii-ix: Petr Aleksandrovič Efremov: kratkija biografičeskija svedenija i spisok ego literaturnych rabot, sostavil N.M. Lisovskij; S. x-xvi: V.A. Žukovskij: biografičeskij očerk

Stichotvorenija V. Žukovskago. T. 1-8. Izd. 4-oe, ispr. i umnožennoe. Sanktpeterburg: Izd. knigoprodavca Aleksandra Smirdina, 1835-1837.

T. 1: Orleanskaja deva — Liričeskija stichotvorenija. 1835. 292 s.

T. 2: Romansy i pesni — Élegii — Poslanija. 1835. 258 s.

T. 3: Ballady. 1835. 274.

T. 4: Ballady. 1835. 224 s.

T. 5: Povesti. 1837. 249 s.

T. 6: Smes'. 1836. 263 s.

T. 7: Sočinenija v proze. 1835. 283 s.

T. 8: Undina. 1837. 243

Stichotvorenija Vasilija Andreeviča Žukovskago. Obščedostupnoe izd. Moskva: V universitetskoj tipogr., 1885. 156 s.

Stranstvujuščij žid. Predsmertnoe izd., po rukopisi poèta. Vstupiteľnaja staťja S.I. Ponomareva. Sanktpeterburg: Tipogr. Imperatorskoj Akademii Nauk, 1885. 112 s.

—> Ogarkov, V. V.: V. A. Žukovskij

Žukovskij, Vladimir Grigor'evič

Stichotvorenija Vladimira Žukovskago 1893-1904. S.-Peterburg: Izd. A. S. Suvorina, 1905. 316 s. (Pamjati dorogogo otca)

PERIODICALS

Bajan. Dvuchnedeľnyj literaturno-chudožestvennyj žurnal dlja semejnago
čtenija pod red. A. Arakina. Charbin,
1923: 1-10

Bezbožnik u stanka: Organ M.K.R.K.P.
(boľševikov). Moskva, 1923: 3-10 (50.000)

**Bjulleten' torgovogo sektora Lengi-
za**. Leningrad, 1925–1927: 3(28)-40

Čisla. Sborniki pod red. I. V. Manciarli
i N. A. Osipa. Paris, 1930–33: 1-8

Golos minuvšego: žurnal istorii i istorii literatury. Moskva, 1921: 9 (2.500)

Grjaduščaja Rossija: ežemesjačnyj li-
teraturno-političeskij i naučnyj žurnal
pod red. N. V. Čajkovskogo, V. A. Anri,
M. A. Landau–Aldanova i Alekseja N.
Tolstogo. Pariž, 1920: 1-2.

Istoričeskij vestnik: istoriko-literaturnyj žurnal. Peterburg, 1881–1914, god
2-8, 10, 11, 13-35

**Knižnaja letopis' glavnago upravleni-
ja po delam pečati**. S.-Peterburg, 1907-
1920. 1 (1907)–10 (1916), 12 (1918), 14
(1920)

Knižnyj ugol: kritika, bibliografija,
chronika. Pod red. Viktora Chovina.
Peterburg, 1918: 1-4

Knižnyj vestnik: žurnal knigo-torgovoj,
izdateľskoj i literaturnoj dejateľnosti v
Rossii. Izd. Russkago obščestva knigo-
prodavcov i izdatelej. S.-Peterburg, 18
(1901)–23 (1906)

Krasnaja nov': literaturno-chudožestvennyj i naučno publicističeskij žurnal.
Moskva-Leningrad, 1927–1934

Kuľtura teatra: žurnal moskovskich
associirovannych teatrov. Moskva: Gos.
izd., 1921: 5 (maj)

Kuznica: organ proletarskich pisatelej.
Moskva: Izd. Literaturnogo Otdela Nar-
komprosa, 1920: 1-2, 4 (10.000)

Letopis' doma literatorov: literaturno-
issledovateľskij i kritiko-bibliografičeskij žurnal. Vychodit dva raza v mes-
jac. Peterburg, 1921–1922: 1-8/9

Mir božij: ežemesjačnyj literaturnyj i
naučno-populjarnyj žurnal dlja samoobrazovanija. S.-Peterburg, 13 (1904):
1-9; 15 (1906): 1-12

Na čužoj storone: istoriko-literaturnye
sborniki. Pod red. S. P. Meľgunova. Berlin i Praga, 1923–1925: 1-13

Niva: illjustrirovannyj žurnal literatury, politiki i sovremennoj žizni. S.-Pe-
terburg, 14 (1883), 32 (1901)

Novaja kniga: bjulleten' petrogradskogo otdelenija gos. izd. Petrograd, 1 (1922):
1-5 – 4 (1925): 18-19

Novaja russkaja kniga: ežemesjačnyj
kritiko-bibliografičeskij žurnal pod red.
A. S. Jaščenko. Berlin, 1922: 1-12; 1923:
1-6

Novyj žurnal dlja vsech. Peterburg 1910:
15-26. Priloženie: Aľbom-gallereja sov-

remennych pisatelej. Besplatnoe priloženie k Novomu žurnalu dlja vsech za 1910-j god. [48 portretov russkich pisatelej]

Pečat' i revolucija: žurnal literatury, iskusstva, kritiki i bibliografii. Moskva: Gos. izd., 1925: 1; 1926: 3, 5; 1927: 1; 1928: 1

Pravda: ežemesjačnyj žurnal iskusstva, literatury, obščestv. žizni. Moskva, 1904: janvar'–aprel'; 1905: nojabr'

Proletarskaja kul'tura: ežemesjačnyj žurnal. Organ vserossijskogo soveta proletarskich kul'turno-prosvetitel'nych organizacij. Moskva: Gos. izd., 1918: 1-10; 1919: 13-14; 1920: 15-16

Russkaja kniga: ežemesjačnyj kritikobibliografičeskij žurnal. Red. A. S. Jaščenko. Berlin, 1921: 1-9

Russkaja letopis'. Pariž, 1921: 1–1925: 7

Russkaja mysl': ežemesjačnoe literaturno-političeskoe izdanie. Moskva-Peterburg, 35 (1914): 1-12; 38 (1917): 1-12; 1921: 1-9; 1922: 1-7

Russkaja starina: ežemesjačnoe istoričeskoe izdanie. Sanktpeterburg, 1870-1904. T. 1-120

Russkij vestnik. Moskva, 1901–1906. T. 271-306

Russkija zapiski: obščestvenno-politīčeskij i literaturnyj žurnal. Pariž, Šanchaj, 1937–39: 1-21

Russkoe bogatstvo: ežemesjačnyj literaturnyj, naučnyj i političeskij žurnal. S.-Peterburg, 1909: 1-2; 1917: 4-7,10

Slavjanskij mir: ežemesjačnyj žurnal literatury, iskusstva i kritiki. S.-Peterburg, 1910: 1-12; 1911: 1-5

Sovremennyj mir: ežemesjačnyj literaturnyj, naučnyj i političeskij žurnal. S.-Peterburg, 1 (1906): 1-3

Sovremennyja zapiski: ežemesjačnyj obščestvenno-političeskij i literaturnyj žurnal. Pariž, 1920–1939. T. 1-69

Spisok izdanij vyšedšich v Rossii 1886–1900. S.-Peterburg 1886–1900 [1886, 1888, 1889, 1892–1893, 1895–1896, 1900]

Vestnik agitacii i propagandy. Dvuchnedel'nyj organ C.K.R.K.P. (bol'ševikov). Moskva, 1921: 9-10 (30.000)

Vestnik Evropy: žurnal istorii-politiki-literatury. S.-Peterburg, 36 (1901)-49 (1914), 52 (1917)

Vestnik rabotnikov iskusstv: ežemesjačnyj žurnal. Organ vseros. profession. sojuza rabotnikov iskusstv. Moskva, 1921: 4-5 (8.000)

Vesy. Moskva, 3 (1906): 9; 4 (1907): 1; 5 (1908): 1-12; 6 (1909): 1-12

Volja Rossii: ežemesjačnyj žurnal politiki i kultury. Pod red. V. I. Lebedeva, M. L. Slonima, V. A. Stalinskogo, V. V. Suchomlina. Praga, 8 (1930): 1-12

Voprosy žizni. 1905. S.-Peterburg 1905: 1-12

Zolotoe runo. 1906: Nojabr'–dekabr'

Index

126